# PROACTIVE
## AND
# APPLIED
# RESILIENCE

## The Sixteen Experiences

GLENN E. RICHARDSON, PHD

# PROACTIVE AND APPLIED RESILIENCE
## THE SIXTEEN EXPERIENCES

*iUniverse books may be ordered through booksellers or by contacting:*

*iUniverse*
*1663 Liberty Drive*
*Bloomington, IN 47403*
*www.iuniverse.com*
*1-800-Authors (1-800-288-4677)*

*ISBN: 978-1-5320-1392-8 (sc)*
*ISBN: 978-1-5320-1393-5 (hc)*
*ISBN: 978-1-5320-1394-2 (e)*

*Library of Congress Control Number: 2017901361*

*Print information available on the last page.*

*iUniverse rev. date: 06/06/2017*

In Appreciation for Love and Support

To Glenwood and Ruth, who served as noble resilient exemplars
and instilled a drive in me to try to make them proud.

To Kat, for a special love and helping to stay the course.

To my children, for continuing to ignite my childlike resilience.

To my university graduate students, who have joined
me along the academic resilient journey.

# Contents and Highlights for
## *Proactive and Applied Resilience*

The solution to every problem, the guidance for every dream, and all that anyone ever needed, wanted, or hoped for reside in the sea of energy, vitality, enlightenment, and power that dwells within you and within the world around you.

This book will help you access that energy, vitality, and wisdom within and around you and help you thrive through adversity and maximize your potential.

## Part 1: An Orientation to Living Resiliently: The Q-Nexus Experiences to Enhance Resilient Capacity

### Preface: A Personal Journey to the Q-Nexus

Every resiliency story has a beginning. What I describe in this section is the greatest life-transforming experience of my life when I was hit by a car and in a coma for ten days and how it set me on the path of resilient inquiry and subsequently allowed me the opportunity to help others live resiliently. Sometimes we learn through positive experiences and sometimes through adversity. I learned skills from this personal life tragedy that strengthened me and gave me purpose. As I describe my story in this preface, I cover and highlight the stages and experiences of the resilient journey.

### Introduction: The Language and Postulates of the Q-Nexus

The Q-nexus refers to our connection with elements in and around us that help us thrive through adversity, resonate with the wisdom within and around, and set us on the resilient path through life. The introduction provides the important foundation for understanding the language, assumptions, and concepts that spark and enrich the most powerful and important experiences of your life—the Q-nexus.

## Part 2: The Resilient Journey

The resilient journey is a process—a process you go through on a regular basis. As resiliency is about thriving through adversity, it is not about the ups and downs of life but rather the downs and ups. You will learn the several steps in making the journey to help assure that you are thriving through life's challenges.

### Experience 1: Resiliency and Resiliency Mapping

Resiliency is the process and experience of being disrupted by life events, adversity, or challenges and, in the humbling lows of introspective enlightenment, accessing innate self-mastering strengths to grow stronger through the disruption. The resilient journey is the framework for the Q-nexus experiences. Every life experience creates a new story that will follow this predictable and controllable resiliency map. You will begin to take control of your life experiences by learning the resiliency-mapping process. As you apply resiliency in your life, what emerges over time is a far more empowered and authentic self.

## Part 3: Discovering Resilient Yearnings and Drives

You need energy and motivation to get through the downs and ups of life. This second experience below will help you discover the vast reservoir of strength, courage, and power that is housed within you and the world around you. This energy within is called resilience. Resilience is a force within everyone that drives him or her to seek self-actualization, altruism, wisdom, peace, and harmony with a source of spiritual strength. You will discover your "acres of diamonds."

### Experience 2: Childlike Resilience

You were born with an amazing reservoir of energy and motivation that was very evident in your childhood. You will learn to rekindle your childlike inclinations to have fun, seek adventure, laugh, and be spontaneous, and then you will learn to harness that energy to enrich your life.

Even as a child, you felt the drive of nobility and wanted to help grown-ups. In return, the grown-up praised (appreciated) you. You continue to have the drive to be helpful and noble as a grown-up yourself, and the mechanism to feel valued is the same. When you help others, you receive praise. You will learn the dimensions of nobility and as a result will increase your self-worth and esteem.

Character resilience is the yearning to live within a chosen set of morals, such as integrity and honesty. You will rediscover your character resilience and learn how to avoid energy-draining experiences.

Ecological resilience is about harvesting the qualities you really want in life from the world around you. You will learn how and why you can be infused with these qualities when you are in natural settings and enriching environments. You will also learn how to create enriching environments with art, pets, aromas, and music.

While ecological resilience provides an external source of energy, universal resilience describes the yearning that comes from within you to discover strength beyond normal capacity. Universal resilience is about the desire to connect with a source of power and wisdom that is beyond how you normally think and reason.

The human body is built to optimize its potential. Your body can tell your mind when to move, what to eat, when to sleep, and when to relax—if you learn the skills of listening intuitively. This experience will help you recognize and act upon your body's messages so that you can optimize your physical capacity.

Volumes of research have been written about personality and the mind. In this experience, we will simply consider the mind as a control center that interprets messages from the resilient drives originating in your body and spirit. Intellectual resilience is the drive to understand these messages and make plans to fulfill them.

The focus to this point has been a journey to understand who you really are and recognize the tremendous potential and resilient drives you have. Part 4 helps you to take leaps of faith and enjoy the harvest of qualities (Qs) and virtues you really want as you embark on the resilient journey.

Your vision or dream for a happy life is the focus of Experience 9. Once you understand the innate drives of your body, mind, and spirit, you will be prepared to answer the age-old questions "Who am I?" and "Where am I going?" This experience will help you formulate a vision of where you really want to go in life. You will discover that your vision remains constant throughout your lifetime. The goals you set to support your vision, on the other hand, are flexible (as well as measurable and accomplishable).

With a vision of where you want to go in life while harvesting the energy from your resilient nature, you can now take action by following your resiliency map. Leaving homeostasis is the experience of venturing. You will learn to venture and increase your capacity to take leaps of faith in this experience. You will learn how to lessen fear and enhance courage.

When you take a leap of faith into a new adventure, you will feel somewhat disoriented with the new experience, resulting in some degree of chaos. Experience 11 will first guide you through exercises that enhance your creativity and then help you apply them to make order in the chaos. You will also learn integrative skills to prepare yourself for the answers to life's disruptions.

The Q-nexus is the key experience during your resilient journey to know what to do and when to do it. The resonating and quickening moments of the Q-nexus may come as dramatic experiences, or they may be subtler, such as when a plan comes together or you have an aha moment.

Resonation is the sense that you are on the right path, making the right decisions, and in harmony with your optimal life plan. Quickening is the enlivening moment when your soul is infused with the qualities (Qs) you really want, enabling you to progress through life's disruptions. The quickening moments may redirect your life course. You will learn about both of these powerful experiences as they constitute the Q-nexus.

Quickening experiences provide direction and energy to overcome your challenges. Through these disruptive experiences, you also have the opportunity to form new, more powerful identities that have greater capacities and enhanced coping skills. You will learn to use your resilient drives to persist and overcome undesirable habits.

Self-mastery is a complex and powerful quality that helps you persist and find peace as you thrive through life experiences. This experience will teach you how to create new identities to add to your arsenal of coping skills, thus empowering you to become what your Q-nexus moment guided you to become. You will learn the steps and skills for creating a specific identity that will best deal with each life challenge. You will also learn persistence. You will learn how to muster grit to endure.

Self-Mastery 2 provides guidance and clarifies a resilient journey along the path with heart (Q-path). This exercise will help you harvest the qualities and virtues you really want.

The challenge of following a path with heart is to keep undesirable thoughts and actions from derailing us along the journey. Self-Mastery 3 will build upon the path with heart model as compared to the path of shadows model. This experience helps you to dissect your undesirable habits, put them on trial, and create a life plan to overcome them by activating innate resilient strengths. We will explore how to transform your shortcomings and bad habits into strengths and develop skills to jump from the path of shadows back to the path with heart.

Resilient reintegration is the experience of incorporating new pieces into your new world puzzle or worldview following disruptions. Resilient reintegration reflects the accomplishment and progression you have experienced along your resilient journey.

Wisdom, or resilient reintegration, is the pinnacle of the process of coping, learning, and becoming stronger through the disruption. It is the wonderful feeling of fulfillment and the infusion of the qualities and virtues you really want. Wisdom is the product of learning and growing from life's challenges. You will see how the Q-nexus moments are key to dealing with all your life issues. You will learn the skills of looking at the world through resilient eyes (Q-eyes).

# PART 1

# AN ORIENTATION TO LIVING RESILIENTLY: THE Q-NEXUS EXPERIENCES TO ENHANCE RESILIENT CAPACITY

Resiliency is a disruptive and recovery journey you take every day. Resiliency is the process of beginning, experiencing, and ending your story that occurs many times each day over your lifetime. Your story of learning, growing, and progressing throughout your life brings you peace and builds the foundation of your legacy. From the simple lessons of how to use an electronic device to life-threatening experiences, each story has the potential to create a humbling experience of introspective enlightenment, allowing you to grow stronger through the disruption.

People are drawn to stories. Whether your parents told you bedtime fantasies growing up or you enjoy a good movie or book now, stories are embedded within the human culture. The adventures are not limited to imaginary characters. Perhaps your friends and family members have told you stories from when they were younger or shared the crazy things that happened to them yesterday. You have also shared similar tales with them. Although people do not always think of their lives as stories, each of our lives is an adventure in the making, and we create new experiences that add to our life stories every day. More importantly, each of us has the opportunity to be the hero of our stories.

You have a story. You have multiple adventures that happen many times a day within your life's story. All the stories are unique, but the essence of your journey through the experience is the same. Each story follows a predictable journey or process. In the journey, there are multiple experiences and choices that can spawn inspiration, hope, and courage. The same story can lead to confusion, hopelessness, and chaos. Your personal stories can be very simple, such as learning a new concept or deciding to pick up this book to read. Your personal tale may also be very complex, such as experiencing a serious health issue or finding yourself in financial chaos. What is important for you is to emerge as the hero of your story. The power and motivation to become the hero is innate within you.

Part 1 includes a preface and an introduction. The preface is the author's personal story about being hit by a car, experiencing a near-death coma, and taking a journey of rehabilitation. The stages of resiliency are highlighted in the story to set the framework for the rest of the book. The introduction will describe the language and postulates of proactive and applied resiliency.

# A PERSONAL JOURNEY TO THE Q-NEXUS

This book will help you, as the reader, to take control of your life story and all the short stories that happen every day. Your adventures describe a journey of progression. In the midst of the journey, you will discover personal insights and strengths. You will learn that there is a best story for you. You have within you an amazing script—a script that is read to you from multiple sources from within your innate wisdom. You will learn about your amazing human spirit that is trying to guide you through your life story. In the story, you are noble. You are the powerful warrior in your crusade to fulfill your full potential. You were born to be magnificent! Unfortunately, what happens in so many lives is that skills, gifts, and talents have been buried under layers of fear, self-doubt, and perceived failures.

Perhaps the best way to explore the nature of this book is to consider an adventure that comes from my life. As the story is told, there will be interruptions with notes. The notes within the story will highlight concepts that will be described for your personal enrichment in subsequent experiences. All life stories go through the stages noted in this story and the concepts that will be described in later experiences. By the time you finish this book, these concepts will become part of your thinking and feeling as you become the hero in your personal story of progression, power, and peace. Here is my story.

I was finally done. It was December 21, the day after my forty-first birthday, and I was exhausted. After my family birthday party, I left the house and drove to the university. I had to finish writing the final chapter for a personal health textbook. The final chapter, entitled "Death and Dying," not only described how I was feeling but perhaps served as an omen and warning of things to come. Following my all-nighter, I had a meeting with some faculty members at the School of Nursing to make final revisions for a grant proposal that was due by the end of the year. I yearned to go home. Students were gone for the holidays, turning the campus into a virtual ghost town. I was finally going to be away from the hassles of work and be with my wife and four children for Christmas. As I walked down the hill toward my car, I breathed deeply as the invigorating winter air filled my lungs. Even with my sleepless fatigue, I felt a great sense of accomplishment and peace.

Note: Stories begin with a time or stage when people have adapted to their life situations. This stage is called *homeostasis* or a *comfort zone*.

I approached the road that divided the upper campus from the traditional academia of the main campus. At the crosswalk, a van had stopped to let me cross the first of four lanes. From this moment until thirteen days later, I have little conscious recall of the events that ensued. I will continue this story based upon the reports from the physicians, police, and paramedics. As I stepped past the van into the second of four lanes, a 1982 Oldsmobile came barreling down the road at 45 miles per hour (in a 30 mph speed zone). The driver, a foreign student who had only lived in the States for a few weeks and had just received a license to drive, did not even slow down. The Olds's bumper struck my lower legs, shattering the bones into small pieces. My body flipped up onto the hood of the passenger side of the car. Since I was lifted onto the side of the hood, the impact caused me to spin. My head struck the passenger-side window and shattered it. The Olds drove on for several hundred yards before the terrified foreign student realized what had happened. I lay in an unconscious heap on the side of the road. The first car to stop, fortunately, was a physician who worked at the nearby university hospital, and he jumped out of the car and held me in his arms. There was little doubt in his mind that I would die. A hundred yards from the crosswalk, as fortune would have it, was a fire station staffed with paramedics. In a short time, I was put into an ambulance and hurried to the university hospital that I had left with feelings of relief only minutes before. Now I was returning comatose in an ambulance, precariously close to death.

Note: All stories require an event or change to really be a story. Life events take us from our comfort zones. Some events are like the event in the story—getting hit by a car. Maybe not life threatening, but unsettling, are other major life events, such as divorce, financial crises, or family conflicts. Other events are minor, such as others forcing us to make a change in plans, running out of gas, or forgetting an item at the store. Desired and optimal changes are leaps of faith into new learning experiences, such a taking a class, reading a book, or looking for a new job. All our stories begin with homeostasis, and then a life event or change happens. The change begins a new chapter of our lives.

The first emergency room physician did not think to check for internal bleeding, but as I ballooned in size, the astute supporting nurse practitioner realized I was in trouble. I was bleeding to death. They had to cut off my wedding ring because I was swelling so much that it was cutting off the circulation. They performed a fasciotomy (an eight-inch surgical slit) on both of my legs to release some of the fluid pressure that was bloating me. I was rolled into surgery on repeated occasions. The first surgery was to remove my ruptured and bleeding spleen. Another surgery was to put rods down my legs and slide the broken bones around the rods so the bones could heal. The surgeon described it as making macaroni necklaces on a string, like we did back in elementary school. They put four round six-and-a-half-inch screws into each of my lower legs for support and left four inches of the screws protruding from my legs. They left my fractured hip to heal without any clinical intervention. They monitored my head trauma regularly. I would be in a coma through Christmas and New Year's Day.

My first recollection was one of discomfort, largely due to a catheter they had inserted into my urethra to help me with bodily functions. My head hurt. I was confused and disoriented. What had happened? I opened my eyes to see my wife, who I recognized. She asked me, "Buzz [my nickname], do you know where you are?"

As I looked around in my intensive care hospital room with the many tubes in my body and machines all around me, I responded matter-of-factly with an academic tone, "It appears to be some sort of clinical setting." I immediately went back to sleep after my left-brain response. I was not awake enough to begin to understand what was happening to me. The next day, I woke again, and my wife was again there shaving my face with an electric razor. This time I could feel the right side of my brain starting to work again. I have always enjoyed a good laugh and joking around. I saw the razor, took it from my wife, and began to use it as a microphone as I started singing "Tutti Frutti." Again, I slipped back to sleep. I guess my wife and the medical staff wondered at that point if the brain trauma was permanent.

As I slowly evolved from my coma, I was awake for longer periods of time and became conversational with visitors. As the reality of the accident started to sink into my mind, I began to wonder what I was going to do. I first felt badly for my wife and children, who were worrying about their husband and father who was in a coma and precariously close to death. I ached for them. I thought about how my poor mother might be feeling with her tender emotions still evident as a relatively new widow. I wondered about my work. I was a department chair at the university and knew faculty and staff would be affected. Following visits from family, colleagues, and friends, I realized that my loved ones would be okay, but I felt badly for the emotional distress they were going through.

I lay in the hospital for another week. It was a time of wondering, pondering, introspection, and remembering. With my strong belief in a God that loved me, I found myself repeatedly in a state of prayer and meditation. I knew my fate was in the hands of some of the greatest medical professionals in the world, but more than that, I felt that I needed the help of a power well beyond the skills of even the greatest physicians. I was in the process of learning that these kinds of events that seem to be beyond human control, especially events as massive and mystical as this, come from a collective destiny designed to redirect my life path.

I found myself questioning my future during the long, dark, and painful nights. As I looked at the four pins sticking out of each of my lower legs, I wondered, *Will I ever walk again? What am I to do? What am I to be? Will I ever be able to teach again?* I had always been an optimist of sorts and assumed that I would fully recover ... but would I? I needed guidance, comfort, and peace to know what to do and to give me strength to recover from this accident.

Note: Your story is a story of change—of leaving your comfort zone. Change can lead to uncomfortable feelings, such as confusion or fear. Although these feelings are often considered to be negative, there is a silver lining because they are necessary for personal growth. Resiliency is the process for becoming stronger through these experiences.

During my week of pondering while in the hospital, my mind kept going back to my only vivid memory of the time in my coma. I don't know if the memory coincided with Christmas Eve or not, but it did coincide with a time when the doctors indicated that my condition was worsening. About this time, I do remember a precious moment—a moment that even when I ponder it to this day, years later, I still feel stirrings of peace and joy.

As I was starting to slip away from this life, I felt like I was basking in a peaceful warmth. I felt so good. To my right, I became aware of some light. I looked and saw a large opening into what seemed like a beautiful oasis, but the opening was covered with a veil. I could see how luminous it was on the other side of the veil, but yet it was somewhat opaque, and I couldn't really make out any forms to know what was on the other side. But from this lighted veil was an energy and feeling of love and peace that overwhelmed my soul. I felt like I was almost melting under the influence of a loving energy that came from that tunnel opening. I bathed myself in this radiant loving light much like I used to do lying on a beaches near my hometown of San Diego.

I remember questioning what was beyond the covering or veil. As I pondered what was happening, I suddenly felt two hands gently slide onto my shoulders. First, the fingers touched the top of my shoulders, and then I felt the fingers slide down until the palms of the hands were firmly resting on me. The hands were strong yet gentle.

The hands were filled with love and energy that filled my soul like an electric current. I never saw a face, but I knew it was my father, who had passed away a couple of years before. His nonverbal message was short, comforting, and penetrating. "Buzz, ole man, you will live. Stay the course." Dad always called me "Buzz, ole man"—it sounds funny to write it, but when he spoke it, it was endearing.

"Stay the course" was part of the counsel he would give me as a boy when we would go camping or when he would take me on his business trips. It was amazing to me the volume of communication that occurred with so few words. The words he communicated to me were accompanied by visions of grandeur, direction, and awe. "You will live" was full of personal and family implications filled with hope. "Stay the course" was accompanied with a vision of both a mission in life with regard to my family and community as well as my academic career. I could look at my children and see the light in their eyes and the majesty of their spirits. In my work, I was just beginning to ponder the concept of resiliency and trying to understand how people grow stronger through adversity. When he said to me, "Stay the course," there was no question as to what that course was—it was to be my life story. It was clear to me that my journey for the rest of my life would be a life carrying a resilient compass. I knew my purpose was to help people to thrive through adversity. I wanted to touch hearts and, more importantly, have people nurture their own hearts. The range of the vision of "Stay the course" was from nurturing my family to touching lives in academia and the community. I have no idea how long the experience lasted, but it was as clear as any experience I had ever had. Many people who have these kinds of experiences share them with others—I did not for many years. Even now, I cannot express the full measure or details of that glorious day.

A few days later, I again woke from my coma, but everything was different. Rather than questioning my future, I was confident. I felt a remarkable relief and freedom from my pain. I felt as though I were a baby again, wrapped in a warm and cuddly blanket. The feelings I had were amazing. The feelings were euphoric. I sensed that I was being consumed by love. It was exhilarating, and I felt more cherished than I ever had before. I learned what real happiness was. I knew from this experience that I would recover.

Note: In a state of humble readiness, you can receive insights to know what to do and when to do it and have the energy to make it happen. These defining moments infuse your soul with the qualities (Qs) you really want in life, including—among others—peace, courage, and wisdom. Your happy and thriving life is one in which you know that each step of your story is in harmony with what is best for you. You have within you an innate script for an optimal life. The gentle reading of your life script is called *resonation*. You will also feel dramatic moments in your story that are very impactful and life changing. Defining moments or life-changing inspiration is called *quickening*. The essence of your amazing life story is to be in harmony with your subtle resonations to truths and answers as well as to act upon moments of quickening.

I knew that I would recover. I knew I needed to pursue the academic path to discover the depth and richness of the Q-nexus and resiliency. My thoughts in the hospital after I awoke from the coma were about the origins of resilience and pondering, *How can I help people become stronger in the face of challenging life events?* I had received an enlightening moment that let me know what I was to do with my professional life. I realized that I needed to live to be able to tell the story of recovery. After twelve days, I left the hospital in a wheelchair to go home.

With Velcro casts on both legs and pins in my legs, I learned to use my arms to lift myself step by step to reach my bedroom on the second floor of my home. I learned to shower by sitting on the floor of the shower with my legs dangling outside. Still, there were dozens of discouraging moments. I had always been physically active and enjoyed sports, but now I was stuck in a wheelchair. But because of what I had experienced, I knew I was on the path that was directed by a strength beyond myself. As weeks passed, I became impatient with my slow healing, even though the doctors told me I had been rehabilitating quickly. I figured out how to drive my Ford F-250 pickup after a couple of weeks with my legs in casts and the pins still in my lower legs.

I had learned that I would live. I knew my mission. I would change my goals from administration and move more deeply into the world of resilience and resiliency. Nothing would deter me. I became a rehabilitation warrior! I pushed the limits.

Note: With each new life experience, you have the opportunity to create a new identity or character for yourself. This book will help you tap into the driving forces housed within you so that you can discover, create, and become the new identities you seek in order to deal with life's challenges. Self-mastery, which embodies persistence and drive, is one of the most important qualities one can have for success. By learning how to maintain motivation even when times get tough, you will be able to break undesirable habits and addictions.

Since the day I gained consciousness in the hospital, I have been passionate about understanding the resilient journey. This journey is one that each of you has the agency to create and live. Each phase of the disruptive and reintegrative journey provides an opportunity for you to tell your story of victory and learning. You will learn that by listening to the prompts that come from within your soul, you can progress throughout your lifetime. Your greatest story is yet to be told. This process is not a quick fix solution but rather a journey. You will go through that journey, experience by experience, each with a skill and insight to help you thrive and fulfill your potential.

The next section of the book is the introduction and will describe the key assumptions you should make about life. The introduction will also teach you the language of resilient living and the Q-nexus.

# THE LANGUAGE AND POSTULATES OF THE Q-NEXUS

*The Q-nexus is the experience of discerning what to do, knowing when to do it, feeling confident that it is the right thing to do, and experiencing an infusion of energy to make it happen.*

As you have faced life's decisions, problems, and adversity, how often have you asked yourself, *What am I going to do?* Many of us have wished that we could see into the future to know which solution would be best for us and for our loved ones. We have often wished for more energy and strength to accomplish the challenges at hand. The experience of harvesting more energy and strength is through the Q-nexus, and we need this introduction to clarify what these terms mean.

This introduction will help you understand the language of the Q-nexus. Since the Q-nexus is a special experience, unique terms have been developed to describe its supportive concepts. The experience will also identify six truths that will lay the foundation for an optimal and happy life.

## UNDERSTANDING THE EMPOWERING NATURE OF THE Q-NEXUS

The Q-nexus experiences are often subtle, but they are also powerful moments that stir something deep inside you and help you embody the feeling you need for the situation at hand. The enlivening moments are best understood by considering how the Q-nexus empowers us.

- When you are afraid, the Q-nexus will help you to channel the energy of fear into the power of courage.
- When you encounter stressors, the Q-nexus will help you embrace those stressors as springboards for growth.
- When you face great adversity, the Q-nexus will help you find strength beyond your normal capacity to thrive.
- When you feel confused at a time of important decision making, the Q-nexus will help you discern, choose, and gain confidence in your choice.
- When you feel down and discouraged, the Q-nexus will help you discover jewels of hope in the mire of depression.
- When you are feeling anxious, the Q-nexus will instill calm and peace.
- When you are held captive by addictions, the Q-nexus will empower you with strength and control.
- When you are angry, the Q-nexus will infuse you with compassion.
- When you are faced with situations beyond your control, the Q-nexus will help you find peace and acceptance.
- When you are concerned about what is right, the Q-nexus will confirm your truth.
- When you are fatigued, the Q-nexus will infuse you with increased capacity to think, perform, and do.
- When you need to create a turning point in your life, the Q-nexus will infuse your heart and mind to know which way to turn.

## WHY Q-NEXUS?

With a sense of what the empowering Q-nexus experience is, we can explore why the experience is called the Q-nexus. Q-nexus moments are when you feel the infusion of the qualities (Qs) you really want or need in life situations. The letter *Q* has been chosen because of several key Q-word concepts (such as *qualities*, *quanta*, and *quest*). The letter *Q* is intuitive and easy to remember and practice. As we walk the resilient journey, the letter *Q* in *Q-nexus* instantly reminds us to connect (*nexus*) with the qualities

(Qs) we need to progress. Let's ponder the significance of the letter *Q* in the words that follow.

- **Qualities:** Underlying what we really want in life are qualities and virtues that are somewhat intangible and difficult to measure. First, consider the qualities and virtues that underlie what you really want in life. A representative list of qualities you really want in life is suggested in table 1.

**Table 1: Qualities and Virtues You Really Want in Life**

| | | |
|---|---|---|
| Enlightenment | Fun | Discernment |
| Meaning | Adventure | Guidance |
| Purpose | Enjoyment | Love |
| Understanding | Fulfillment | Self-worth |
| Hope | Spirituality | Value |
| Honesty | Happiness | Peace |
| Comfort | Courage | Inspiration |
| Pleasure | Confidence | Character |
| Wisdom | Power | Energy |
| Morality | Freedom | Strength |

- **Quanta:** Another way to view what we really want in life comes from theoretical physics, specifically the field of quantum physics. In this field, the vitalizing light and energy that bring atoms and everything in the universe to life are called *quanta*. Through the eyes of an experimental physicist, quanta are the substances that ignite the qualities (Qs) you really want (Greene 2003).
- **Quintessence:** From ancient philosophies, we learn of *quintessence*. Quintessence is the fifth and highest element that runs through the other basic elements of air, fire, earth, and water. It is the vitalizing, pure, and refined substance that permeates and enlivens all nature and the cosmos.
- **Quickening:** When we are infused with Qs, such as love or courage, *quickening* provides a renewed sense of energy that brings us to life. This experience is likened to the first indications of

life from a baby in a mother's womb—an experience known as *quickening*. Therefore, the revitalizing experience of receiving an infusion of Qs is also called *quickening*.

- **Qi:** Eastern philosophies embrace the concept of vital energy that runs through everything in the universe, including ourselves. This energy is called *qi*, or *chi*, and it connects us to everything. Qi is the energy that is the source for Qs.
- **Questioning:** Oftentimes we are so focused on finding solutions to problems that we fail to live the questioning journey. As we will see, questioning is a precursor to humility and readies you to receive Qs. Questioning in itself is revitalizing and necessary to progress in life.
- **Quest:** The most important quest in life is the journey to identify, discover, and experience the infusions of qualities virtues (Qs) you really want in life. *Quest* is another wonderful Q-word.

There is another important concept that is not exactly a *Q*-word but rather a *Q*-homophone—the concept of *cues*.

- **Cues:** One of the most important skills you will learn is to discern the messages that come from a source of wisdom that is beyond your normal consciousness. Those messages come in the form of cues that prompt thoughts or actions. Some call these hunches, gut feelings, or intuition. You will learn to discern and trust your intuitive natures. Cues that come from the human spirit come as soft cues.

## Qs: What Do You Really Want?

We should now understand that the letter *Q* is part of the Q-nexus, and before focusing on the nexus, let's take the opportunity to identify the Qs that you want.

## ACTIVITY #1: THE Qs YOU WANT

To formulate your own list of Qs, try the following exercise:

1. List five material or tangible things that you want in life. List practical, real, or imaginary items in the left column of the table below. For example, if you want an academic degree, a new romantic partner, new clothes, or a new car, list it.

2. In the second column, next to the desired tangible item, answer the question "Why do I want that?" You can reflect upon the list of Qs above or identify your own Qs. For example, you may want an education to feel power, confidence, wisdom, or worth. You may want a new romantic partner for companionship and love. You may want new clothes to feel valued, to belong, or to be comfortable. You may want a new car for feelings of safety, adventure, or for pleasure.

| Tangible Wants | Why I Want That? |
|---|---|
| Academic degree | To feel more confident and wise; to feel more powerful; to feel more self-worth |
| New car | To feel safer; to have more adventures |
| 1. | |
| 2. | |
| 3. | |
| 4. | |
| 5. | |
| 6. | |
| 7. | |
| 8. | |

You will hunger for these Qs throughout your life—the means to capture them will vary during life's journey. The richness and depth of the Qs you have listed makes the letter *Q* a meaningful symbol for the qualities and virtues that you desire. In essence, the Qs can be summarized as follows:

1. Tiny universal energy packets are the building blocks of life.
2. The energy packets are within us and within everything in the universe.
3. The universal energy packets infuse our souls, which energize the desired virtues and qualities we can feel (Qs). The Qs will guide and nurture us on our progressive quest to optimize our human experience.

For example, if you are having a troubling day and you feel stressed and discouraged, then the process will be for you to practice a skill that will allow you to access the energy units from the world around you. Perhaps you will just step outside in nature and realize that there are energy units in nature all around. As you practice some skills to feel the infusion of energy packets, you will feel the Qs you need for each moment. You may need peace, comfort, and calm. As you absorb the peaceful energy from nature and feel an infusion of the qualities (Qs) you need to handle the situation at hand, the Qs will help guide you to do what you should do to better the situation.

Other examples are:

- To venture into something new, you may need the Qs of courage and wisdom.
- To think through a difficult problem, you may need the Qs of peace and purpose.

These are examples of Qs and Q-infusions you may need (depending on the experience and the situation) from within yourself and from your environment to progress along the resilient journey.

This may be unclear now, but the skills and concepts will be explained throughout the book.

# WHY ADD "NEXUS"?

Nexus means *connection*. Q-nexus, then, is the experience of connecting to the universal energy packets, which results in feeling the Qs you really want. The feeling of the Q-nexus, or connection to the Qs, may come as a stirring moment of energy and hope. The connections may also come in a subtler sense of knowing that you are on the right path—a peaceful state. Consider the feelings as per the definitions of Q-nexus.

> The Q-nexus is the experience of resonating with desired virtues and qualities, being aware of their subtle companionship, and knowing that you are following a path of personal progression.

Some people experience the Q-nexus by feeling a sense of rightness and purpose throughout each day. Life is about progression, and the best way to progress is to acquire the Qs you want in life—confidence, wisdom, peace, joy, and so on. Many people feel themselves progressing as they steadily acquire Qs. The Q-nexus may come more forcefully as per the following definition.

> The Q-nexus is also the quickening or enlivening moment when infusions of qualities and virtues stir the soul, enabling one to progress through life's disruptions.

In times of decision making or despair, a jolt of inspiration fills your entire soul with meaning, or courage, or whatever Q you need. These quickening moments are almost magical as they fill your heart and mind with direction and the confidence to do what you need to do, or feel how you need to feel, based upon wisdom that is beyond your normal thinking. For a practical view of the Q-nexus, consider the following true story.

> Ruth was baking in the kitchen, and her ten-year-old son, Buzz, was helping. This was a great time to talk and laugh while baking homemade bread together. They were talking about funny things that had happened at school

and Cub Scouts. In the middle of the laughter, suddenly Ruth had a thought. *Where's Victor? I've got to find Victor!*

Victor was Buzz's little brother.

Buzz, enjoying the time with his mom, simply responded, "He took off and went outside somewhere." Buzz, not wanting to disturb the bonding moment, kept talking as though his mom had never asked the question.

Ruth felt the power of a mother's intuition and again asked Buzz with more power, "Do you know where Victor is?"

Buzz knew he had to respond when his mother's voice reached a certain tone—she was at that tone and beyond. "The last I knew, he was going to play Superman in the front yard," Buzz explained with some disappointment.

Ruth threw off her apron and bolted for the front door. As she opened the door, she looked quickly at the two large trees in the front yard. As she glanced at the shorter of the two trees, she caught a glimpse of Victor, who had climbed high into the tree, lunging out as if to fly. He had a sheet tied around his neck that served as his cape. As Victor flew from the tree branch, gravity brought a quick reality, and Victor fell through the branches. His makeshift cape caught on a branch, which broke his fall but at the same time served as a noose. Victor started choking and gagging as the cape tightened around his neck. Ruth rushed to the tree, supported Victor, and loosened the cape. As Victor ran into the house, shaken but relatively unharmed, Ruth began to tremble as she pondered, *What would have happened if I hadn't heeded my prompt?*

Why, in the middle of having quality time with Buzz, was Ruth prompted to find Victor? If she had waited five more minutes, Victor may have died. You can have access to prompts with significant power to change your course of action, guiding you along a better pathway. The guidance, direction, and insights are the Q-infusions during the experience of the Q-nexus.

## SIX TRUTHS OR POSTULATES

Resilience and resiliency are based upon several truths or assumptions. These truths provide the foundation for the resilience experiences that are included in the meat of the book. The six truths in life are also called *postulates*. A postulate, as it pertains to thriving through life challenges, is a universal truth that is innate and consistent with all people. The assumed truths are logical and congruent with common sense. It will be important to embrace these postulates as the foundation for all the training. The six postulates we will treat in this book that are foundational in the acquisition of resilience are (1) innateness, (2) resonation, (3) progression, (4) faith/belief, (5) agency, and (6) love.

## 1. THE POSTULATE OF INNATENESS

A constant among the many academic, philosophical, and religious thoughts is that housed within each person is a potential to access strength and insight well beyond normal capacities. In psychology, Carl Jung spoke of a collective unconscious mind that housed the wisdom of the ages in each person. In Eastern philosophies, the thought is that we are walking in a sea of energy and insight as described as *qi*. In physics, we are part of a sea of energy and wisdom that fills multiple universes called *strings*. In theism, many believe that God's Spirit fills the immensity of space and that our spirits can access his spirit. The postulate of innateness suggests that we can have access to the magnificent sea of wisdom.

Our conscious mind is a tiny percentage of our total potential capacity. We have the potential, through different sources, to access insights, strengths, and talents that are housed within us. We also have the mechanism and potential skills to access the truths in a universe of energy, wisdom, and strength. Here, in essence, is the postulate of innateness.

The solution to every problem, the means to every dream,
and all that anyone ever needed, wanted, or hoped for resides
in the sea of energy, vitality, enlightenment, and power that
dwells within you and within the world around you.

## 2. THE POSTULATE OF RESONATION

The language of the universe is really in a form of vibrations or frequencies (Greene 2003). If you want to know a truth, then you will vibrate at the same frequency as the truth. Not everyone resonates to the same truth. Perhaps the best way to understand how resonation works comes from a personal account of my elementary school years.

> My first-grade teacher was Miss Slack. One day, she stood in front of the class and talked about sound. She struck a tuning fork and asked if we could hear it. We could. She then explained how the sound waves were making our eardrums vibrate, which transmitted messages to our brains. To make the point that sound was something real, she again struck the tuning fork. She then brought up a second tuning fork that was not vibrating. She placed the new tuning fork about six inches from the vibrating fork. The second tuning fork started to vibrate just by being next to the vibrating tuning fork. She stopped the vibrations from the first turning fork, and the second one kept the sound alive.

When trying to make good decisions in your life, the best choice is the one to which you resonate. You will feel the rightness of your choice with soft gentle vibrations in your soul much like the second tuning fork. Another detail of Miss Slack's tuning fork experiment was that the second tuning fork was the same size as the first. If the tuning fork had been bigger or smaller, the second tuning fork may not have vibrated. The metaphor for us suggests that we are walking in a world of wonderful truths, but we must be in a state of readiness to receive the truth in its fullness. If we are smaller than the source of truths (low self-worth), then we will not be able to handle all the truths that come from the vibrations. If we are too big, relying on our "expert" mind and conscious logic, and think we know more than the truth, the vibrations will have little impact.

Within each of the experiences in this book, as we talk about the resiliency process, there will be opportunities to resonate to the rightness of the experiences. The postulate of resonation will be referenced throughout the book. Here, in essence, is the postulate of resonation:

> Every truth and every best answer will be disclosed through the universal and subtle vibrational language of resonation.

The how-tos of resonation will be discussed in more detail in Experience 13.

## 3. THE POSTULATE OF PROGRESSION

Progression states that through Q-nexus experiences, you can progress throughout a lifetime. Progression is the experience of harnessing wonderful qualities and virtues, over time, even into your senior years. When you have positive experiences, you can harvest confidence, love, and wisdom to keep within your treasury of Qs.

Unfortunately, you will not be able to progress in all dimensions of your life. Physically, the difficult reality is that you will peak at midlife or earlier, and, as you enter your later years, your physical body will begin to get slower and become weaker. So physical progression throughout your life is not really feasible. Figure 1 shows physical progression, and at midlife, we see decline.

**Figure 1. Physical Progression**

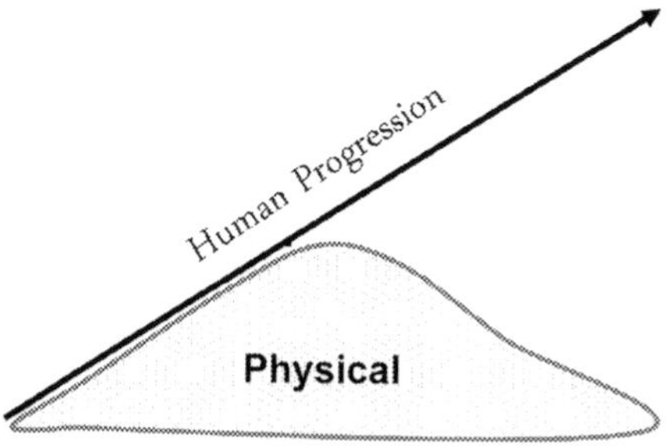

Human Progression

**Physical**

Mentally, you learn very quickly in the early years. Again, as we age, learning becomes slower. It is difficult to make a case for intellectual progression throughout a lifetime if we just think of our learning capacity.

### Figure 2. Intellectual Progression

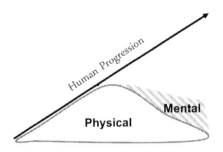

So how do we progress throughout a lifetime? The answer is in the infusion of Qs. These might be called spiritual qualities. Consider the following questions:

> Can you ever have enough peace? (Peace is learning over time to be happy with who you are, living within your chosen moral framework, and fulfilling your purpose in life.)

> Can you ever have enough integrity? (Integrity is having contentment that you are doing what you say you will do and "walking your talk.")

> Can you ever have enough happiness?

> Can you ever have enough wisdom? (Each life experience brings some wisdom about life—if you improve your life, your wisdom will increase.)

You can continue to ask the same questions for all the Qs. The postulate of progression suggests that the way to progress throughout your life is to harvest as many Qs as you can—to have as many Q-nexus experiences as you can. The process of accessing and experiencing the Q-nexus, the infusion of the Qs, can and should occur throughout life.

Many of us have had experiences visiting with loved ones in their final days of life. Some may be bitter and angry, but others show Qs in their countenances. You can see wisdom, compassion, caring, and peace in their eyes. They are focused on the happiness of their surviving loved ones. The infusion of Qs is the means to experience progression throughout a lifetime.

**Figure 3. Spiritual Progression**

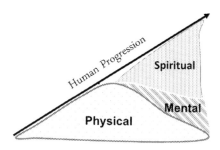

In essence, the postulate of progression is this:

> Adventure upon adventure, wisdom upon wisdom, compassion upon compassion, and Qs upon Qs are requisite to a life of fulfillment, happiness, and enchantment.

## 4. THE POSTULATE OF FAITH/BELIEF

All the good ideas, all the desires, and all the good intentions will fall by the wayside if you do not have the faith or belief that you can make them happen. The first step into a new experience may be the most challenging and requires a strong belief or faith to take the step. Leaps of faith are the means to access the desired Qs.

The concept of faith has been an important postulate for centuries as evidenced in spiritual literature throughout history. The concept of belief or faith is evident in the Eastern philosophies and religions. In modern times, Robert K. Merton (1948) coined the term *self-fulfilling prophecy* and described it as "a process whereby a belief or expectation, correct or incorrect, affects the outcome of a situation or the way a person or a group will behave." One of the most powerful concepts to help people to change their behaviors comes from Albert Bandura (1982), who identified the concept of self-efficacy as "our belief in our ability to succeed in certain situations." More recently, a popular theme in self-help literature identifies the concept of intentions (Dyer 2004). Dyer summarizes this concept by a quote he takes from Neville Goddard: "Make your future dream a present fact, by assuming the feeling of the wish fulfilled."

In essence, the postulate of faith is as follows:

> The art of faith is initiated with resonation (confirming rightness), is followed by belief (creating a vision of accomplishment), is loaded with courage (taking the leap of faith), and is ripened through action (doing). If faith can move a mountain, you will need to start digging and believe that a magical force will pitch in to help haul the dirt.

## 5. THE POSTULATE OF AGENCY

We learn from many theories and philosophies that we have the potential to grow into someone who will feel fulfilled and will be able to touch the lives of many people. You are essentially growing into an energy field that will guide you, through resonation, into what your best self will be. Yet, with all the subtle and soft yearnings and driving forces, your mind can override all those yearnings. You have "agency," or choice, not to follow the "best" path but an alternative path that lacks progression. You choose what you will become. In essence, the postulate of agency is as follows:

> The mind is charged with the challenge of discerning between a progressive path with heart (harvesting Qs) or a stagnating and draining path of shadows. In a world of opposing forces, you have the power to choose your destiny.

## 6. THE POSTULATE OF LOVE

To follow a path that will be fulfilling and happy, we need love. Love, in a nonemotional sense, means connection or nexus. A common theme throughout the Q-nexus adventure of growing and thriving is the postulate that you should love yourself, love others, and love a force beyond normal capacity. Love means to be connected to all your innate potentials and motivations. Beyond being connected to self, you want to be synergistically connected to others and be engaged in common causes. You also want to be connected to a strength beyond normal consciousness (spiritual source of strength) that will help you make happen what you need to make happen. In essence, the postulate of love is as follows:

> Loving (connecting to) your true self with all your subtle progressive yearnings allows you to create genuine loving (connecting) relationships under the guidance and love (connection to) of universal wisdom.

## THE Q-NEXUS: THE APPLIED THEORY OF EVERYTHING

On a personal note, I want to mention that since I began to study resiliency and later resilience at the university, I used to joke that the metatheory of resilience and resiliency that I wrote for the *Journal of Clinical Psychology* in 2002 was the "applied theory of everything." Initially, I was playing off the string theory that physicist Brian Greene proposed to be the "theory of everything" (Greene 2003). As the years have passed, it has become clear to me that the Q-nexus, which embraces both resilience and resiliency, is the "applied theory of everything." There is a best way to deal with any life problem, opportunity, or challenge. The Q-nexus is the mechanism to discover that best way. Experience 1 in the next chapter will focus on the resilient journey—the journey that leads to the Q-nexus and the infusion of Qs.

# In Summary

- The Q-nexus is the experience of resonating to desired virtues and qualities that comfort and guide you in your life.
- Qs are the qualities and virtues you really want, and nexus is the connection to sources for those qualities and virtues.
- The Q-nexus is the infusion of those qualities you really want.
- The Q-nexus experiences are often subtle, but they are also powerful moments that give you guidance and direction in life.
- Innateness: You have within you a vast reservoir of identities, skills, and potentials that are within you.
- Progression: To be fulfilled and progress, you need to harvest Qs throughout your life.
- Resonation: Truths, rightness, and directions in life will be accompanied by energizing and warm vibrations.
- Faith/Belief: There is tremendous power when you have strong intentions and faith to progress.
- Agency: You have agency in your life choices and your attitudes.
- Love: You will find joy through love (connections) to yourself, to others, and to your source of spiritual strength.

# PART 2

# THE RESILIENT JOURNEY

Resiliency is the process and experience of being
disrupted by life events, adversity, or challenges, and,
in the humbling trough of introspective enlightenment,
accessing innate self-mastering strengths to grow
stronger through the disruption.

I don't expect you to grasp the full meaning of the introductory
definition of resiliency, but by the end of part 2, you will. The
definition is basically saying that things happen to you by choice or
through unexpected events, but that each time "stuff happens," you can
become more resilient. Let's start with your story of resilience.

Your life story follows a predictable plot. Simply, it is a journey of
challenges and opportunities for growth. When you understand the
resiliency process, or what we call the resilient journey, you will be able
to feel a sense of control regarding the outcomes of your life story. This
experience will describe resiliency as a nine-step journey that will allow
you to prepare for life's disruptions—both the ones you plan and the ones
that blindside you.

It may be easy to recall times when you willingly took on new
challenges, experienced disruptions, and had positive outcomes. You can
reflect upon common events, such as going to school, taking a new job,
getting married, or meeting a new friend. This is a choice, because you
had the agency to make the choice, you were able to learn, expand your
worldview, and likely learn new skills.

Perhaps it is harder to think of times when unwanted disruptions led to positive growth. With your first fender bender, you learned how you work through the process of negotiating with an insurance company to get your car repaired. When you have had unexpected demands placed upon you at work or home, you have learned to manage and systematically plan your way through the demands. When you had unexpected health care problems and accompanying bills, you learned to save for unexpected financial demands in the future.

As you learn about the resiliency process, you will see that even when devastating life events occur, such as the death of a loved one, you still have the power to find peace and other Qs in those difficult times. Your life perspectives and choices impact your story's potential for a positive ending.

# RESILIENCY AND RESILIENCY MAPPING

> *Resiliency, with its accompanying skills of resiliency mapping, is the experience and choice of planning how you will thrive through life's disruptions.*

In the preface, I shared with you a personal story of getting hit by a car, and I gave some hint as to the nature of the resilient journey. Within Experience 1, we will learn the steps and experiences of the resiliency process or model (Richardson 2002 and Richardson et al. 1990) and how to do resiliency mapping. Resiliency is a process that initially will result in being disrupted by life events, adversity, or challenges. The resulting humbling trough that is often felt as hurt, loss, or fear can turn to introspective enlightenment, allowing you to access innate self-mastering strengths to grow stronger through the disruption.

The resiliency process, or resilient journey, can be described in nine phases. It is somewhat complex, so we can go through this a step at a time.

# STEP 1: ECOBIOPSYCHOSPIRITUAL HOMEOSTASIS (COMFORT ZONE)

Homeostasis is a moment in time when you have adapted to your life situation. *Homeostasis* is a fancy term that suggests balance and normalcy. It is a state when you have adapted to your body, mind, spirit, and life situation. Homeostasis, metaphorically, is like preparing to sail to a wonderful destination, but at this point, you are anchored at the dock in a safe harbor, not going anywhere. Let's start to look at the resiliency process model.

The first dotted arrow on the resiliency map reflects the postulate of progression. As we have already discussed, your life is an opportunity to progress throughout your lifetime, harvesting Qs along the way. Let's start with homeostasis, which some people refer to as a *comfort zone*. In figure 4, it is labeled *ecobiopsychospiritual homeostasis*. Don't be bothered by the twenty-five-cent word that introduces the first stage; you'll understand by the end of this section. Homeostasis—a comfort zone—can be applied to each dimension of your life and is shown as the first part of the resilient journey in this figure.

**Figure 4. Ecobiopsychospiritual Homeostasis**

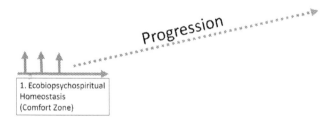

Progression

1. Ecobiopsychospiritual
Homeostasis
(Comfort Zone)

Let's break ecobiopsychospiritual down into its component parts: *eco, bio, psycho,* and *spiritual.*

- ecological homeostasis
- biological homeostasis
- psychological homeostasis
- spiritual homeostasis

**Ecological homeostasis** suggests an adaptation to your environment. You live where you live, work where you work, and play where you play. You have chosen or have been compelled to choose, to live in a certain place. The environment may be enriching or less than enriching, but you have adapted to it.

**Biological homeostasis** indicates that you have adapted to your state of physical health and appearance. You look like you look. You may be underweight or overweight. You may have certain physical conditions to which you have adapted, such as a sore back from an old injury. You are used to your physical talents, such as knowing you have a good singing voice. You may have adapted to your level of physical coordination or fitness. You have adapted to your physical appearance.

**Psychological (intellectual) homeostasis** implies that you know what you know at this point in time. You have learned enough math to do a budget. You have learned to read. You have learned enough to perform duties as a student or an employee. You have learned to use electronic devices. You have developed a personality that best helps you in living your life. At this moment in time, you know what you know. This is your intellectual state of homeostasis.

**Spiritual homeostasis** also portrays a state of adaptation. Simplistically, we could say that you have adjusted to your beliefs. If you have identified a source of spiritual strength, you are content with your degree of closeness and intimacy with that source. Your ability (or inability) to access the Qs that come from that source is consistent. You will learn in the next experience about the motivational and driving forces that really make up who you are. If you combine your ecological, biological, psychological, and spiritual states of homeostasis, you end up with *ecobiopsychospiritual homeostasis*, the first phase of the resiliency process.

It is important to recognize that because of your previous life experiences, you have learned to cope and thrive through many of life's changes and challenges. With each challenge, you have collected resilient qualities (Qs) and developed physical and mental skills. In the past, you have had experiences that produced compassion, courage, and persistence. You can reflect upon those times and incorporate the wisdom you gained into your state of homeostasis. Going through these stages, I am again going to reference the traumatic accident that I shared in the preface of this book.

Referencing my personal homeostasis before my accident, I had always dreamed about being a professor. I remember as a young man going to college for the first time. I walked on campus and felt a resonating feeling of home and of my future. I have loved every campus I had ever visited. Now I was at the University of Utah, not only teaching but also happy to be a department chairperson. I worked with great faculty, and I loved my students. I had just built my own home, married, and had four great kids, ages one to ten. I was doing a lot of service work in my church.

## Step 2: Life Events, Stressors, and Challenges

*Life events* are experiences that come from external sources or your perception of external stressors. Many life events are stressors that blindside you and force you out of your adapted state of homeostasis. For instance, you may need to help someone in a crisis, deal with a broken household item, accomplish additional work, face an argument with a loved one, experience hurt or injury, or even receive an unexpected (and unwanted!) bill. These life events often require you to change your plans.

Life events can also be positive. For instance, if someone offers you tickets to a musical production, you still have to deal with a change in schedule, but the life event is a good one. A friend may call and want to get together—a good event that changes your plans. You may choose to venture into a new life event, such as taking a computer class or even going back to school.

Change and challenges may occur socially (someone wants your help), ecologically (there is a strange smell in your home), biologically (you trip and hurt yourself), psychologically (you don't know how to fix your computer), and spiritually (you do something outside of your moral framework). Life events are usually generated by outside sources. But sometimes an event is happening and we misunderstand the event. We assume it is something that will affect our lives, but in reality, it does not. For example, a boss at work begins to describe a difficult project, and you are assuming that it will derail your plans to work on another project. You worry and stew over how this is going to affect your life. You are experiencing a disruption. In the end, you learn that the boss assigns the project to someone else. Your disruption was your own misperception.

> In my personal story, the obvious and unforeseen experience of being hit by a car was the event that propelled me out of my state of ecological, biological, psychological, and spiritual homeostasis.

**Figure 5. Life Events, Stressors, and Challenges**

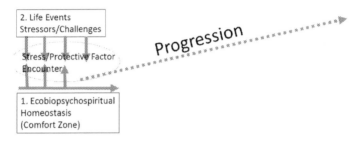

Figure 5 shows the downward arrows for the life events (#2) and then shows arrows that point upward that represent resilient qualities (Qs). These upward arrows are skills and protective factors you have developed already in your life that have allowed you to be in homeostasis or in a comfort zone. If you have coped with similar life experiences in the past, then you may not be affected by the event. For example, you may remember the first time you went to class in high school. This was a new experience, and you were nervous and unskilled. By the time the class had met several times, you had adapted and became comfortable going to class. You were no longer bothered by the experience of going to class because you had developed skills through experience. You gained resilient qualities of confidence and understanding.

Notice that there is an arrow coming down from life events that has no opposing arrow. This represents an event that you have not encountered previously and for which you have no experience. The encounter between the new experience and your lack of coping skills for the experience will result in change. The change may be an opportunity or it may be something you didn't want to happen. Either way, you will be disrupted from your normal comfort zone.

## STEP 3: VENTURING

Venturing is the experience of leaving homeostasis (comfort zone) in light of the life event. You find yourself in a new experience. Venturing, whether good or bad, is to take the leap of faith into new territory. Figure 6 shows a downward arrow that launches the resilient journey by venturing (#3).

Venturing by choosing to take a leap of faith is the most desirable means to leave homeostasis. Venture is your creation and of your choosing. Venturing emerges from your innate resilient drives to progress and improve your life experience. You may have innate drives to play, to learn, to serve, and to have new experiences. If you respond to resilient cues, then you will find yourself venturing and taking leaps of faith into new adventures. Venturing may remind you of your childhood, when you dared to do so many things.

Sometimes your venture begins not because you choose to venture but because you are blindsided by life events as described above. You are pushed out of homeostasis because you got a flat tire on your car or a child misbehaved as per the examples in Step #2.

Living out of character is the experience of leaving homeostasis because your thoughts and actions conflict with your moral sense of what is right and wrong. For example, if you lie, cheat, or steal, which are actions that likely violate your moral framework, you will find yourself leaving the peace of homeostasis and venturing into the emotional and disruptive turmoil of guilt.

**Figure 6. Venturing**

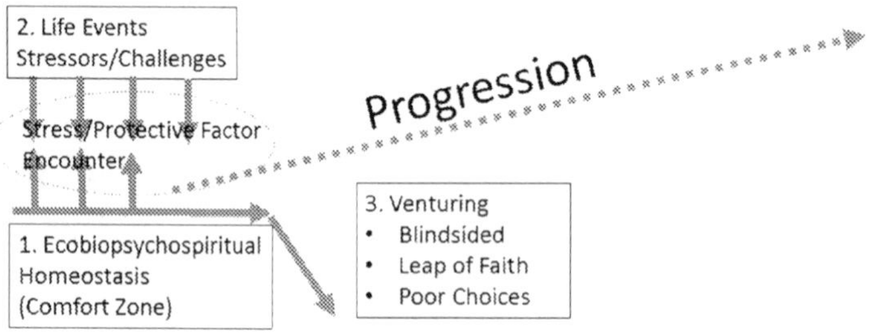

# STEP 4: DISRUPTIONS

The outcome of being blindsided by life events, leaping into new adventures, or stepping outside of your moral framework is disruption. As you leave homeostasis and find yourself in uncharted waters, a range of mixed emotions may surface. Stage #4 of the resilient journey shows a disruption after having been taken from your state of homeostasis as shown in figure 7.

**Figure 7. Disruptions**

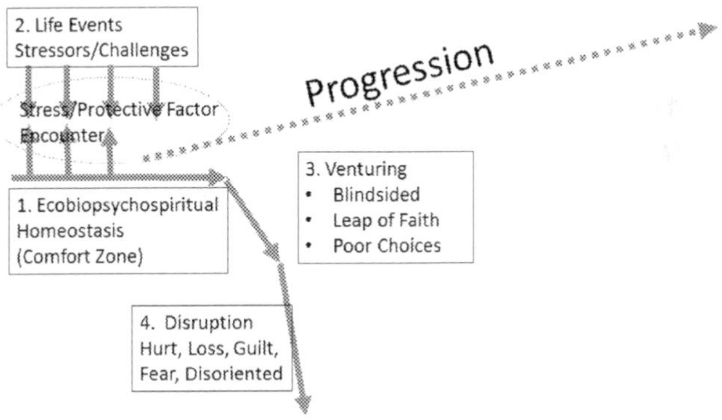

When blindsided by life events, your disruption will be sensed as hurt, loss, guilt, fear, or some other sense of disorientation. In disagreements with loved ones, you feel the loss of closeness you had prior to the disruption. You may feel a loss of predictability or comfort when you move to a new place. Even when unexpected opportunities come your way, you still feel some discomfort in having to change plans, although the potential to receive positive Qs outweighs the negative.

When venturing into new experiences, you plan for positive outcomes but often have a sense of fear or discomfort as you engage in something new. You may feel the Qs of excitement in the new adventure, but at the same time, you feel some loss of homeostasis.

If you choose to think or behave outside of your moral framework, your disruption will be experienced as guilt. You will sense the loss of energy and excitement in your life that generally accompanies you.

There is a dynamic interplay between life's disruptions and your state of homeostasis. If you have already established the Qs of confidence, hope, and adventure, then some of the disruptions you experience may seem insignificant. If the experience is entirely new, then the disruption is more likely to have an impact on you. My story continues with the disruption.

> After waking up from the coma and seeing the long screws protruding from my legs and realizing that I had lost two weeks of life, the academic part of me felt guilty for wasting so much time. I was writing a book and had deadlines. Then the reality of my situation began to sink in, and I realized that I had almost lost my life. I then realized what my family had been through for two weeks not knowing if I would live or die or if I would be able to be normal. The thought broke my heart, and I wept and wept alone in my hospital room. When the kids came up to see me, they were nervous and unsure of how to act. Before the accident, they would run to me and we would wrestle, joke, and play. Now I didn't look good—I didn't even look like their dad. I had been beaten up so badly by the car. The children were confused and didn't know whether to hug me or not because it might inflict more pain. Several thoughts, emotions, and questions were running through my mind. I was trying to wrap my arms around what had just happened. Could I have avoided being hit by the car? Everyone was going through so much emotional pain. *What have I done? I was so stupid to get hit by the car. Why had I inflicted so much emotional pain on everyone? I am supposed to be the helper, not the helped. I am not a victim. Why is this happening to me? Will I ever feel better? Will I ever be normal again? What is my life going to be like?*

## STEP 5: READINESS SKILLS FOR THE Q-NEXUS

When disruptions occur, you seek insights that come from beyond your normal capacity. To receive these insights, you will need to be in a state of openness or humility—the desired outcome of disruptions. In your quest for strength, insight, and enhanced capacity, you first need to be receptive to insights. Figure 8 (#5) represents the next stage of the resilient journey.

## Figure 8. Readiness Skills

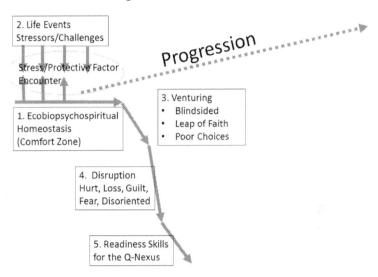

In traumatic situations, it is a natural process to be humbled, and it is natural to be receptive to insights. When taking leaps of faith, sometimes we need to learn techniques, practices, and skills that help you prepare yourself to receive answers to your questions. These help to experience emotional readiness and openness. Such practices as meditation, art therapy, music therapy, journaling, storytelling, aerobic exercise, and reading inspiring literature can help you to attain a state of openness to ready yourself to receive insights. The academic literature is beginning to cite more and more studies demonstrating the effectiveness of tai chi, yoga, mindfulness, and other modalities in healing and providing insights. At the same time, the ability to practice these techniques requires humility, openness, receptivity, a beginner's mind and heart. Experience 11 will discuss these techniques in more depth.

> I knew I was in trouble. I got rid of my natural professorial mind-set of questioning everything and instead listened carefully to the instructions the doctors gave me. I had never been in a situation like this, and I had an open heart and mind, desperate to get better. More importantly, I pondered. I prayed. I believed. I sought peace.

# STEP 6: THE Q-NEXUS (RESONATION AND QUICKENING)

In the trough of disruption, you will find yourself in the optimal state of openness and humility, primed to experience the Q-nexus. Figure 9 shows how the resilient journey has progressed.

**Figure 9. The Q-Nexus**

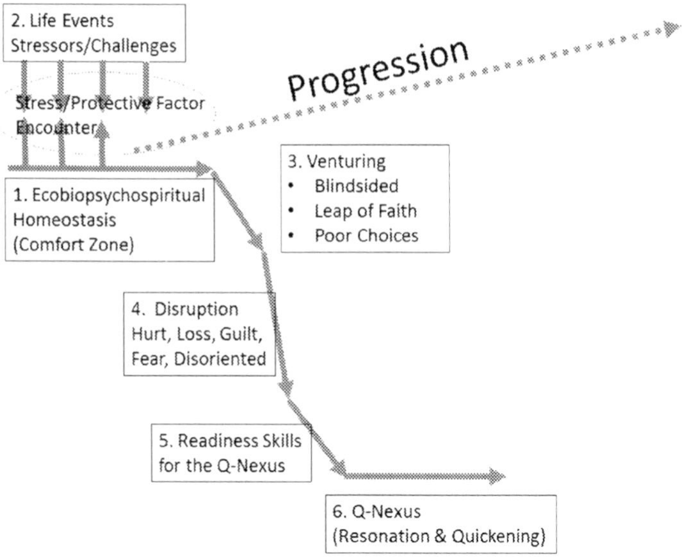

The postulate of resonation, which was described briefly in the introduction, is the key to experiencing the Q-nexus. While resonation is a gentle prompt that lets you know your thoughts and actions are on the right path, quickening is more compelling. As you will learn, quickening is a sudden insight, a burst of understanding, or a gestalt. Pure Q-nexus experiences, if accompanied with the peace and joy of rightness, are significant. This is a moment of synchronicity when everything comes together. This is a time when you feel the infusion of knowing what to do and how to do it. This is a moment of guidance and direction. You are filled with confidence and courage. It may come in the form of an impactful dream. It may be feelings that come in response to a fervent prayer. It may be a moment of clarity or insightfulness. These are the moments when you feel the infusions of Qs, the qualities and virtues you really want in life.

After I had started to think more clearly after the head trauma I had experienced, I moved past the emotion of fear. I felt a calm resonating feeling that I would be okay. I imagined myself going through rigorous training, much like my years in high school and college athletics. I was going to be a rehabilitation warrior! I imagined myself becoming a better father. I had a good relationship with the children, but now being close to them became a quest. At the same time, the long-term vision of having my area of academic expertise change from just stress management to developing courses and doing research about the resilient journey became clear. These insights filled my soul, and I could not escape them. My life was to be one of doing resiliency teaching.

## STEP 7: IDENTITY FORMATION

Quickening from the Q-nexus gives you the insights and peace to move forward. With each new Q-nexus experience, you have the opportunity to create a new identity. You can see the continuation of the resilient journey in figure 10.

**Figure 10. Identity Formation**

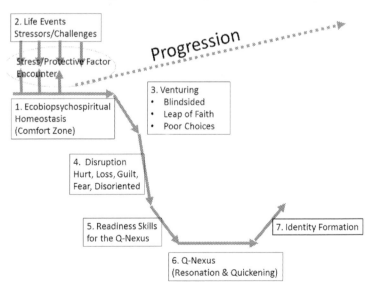

41

The new identity is one that is a product of the insights you received from the Q-nexus. It is an identity that is within you and part of who you really are and is necessary to fulfill your potential. It is the identity that will most effectively deal with the life event or venture you face. You may need to discover the warrior inside of you, or perhaps the peacemaker. You may need to find the teacher within you, or perhaps the student that will thrive most effectively. You may need to discover the leader, or find the follower. The specifics of how to form an identity will be detailed in Experience 13.

> I had three primary identities I was creating. One was a short-term rehabilitation warrior. With each new exercise, I imagined myself doing more. The second identity was as an ideal family man. Thirdly, I created a resiliency researcher and teacher.

## STEP 8: SELF-MASTERY

Once an identity is formed, it may take a few moments or perhaps days and weeks to have that identity become part of your nature. In the resilient journey, you can see in this figure how self-mastery is the quality that brings you out of the disruptive trough.

### Figure 11. Self-Mastery

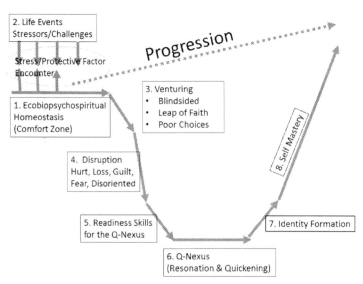

Experiences 14 and 15 will describe how self-mastery embraces quickening moments of enlightenment and uses them to power you through the creation of new identities and resilient reintegration. Self-mastery embraces the powerful qualities of persistence, drive, and a strong work ethic. It is the ability to overcome undesirable behaviors and thoughts that impede progression. Self-mastery persists until the task of personal change is complete.

> I wanted to go home from the hospital. Once the doctors discharged me, I went home and pushed the limits. I scooted around on my bottom going up and down stairs because I couldn't walk. I strengthened and trained my arms to help me become more ambulatory. I tried to walk every day. I would force myself to take one step at a time, and I began to be somewhat mobile.
>
> The third identity I was creating was that of a resiliency researcher. I kept analyzing what I was doing and what I could do to rehabilitate faster—in body, mind, and spirit. Life itself became a laboratory. I began to review all the literature I could find on resiliency.

After quickening occurs and you know the identity you should assume, you have a choice of three different outcomes, or ways to reintegrate. Understanding these outcomes and thinking about "what could be" will help you gain perspective on your present situation.

## STEP 9: REINTEGRATION

With insight received from the Q-nexus and the drive and persistence of self-mastery, you can begin to celebrate the creation of a new identity. For example, you can transform a self-centered identity into an altruistic identity. You can change from being a sedentary person into a physically active person. Whatever identity formation you have created and is now part of you, you have the option of becoming that identity. You can see it, feel it, and know how to live it, but without persistent effort in the direction of resilient reintegration, it is easy to give up and go back to your old ways.

If you give up, you deny yourself the opportunity to grow through the experience. You can consider the choices (9A, 9B, or 9C) as you again revisit the final stage of the resilient journey.

**Figure 12. Reintegration**

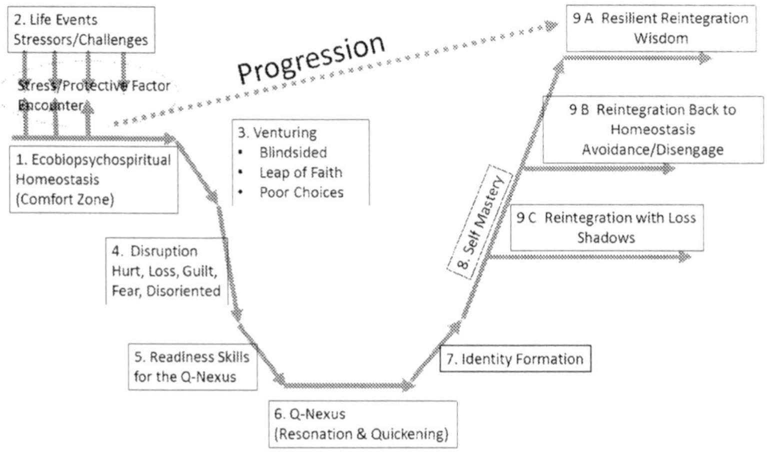

## OPTION 9A: RESILIENT REINTEGRATION

Resilient reintegration is the desired outcome of the resiliency journey. It is learning and growing through adversity and life events. You create a new identity that will thrive through the experience. Optimally, you will embrace the change, opportunity, or life event and gain Qs from the experience. If you choose to persist in the new identity, you will harvest qualities of resilient reintegration. Resilient reintegration implies that in the aftermath of disruptions, you will rebound stronger with more skills. This path enables you to progress in life. Each new experience helps you learn and grow. The reality is that you have several new experiences every day, and with each, you have the choice to gain some wisdom. Life is about a variety of human experiences—some familiar, some comfortable, some enlivening, some disruptive. As described before, resiliency is about bouncing back stronger from challenges or disruptions. Every disruption can potentially result in wisdom. We grow in wisdom and progress throughout life as we live it resiliently. This is shown in figure 13 as progression—wisdom upon wisdom with each disruption. You can also see that to resiliently reintegrate, the capacity enhancing quality is self-mastery. You will need to persist, overcome the temptation to quit, and thrive until lessons are learned. Resilient reintegration is to persist until your new identity is part of who you are and you can reflect upon what you have accomplished.

> The year following the accident, I stepped down as department chair and began to focus on the study of resiliency. Resilience and resiliency have been my professional passion since that time. I continue to receive insightful Qs as I learn and grow from following the guiding path I received years ago in my coma. I am grateful to have recovered and enjoy an active physical life. I am so grateful to be in a position to try to touch the lives of my students.

## OPTION 9B: REINTEGRATION BACK TO HOMEOSTASIS (COMFORT ZONE)

Reintegration back to the comfort zone is to ignore the insight and direction you received during the Q-nexus (Step #6 on the model). You envisioned an identity and knew it would make you stronger. Then in the follow-up, you lost the vision or decided it was too difficult and did not follow through to resilient reintegration. You may have even tried for a while but then disengaged as shown in the figure. You decided to just get past the experience and not embrace the life lesson. You simply returned to what is comfortable.

Reintegration back to the comfort zone is not always an option. You may have had an injury and continue to experience chronic physical pain. You may have divorced. You cannot go back to the comfort zone. But you can grow from the experience or recover with loss. Each time you "just get past it" without growth, you will stagnate and thwart your progression in life. If a similar experience happens again, you will not have the experience or resilient qualities to prevent disruptions a second time.

# OPTION 9C: REINTEGRATION WITH LOSS (SHADOWS)

Sometimes you learn what you should do and the identity you want to have, but you choose not to do it. Perhaps it seems like too much work or you just don't like to change. In the process of avoiding the new identity, you give up. You give up Qs as you lose confidence, hope, courage, and your positive self-esteem. When the Qs leave, they are often replaced by secondary emotions of bitterness or anger. We call these *shadows.* Oftentimes when we go against what we know will be good for us, we get angry with ourselves and project that onto the world around us. We have caught a vision of what could be, from the Q-nexus experience, and then give up and become disgruntled.

Some people skip past the enlivening moments of the Q-nexus stage, and rather than taking time to ponder the riches of the new experience or challenge, they instead move quickly from the hurt and loss of disruptions to shadows like anger. "If they hurt me, then I will hurt them" is the mind-set, totally ignoring the opportunity to learn from life's disruptions. Instead of acting wisely as per resilient reintegration, they reintegrate with loss.

## PROGRESSION, STAGNATION, OR DIGRESSION

The next figure shows how each of the three choices of reintegration influence your progression in life. When you choose to learn and grow from your disruptions, you will experience progression. Insights, wisdom, knowledge, skills, and strengths can be built upon previous insights, wisdom, knowledge, skills, and strengths. Progression can happen daily as well as via extended experiences over time.

If you choose to just get past disruptions and attempt to return to homeostasis, you will experience stagnation. You get insights about ways to better fulfill your potential but choose not to. Again, you can see this on figure 13 as *stagnation.*

If you continue to lose Qs because of failed attempts to progress, you begin to lose hope, confidence, and esteem. You quit trying and become bitterer and even more withdrawn and unhappy. Reintegration with loss is shown in the figure as digression or emptiness (losing Qs) upon emptiness (losing more Qs). It can quickly become a negative feedback loop or a negative spiral.

**Figure 13. Progression, Stagnation, or Digression**

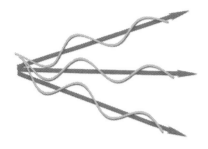

## PUZZLE METAPHOR

We can look at progression as a worldview puzzle that begins at birth. As you enter the world, you experience your first disruption—the change from the watery and warm comfort of the womb to the world of air and cold. The first piece of your life puzzle after birth is now all of a sudden, you are having to use your lungs to breathe. You meet Mom and Dad (two new pieces). You continue to be bombarded by new pieces of input from the external world and internal world that disrupt and reform your worldview puzzle. By the time you leave the hospital, you already have been disrupted with many pieces added to your worldview. You have added the experiences of being wrapped in a blanket, seeing nurses, viewing strange surroundings, and being put in a car in order to go home. Then more and more pieces of the world are thrown at you. You ride in a car for the first time as you ride home. You are greeted by new family members. You are placed in your new room. You learn that when you cry, you get attention, and another piece of your worldview puzzle falls into place. Each of these disruptions requires a subsequent reintegration. Your worldview gets bigger and bigger, and you learn to negotiate life with new skills and insights.

As you try to navigate through life, you will continue to have disruptions. In childhood, your disruptions were learning to play, to make friends, and to study for school. As adults, you learned a trade or role in life through repeated disruptions, but in the process you acquired skills you didn't know before the disruption. Each experience is a learning disruption that you can choose to have as part of your worldview of life. Conversely, many experiences you can forget and choose not to learn and not have as a part of your life. Without growing or progressing, your worldview doesn't change. If you become bitter and angry, your worldview becomes smaller—not by experience but by the loss of Qs.

## Jake and Suzie Example

To put this model into a real-life situation, let me tell you a story of Jake and Suzie.

> When Jake and Suzie got married, Jake worked as a teller at a bank, and Suzie worked at a popular clothing store for women. The only argument the couple ever had was over finances. At the end of each month, they would overspend a few dollars, and it would result in a blaming and denying discussion for not living within the budget. After the argument was resolved, they would kiss and make up. This went on for a long time. Jake took a higher-paying position as a manager at the bank, and Suzie was also promoted to be a manager at the clothing store. Even with a higher income, the monthly financial arguments continued. Note that at the end of each argument, they would kiss and make up but did not make any changes in their financial planning. They reintegrated back to the comfort zone—and learned nothing from the disruption. Finally, one day, Suzie said to Jake, "I don't want to argue over finances ever again." Jake, in jest, said, "What are we going to do at the end of the month if we don't argue over finances?" Jake and Suzie spent a Saturday wandering in the park, discussing options and brainstorming solutions. They finally decided to split their accounts into three different areas—one for Jake, one for Suzie, and one for both. The "both" account was for living expenses, and then each had his or her own account. This is not that much of a revolutionary budget plan, but the result was that they rarely ever argued over finances again—they resiliently reintegrated. Jake and Suzie surfaced with new identities as more responsible budgeters.

In Jake and Suzie's scenario, you can see that for years they reintegrated back to the comfort zone. Finally, they reintegrated resiliently. The option that could have happened would be the choice to attack each other's character during the arguments. They could call each other names and blame each other for the financial problems. They could cite the other person's irresponsibility or express their distrust. Qs would be lost, and the relationship could digress and become dysfunctional—reintegration with loss.

## PERSPECTIVES FROM THE RESILIENCY MODEL

The resilient journey is more complex than it appears. Every dimension of your life is accompanied by a resilient journey; the more dimensions you have, the more resilient journeys you will take. Consider the following resilient journey perspectives:

Multiple Roles: Each role that you have in life could be mapped onto a model of the resiliency process as shown in figure 14. X1, X2, and X3 will represent a different role or facet of your life. Each $X$ is in a different place on the resiliency map. For example, each $X$ could represent the following:

- X1 is the case of a disagreement with a family member. Let's assume that you are on the back end of the disagreement, and you have recognized through the Q-nexus experience that you need to be more compassionate and understanding. You have rehearsed what your new compassionate identity will look like. Now, with this disagreement, you are on the road to resilient reintegration at the point of self-mastery.
- X2 is another facet of your life. At this moment in time, for example, you are really happy at your work. You understand what you need to do each day, and you do it well. Your coworkers and bosses like you. They approve of what you are doing. You are in homeostasis.
- X3 may be related to another dimension of your life. Let's say that in the evening you are working on acquiring a professional certification with an online training program. You may be having difficulty understanding what you are supposed to do and are discouraged by the content of the required class. You feel a loss of

confidence and are confused. You find yourself in a disruption on the resiliency mapping model.

## Figure 14. Resiliency in Multiple Roles

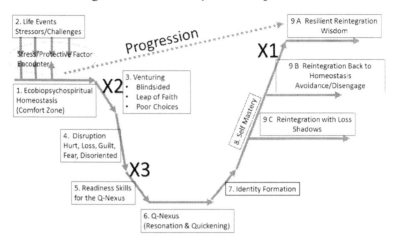

## SECONDS TO CENTURIES

The time that is required to go through the resilient journey will vary depending upon the nature of the disruption. At the short end of the range, it may only take seconds to add new pieces of information to your worldview puzzle. For example, imagine you are watching the news and one of the stories is about someone who performed kindly acts toward less fortunate citizens. You would experience a disruption in the form of positive emotions associated with altruism. You may even take this a step further by preparing yourself to perform acts of kindness at a future time; this could be as simple as envisioning yourself helping others in your mind's eye. In just moments, your worldview expands to have this become part of your nature.

The resiliency process is not always so quick. For instance, learning how to create a web page might take several hours. Recovering from an argument may take a few days. Earning an academic degree may take a few years. In my personal example, rehabilitation was eight months. Complex social, political, and cultural resilient journeys may take years to resolve after disruptions. It took more than eight years to gain independence in the American Revolutionary War.

Whether the resilient journey takes seconds or centuries, the process is the same. Often, when there are big changes, they are comprised of multiple smaller changes. For instance, the disruption of learning how to use a new computer program includes several smaller disruptions: getting access to the program, learning the program's purpose, understanding how to input data, and learning how to generate the output.

## TRANSCENDENCE AFTER TIME HAS PAST

Sometimes people reintegrate with loss after a life event as they bury the experience under layers of disappointment and hurt. When this occurs, feelings of bitterness or sadness become their new state of homeostasis as they mourn the initial hurt. Getting out of a maladapted state of homeostasis sometimes requires going through another disruption— taking a leap of faith into learning how to grow from the experience.

> I once did a resilience program for a large government organization. When I reached the part of the program that talked about forgiveness, one woman came to me after the training and shared her story. She said, "I was sexually abused three times in my teen years by three different men during a four-year period. Each of the men knew my family. Each threatened to kill me if I told anyone. I was afraid to tell anyone. It has been twenty-five years, and I think I have forgiven them, but I do hope they burn in hell." Her bitter edge was evidence that she had not recovered from these tragedies. After going through the forgiveness exercises, twenty-five years later and with some additional counseling, she was finally able to forgive. Afterward, you could see the Qs in her countenance.

You can still resiliently reintegrate even after time has passed.

## APPLICATIONS BEYOND THE SELF

The resiliency experience applies both to you personally and to your interdependent relationships. In one sense, you are living in your own personal world of thoughts, learning, experiences, and spiritual insights. At the same time, you function among family, friends, organizations, and even in your country. Each group is likely to experience life events that cause disruptions that affect everyone in the group. Because of different life experiences, the impact upon each member of the group may vary, but still there is an impact. For example, if an elderly grandmother suffering from an illness dies, the whole family is affected but differently. One of the children may celebrate her life and is grateful for the positive influences. Another child will grieve and feel regrets for not being a better child. Even with a different disruptive experience caused by the same experience, the family or organization has the opportunity to work together to resiliently reintegrate and can seize the disruption as a growing opportunity.

In a positive way, if a member of a family graduates from college, the whole family celebrates. If a company creates a new product that is well received by the public, then the whole company celebrates. In the Olympics, when the United States produces winners, the whole country celebrates. Conversely, if one family member physically hurts him or herself, the whole family is affected and rallies in support. Embezzlement by one employee in a company can affect the levels of trust and mood of everyone at the office. Such national tragedies as 9/11 or mass shootings affect the whole country.

## RESILIENCY MAPPING

You can use resiliency mapping to think through your life experiences. If you have been blindsided by life events, resiliency mapping provides a framework that empowers you with some control. The nine phases of the resiliency map are shown in the figure. You can use resiliency mapping when reacting to being blindsided, or you can use it proactively when venturing.

## Figure 15. Resiliency Mapping

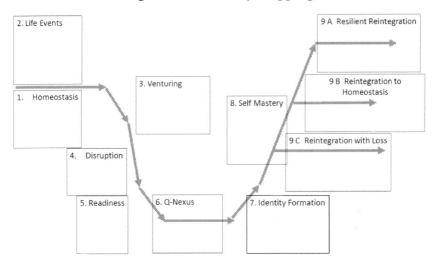

## PROACTIVE RESILIENCY MAPPING

When you feel the need to progress and move forward in life, you venture out to learn or try something new. You venture or take a leap of faith into a new experience. Before taking the leap, you can do resiliency mapping to better understand the disruptions, the feelings, the insights, and the self-mastery you are about to experience. You will be asked in the mapping process to consider what you could do to make you happier, more skilled, or have a better relationship. Activity #2 will guide you through the process of taking leaps of faith into ventures that will help you to progress.

## ACTIVITY #2: PROACTIVE RESILIENCY MAPPING

1. **Homeostasis:** Consider your current ecological, biological, psychological, and spiritual (ecobiopsychospiritual) state of homeostasis. You have a routine, and you may be happy with it, or perhaps you have just adjusted to a challenging situation. What is your state of adaptation with a particular situation in your life? Describe your adapted state in box #1.

2. **Life Events:** The life event is what you have chosen to do to improve your life situation. Even if you are content with your situation, in all likelihood, you want to improve something about

your personal health habits, your relationships at work or at home, your living situation, or your finances, among several progressive opportunities to improve your life. The postulate of progression compels you to look for opportunities to improve yourself, and you may just want to learn a new skill. You may also have some difficult challenges that will require disruptions in order to become more resilient. In box #2, enter what you wish to improve in your state or situation.

3. **Venturing:** As you consider doing something to improve your situation, imagine the courage and drive you will need to take the leap of faith. Prepare to take the leap. Remember the postulate of resonance—each step should feel right. Then take action. Describe your venture in box #3.

4. **Disruption:** Anticipate that as you take the leap of faith, you will be leaving homeostasis and may feel disoriented and confused. In box #4, write how you might feel. Disruption leads to openness and humility as you ponder the changes you are making.

5. **Readiness:** Begin to practice activities that will lead to insights and an infusion of Qs. You may try meditation, prayer, meditative walks, mood-specific music, imagery, journaling, talking with others, or other activities that help you get into the right mind-set for receiving ideas and Qs beyond your normal thinking. Write what you will do to create a state of openness in box #5.

6. **Q-Nexus (Quickening):** During the process of venturing and readying, be open to ideas, inspiration, insights, and aha moments. With the quickening moment, you can catch the vision of what you can do. With a vision or insight in your heart and mind, write your impression in box #6.

7. **Identity Formation:** The insights from quickening should help you recognize that you will be able to add a new identity to your existing arsenal of identities. What is the identity that will best fulfill the outcome you desire from your venturing? Write a description of that identity in box #7.

8. **Self-Mastery:** In box #8, describe how you will be persistent and diligent in maintaining your new identity so that you will thrive in your new venture.

9. **Reintegration A–C**

   **9A: Resilient Reintegration:** This is the most desirable type of reintegration and the goal of the resilient journey. Imagine how your venture will lead to thriving and the addition of a new identity. Imagine how your level of homeostasis will be better and how your experience will cause you to progress in life. You will need to consider your self-mastery and drive to resiliently reintegrate. Describe the Qs you will gain and write them in box #9A.

   **9B: Reintegration Back to Homeostasis:** What would happen if your venture wasn't effective? You decided to give up and go back to where you were before you just tried to be proactive. How would you feel? Write your response in box #9B.

   **9C: Reintegration with Loss:** To complete the picture, what would happen if you tried and failed in this venture? What would it be like to lose hope and optimism by not succeeding? How would it affect you to feel hopeless in your old situation? Write that outcome in box #9C.

## REACTIVE RESILIENCY MAPPING

You can also do resiliency mapping when you are blindsided by life events. You are thrown into an unpleasant situation, and by the time you have a moment to think through the experience, you may be partway through the resilient journey. At this point, you will already be in disruption when you begin to map an event that blindsides you. You can start where you are and then work your way back to homeostasis. Reflect again upon resiliency mapping.

1. **Disruption:** It is likely that a life event has already occurred by the time you have a chance to do resiliency mapping. In this case, you are probably in the midst of emotions that include loss, hurt, and disappointment. Express your emotions in box #4.

2. **Life Events:** After you acknowledge the disruption, think back to the life event that triggered the uncomfortable emotions. Discuss the origins of the disruption in box #2.

3. **Homeostasis:** Backtrack in the mapping process again as you consider your state of homeostasis before the event. Reminiscence of the old comfort zone will help you consider whether you want to go back to that state or if, by being blindsided, you will want to progress and grow from the experience. Describe homeostasis as it pertains to the event in box #1.

4. **Venturing:** First, consider whether this is something that is important enough for you to experience a disruption. Second, is there something you could have done to prevent the event, or did someone else cause this? What new skill do you need or what do you need to learn to become stronger? Make sure you understand why you were forced to leave homeostasis. Now that you have backtracked to the origin of the experience, you can venture into handling the event in a positive manner. Write your thoughts in box #3.

5. **Readiness:** As you reflect upon the origin of being blindsided and then consider the first three boxes on your resiliency map— homeostasis, the life event, and venturing—you can now ponder your readiness to turn the life event into an opportunity to progress. You will ponder your contributions to the life event and consider what you could have done to avoid the life event and created a different situation. Humble yourself and be open to ideas as to how to make the event a positive. Practice readiness techniques, such as reading self-help literature, meditating, praying, walking, drawing, and other pensive skills. Describe what you do in box #5.

6. **Quickening:** Be patient and believe that an idea, a gestalt, or an aha moment will occur and you will know what to do to get out of the disruption. You will sense that you need a particular Q, or a new identity that has the desired Q. Write your desired insights in box #6.

7. **New Identity:** Once you realize the new identity you need, create that identity in your mind. You might choose to imagine a hero that has the desired quality. On the other hand, you could watch

yourself using the new identity to deal with this life event in your mind's eye. Describe your new identity in box #7, and continue to rehearse the identity in your mind.

8.  **Self-Mastery:** In box #8, discuss how you will demonstrate self-mastery. Describe how you will persist until the new identity becomes part of you. Reflect on the intrinsic rewards associated with the new identity.

9.  **Reintegration A–C**

    **9C: Reintegration with Loss:** Think about what could happen in your life if you became bitter, angry, or vindictive. Write about the negative impact in box #9C.

    **9B: Reintegration Back to Homeostasis:** In box #9B, write what could happen if you tried to ignore the event and just got past it.

    **9A: Resilient Reintegration:** In box #9A, describe what your life would be like with the new identity, skills, and experience. Describe how it will make you stronger and wiser.

By now, you should have an understanding of how your life story unfolds—one of new experiences, continually learning, growing in wisdom, and practicing what one has learned so far—as applicable to the life situation. You need to determine what you need to do to resiliently reintegrate when the events are disruptive. In all cases, you should also recognize that each life event holds the potential for a positive outcome. Even when serious life events occur, you have the opportunity to experience Q-infusions and resiliently reintegrate.

The next section of this book is Experience 2: Discovering Resilient Yearnings and Drives. In this section on resilience, you will discover who you really are. You will introspect and feel your energy and motivation that will help you to thrive through adversity and challenge. To consistently progress, you need to access innate sources of energy and power, called resilience, described in Experiences 2–9.

# In Summary

- Resiliency is the process and experience of being disrupted by life events, adversity, or challenges, and in the humbling lows of introspective enlightenment, accessing innate self-mastering strengths to grow stronger through the disruption.
- With every change and new experience, you go through the predictable resiliency process, including homeostasis, life events, disruptions, readiness, quickening, identity formation, self-mastery, and wisdom.
- You have a choice about the outcomes of the resiliency process, including resilient reintegration, reintegration back to the comfort zone, or reintegration with loss.
- You can use resiliency mapping to chart the outcomes for both proactive leaps of faith and also when being blindsided by life events.

# PART 3

# DISCOVERING RESILIENT
# YEARNINGS AND DRIVES

*Resilience is a force within everyone that drives him or
her to seek self-actualization, altruism, wisdom, peace,
and harmony with a source of spiritual strength. It is the
energy and motivation to resiliently reintegrate through
your resilient journey.*

Part 3 describes the most remarkable adventure you will ever
experience. It is the journey of discovery of vast reservoirs of
strengths, potentials, gifts, and wisdom that are housed within
the treasury of your soul. Discovering your resilient yearnings and drives
can change your life by helping you discover the nature of your human
spirit or heart. You have a treasury of gifts, strengths, and talents housed
within you, but it may be buried deep inside. By embarking on a resilient
journey of discovery (which you learned about in Experience 1), you will
be able to unearth this treasury.

Before we begin this new journey of discovery, let's consider the story
of Ali Hafed, a rich Persian farmer as told by Dr. Russell H. Conwell. Dr.
Conwell, a Union officer in the Civil War who later became founder and
president of Temple University, learned this story from his guide when he
traveled through ancient Persia.*

---

* The original story can be found on the Temple University website.

Ali Hafed owned a large farm made up of orchards, grain fields, and gardens. He was well respected in the community and was very wealthy. He had a wonderful family and was leading a life of contentment. One of the best informed men of his time was a Buddhist priest who often visited and provided counsel to the people in Ali Hafed's community. One day the priest came to visit Ali. After passing some time with Ali and his family, telling them how the world was made, the Buddhist priest told Ali in the glimmer of an evening fire that the most precious thing in the entire world was a stone that was a gift from the sun. This stone, called a diamond, contained a drop of sunlight whose glitter would warm any heart. The old priest told Ali that if he had one diamond the size of his thumb, he could purchase the entire community in which he lived. And if he could find a handful of diamonds, he could place his children upon thrones.

The words of the old priest seemed to attack Ali Hafed— he was consumed with the thought of diamonds. He could hardly eat or sleep because of his visions of finding diamonds. In one day, without losing anything, Ali Hafed changed from being a contented and wealthy man to becoming a discontented and poor man. He had lost nothing but had heard of this wonderful stone called a diamond. Now he wanted diamonds more than anything in the world.

He asked all over about where he could find diamonds. Neither the Buddhist priest nor anyone in the community knew. The priest said that somewhere in the world there is a place with plenty of diamonds. Ali Hafed made up his mind; he had to go and find them.

He sold his beautiful farm and left his family in the care and keeping of family members. He left much of his money with his family but took what he thought would be enough money with him to fund his journey. He purchased camels, packed them with food and supplies, and hired several servants to accompany him on his quest. Ali Hafed searched all over the known world of that time. He searched the Middle East and then up into Europe. Time passed, and his search became futile. By then, he had to let the servants go because his money had been depleted. He sold his camels to purchase food. After years of searching, he found himself standing between the Pillars of Hercules in Spain overlooking the sea. Ali was in rags, wretchedness, and poverty. He longed for his family, and he wanted to go home, yet he had no means to return. He was destitute because of his failure to find diamonds. As a huge wave came toward him, the poor, afflicted, suffering Ali Hafed threw himself into the sea and sank beneath its foaming crest, never to surface again.

Meanwhile, back at home, the man who had purchased Ali Hafed's farm was letting his camel drink from the garden brook. As the camel splashed its nose into the shallow water of the clear stream, Ali Hafed's successor noted a curious flash of light coming from the white sands of the stream. He pulled out a stone that had an eye of light reflecting all the hues of the rainbow. He took the stone into his house and laid it on the mantel. Sometime later, when the same old priest came to visit Ali Hafed's successor, he saw the beautiful stone flashing from the mantel and asked, "Where did you find this stone? It is a diamond." Excitedly, they both rushed out into the garden and stirred up the white sands of the brook with their fingers, and lo, there came up other beautiful gems, one after another, and some of them were even more valuable than the first.

This story is said to be a historically true account of the discovery of the great Golconda diamond mine. At the very time that Ali Hafed was longing for diamonds, he was living on top of one of the greatest diamond mines in the world. If he had just looked in his own backyard, he would have found his diamonds—acres of them. Instead, Ali Hafed descended into poverty and starvation, ultimately taking his own life in a strange land.

Metaphorically, you have within you acres of diamonds or resilient terms, acres of gifts, strengths, and talents that have yet to be explored. Years ago, researchers focused on the risk factors that people are experiencing, and then they tried to fix those problems. They would have discussed such potential problems as poor parenting, broken homes, negative peer influence, poverty, drug use, and other factors that could contribute to poor outcomes. More recently, there has been a refreshing paradigm shift in mind-body medicine, positive psychology, and positive health among many academic disciplines that shift from focusing on risks and toward identifying protective factors housed within the human spirit. Researchers now explore the vast reservoirs of strengths, gifts, and talents that individuals and groups innately possess to help them thrive through adversity. The strengths are resilient qualities. Academia now recognizes that each individual soul possesses acres of diamonds (Padesky and Mooney 2012 and Richardson 2002). They may be buried, but the diamonds are still there.

Part 3 is about discovering your resilient yearnings and drives, which are your diamonds. The next several experiences of part 3 are about discovering those diamonds within you and the world around you. Each of the diamonds is a potential new experience to enhance your own resilience. This section of the book will show you how to find the energy and motivation through your childlike nature and how to use that energy to power yourself through the resiliency process. You will learn about the diamonds of nobility that enable you to feel valued, important, and confident as you navigate your resilient life. You will explore the energy-saving diamonds of character. You will learn to find diamonds that cannot be seen by the eye, hear subtle messages coming from your body, and manage your mental control center. Let's begin with your childlike nature in Experience 2.

# CHILDLIKE RESILIENCE

> *Childlike resilience is the experience of thriving through life's challenges by using the energy from one's sense of adventure, play, spontaneity, and fun.*

I n pursuit of your innate resilient diamonds, let's start by exploring the Qs of childhood and your childlike nature. The Qs of childhood are vital sources of energy that enable you to thrive through life's challenges. As children, we sought fun and laughter, play and entertainment, love and protection. Unfortunately, many people no longer know how to play. Instead, they focus on problems, hold grudges, and let work become drudgery.

*Childlike resilience* is the yearning and drive to play, laugh, have fun, seek adventures, and be creative. Childlike resilience is the rich reserve of energy in every soul that can be channeled into overcoming life's challenges with hope and optimism.

Your childlike nature and energy can help you make almost any situation enjoyable; you just have to remember to look for the diamonds originating from your childlike Qs. Perhaps all you ever really need to know comes from your childlike drives, as masterfully described by Robert Fulghum (1988).

All I really need to know about how to live and what to do and how to be I learned in kindergarten. Wisdom was not at the top of the graduate school mountain, but there in the sand pile at Sunday school. These are the things I learned:

Share everything.

Play fair.

Don't hit people.

Put things back where you found them.

Clean up your own mess.

Don't take things that aren't yours.

Say you're sorry when you hurt somebody.

Wash your hands before you eat.

Flush.

Warm cookies and cold milk are good for you.

Live a balanced life—learn some and think some and draw and paint and sing and dance and play and work every day some.

Take a nap every afternoon.

When you go out into the world, watch out for traffic, hold hands, and stick together.

Be aware of wonder ... And then remember the Dick and Jane books and the first word you learned—the biggest of all—LOOK. Everything you need to know is in there somewhere.

As you reflect upon your childhood years, you may remember how you worked through life experiences with natural coping skills. When you were upset—such as when another child took a toy from you or your parent had you stop playing—you recovered in a very short amount of time. You rarely held grudges. You were not afraid to try new activities and learn new games. You would jump from trees or high places for the thrill. You were creative, loved to draw, and were skilled at self-entertainment. Your imagination was vivid as you played with imaginary friends and dolls. Cars and animals could be made of anything.

When you played with dolls or LEGOs, you were totally engaged. In current psychology, this experience of having your body, mind, and spirit all engaged in an activity is called a *flow state* (Csíkszentmihályi 1997). Many modern-day positive approaches to therapy endorse mindfulness, or being in the present, as an important skill. As kids, being present was easy.

What happened to us since childhood? Unfortunately, many of us have grown up and buried these wonderful qualities. The childlike Qs are still within us but might be suffocating under layers of challenging experiences and adult expectations. As we try to thrive as adults, we may find ourselves multitasking, following rigid schedules, unable to focus because of so many demands. When we are offended, we often worry and feel hurt for long periods of time. Sometimes we dissociate ourselves from others and feel awkward around the offender for days or weeks. These things didn't happen in kindergarten.

This experience is about rediscovering your childlike Qs and learning to use them responsibly in adult life. Childlike resilience encompasses the yearnings for adventure, play, and fun. To begin, let me take you through an exercise to help you rediscover your childlike resilience. With this exercise, I want you to remember some pleasant memories. It is from these memories that you will be able to discover your childlike Qs.

## ACTIVITY #3: CHILDLIKE REFLECTION

**Step 1:** In your imagination, go back to your childhood and remember happy times. I recognize that some of you may have had difficulties in your childhood, but there were probably times when you were able to play and have fun. Write down five or six of your favorite things that you did as a child. Before you choose, let me help trigger your memory by asking a few questions that may have been associated with your childhood experiences.

- Did you like to play in water (bathtubs, pools, lakes, the ocean, water hoses, squirt guns, water balloons)?
- Did you like playing with friends (clubs, sleepovers, group games)?
- Did you like to travel (family vacations, amusement parks, games in the car, getting on trains or planes)?
- What childhood games and toys did you like to play with (dolls; electric trains; Monopoly; chemistry sets; craft sets; playing house; Red Rover; Mother May I?; Red Light, Green Light)?
- What active games did you like to play (tetherball, kickball, dodgeball, climbing on the monkey bars)?
- When did you feel safe and comfortable (in someone's arms, when alone in your room, in the yard, at church)?
- Did you like adventures (sleeping out in the yard, hiking, riding bikes, playing night games)?
- Who did you like to visit (a grandparent, a neighbor, an uncle or aunt, a friend)?
- What did you like to create (drawing, painting, building with blocks, other types of art)?

List the activities in the chart that follows Step 3.

**Step 2:** After you have identified five or six things that you liked to do, consider the Qs that come from your childlike nature. To clarify this step, consider the following example from my own life:

> When I was a kid, we lived on a small five-acre homestead near San Diego. We had a couple of horses, raised a few chickens, raised our own beef, and had a huge garden. At that time, we had to build a septic tank, which required digging a huge hole in the ground, and after a tank was buried, there still remained a wonderful dirt pile. I used to spend hours out on the pile of dirt by myself, building communities. I had some toy cars, and I would build roads and dig little caves for the houses. It was a beautiful creation. Then when it would rain, it was a blessing,

because that meant I got to fluff the dirt and rebuild the community in a whole new way.

One of my favorite childhood activities was digging in a dirt pile. Why did I enjoy it? It was fun. It was creative. It was play. It triggered my imagination. It was mindful. Therefore, in column 2, I would write *creative* to represent the Qs I experienced during this activity.

**Step 3:** After you have identified the childlike urges that come from the human spirit, ask yourself, *What am I doing now, as an adult, to fulfill those same needs?*

> As I pondered what I am doing now to fulfill my creative needs and trigger my imagination, I realized that my work as a professor is creative and imaginative. It is play for me to put theories and concepts together—almost like creating a community in a dirt pile. How do I fulfill the creative needs as an adult? My "dirt pile" is now my computer. I love to think about the future. I don't care about "what is" as much as "what could be." Sitting down and writing an article, a book, or a training manual is just as fulfilling as playing in the dirt. However, I still love to sit in a freshly dumped pile of dirt and feel its warmth in my hands.

| Step 1:<br>Activities I Did as a Kid | Step 2:<br>Qs or Feelings from Doing It | Step 3:<br>What Am I Doing Now? |
|---|---|---|
| 1. | 1. | 1. |
| 2. | 2. | 2. |
| 3. | 3. | 3. |
| 4. | 4. | 4. |
| 5. | 5. | 5. |
| 6. | 6. | 6. |

# CHILDLIKE QS

Hopefully Activity #3 helped you identify childlike Qs. One way to be happier in life is to make sure you create and embrace opportunities to feel and express those qualities and virtues. In addition to the childlike Qs you identified in Activity #3, there are probably other childlike Qs you'd also like to feel. Activity #4 will help you think about ways to have more childlike Qs in your life now.

## ACTIVITY #4: CHILDLIKE FEELINGS

Consider the following list of childlike feelings. You may have recalled some of these in Activity #3, while others might be new. To the right of each childlike Q below, plan some experiences that would help you feel the infusion of those Qs in your life now.

| Childlike Qs | My Plan to Experience the Qs |
|---|---|
| 1.  Feel the sense of adventure | 1.   On my way home from work, I am going to stop and explore a botanical garden that I have never visited before. |
| 2.  Wanting to have fun | 2. |
| 3.  Desire to play | 3. |
| 4.  Need to be creative | 4. |
| 5.  Longing to learn | 5. |
| 6.  Urge to laugh and find humor | 6. |
| 7.  Find joy of being spontaneous | 7. |
| 8.  Being open and teachable | 8. |
| 9.  Needing to be genuine | 9. |
| 10. Taking chances or risks | 10. |

# CHILDLIKE Q-SKILLS

When applied correctly, enhancing and activating your childlike nature can help you discover the renewed energy that comes from finding humor in life events. It can help you to see life as a challenge or adventure. You will be able to use your childlike creativity to develop skills to increase your energy to be used in daily life. The skills of Q-breathing, Q-imagery, creativity, and games will help you enhance your childlike qualities.

## Q-BREATHING

Q-breathing is the experience of focusing on a desired Q and using your breathing to have that quality energize your entire being. In the case of childlike Q-breathing, the Qs listed in Activity #4 can be the focus of your breathing. Activity #5 will help you practice childlike Q-breathing.

## ACTIVITY #5: CHILDLIKE Q-BREATHING

Try childlike Q-breathing by taking the following steps:

1. Identify one childlike Q that you would like to feel (listed in the table above).
2. Get into a comfortable position and breathe naturally.
3. If you can, breathe in through your nose and out through your mouth. Breathe diaphragmatically by letting your stomach rise and fall with each breath.
4. With each inhalation, imagine that each breath contains little particles of the childlike quality you identified. For example, you may be imagining little particles of adventure with each inhalation.
5. As you breathe in, feel a gradually increasing sense of the quality you identified. You can imagine it filling your lungs and then moving slowly throughout the rest of your body.
6. Continue to breathe in the quality, but now, with each exhalation, begin to expel all the barriers to fulfilling that quality. For example, with adventure, your exhalation might be ridding yourself of fears. You breathe in adventure and exhale fear.
7. Continue to breathe in the feeling of your chosen Q, and then let it go to your heart, and then your mind, and then your whole body.
8. As you feel the quality within you, you may want to apply that quality to a real-life situation that would benefit from the quality. Imagine that with each inhalation, you can effectively make a life

situation better with the quality. For example, imagine that you use an adventurous spirit to successfully cope with a work situation.

## Q-IMAGERY

When you were a child, your imagination allowed you to escape to far-off destinations and live in fantasy worlds. That same skill can allow you to find joy in life now, even in difficult circumstances. As a child, you could see colors, hear sounds, taste foods, touch animals, and smell the roses in your mind. With those same skills, you can use your imagination to feel energy from humor, play, and fun. For example, when sitting in a boring meeting, you can imagine that people are wearing comical outfits. When traveling, you can imagine that you are anywhere: in a parade, at Disneyland, in the mountains, or at the beach. In all these, we invoke the power and joy of imagination. You can imagine that you are singing songs around a campfire. Your imagination will allow you to walk along busy streets in the city yet feel like you are strolling along a beach in Hawaii. You can imagine that people in other cars are friends and smile at them. Your ability to imagine is a gift from childhood that lets you create wonderful scenarios and enjoy them in the routine of everyday living.

## ACTIVITY #6: CHILDLIKE Q-IMAGERY

With your amazing ability to imagine, take the opportunity to visualize scenarios that accompany the yearnings and drives of the childlike nature. In the first column are some of the Qs of your childlike nature. In the second column, create an imaginary scenario where you can experience these Qs in your imagination. Be sure to imagine the sounds, smells, sights, tastes, and physical feelings of the scenarios. Give a brief description of the scenario in the second column where there is an example.

# CREATIVITY

In a normal day at home or at work, look to your creative nature to spice up your daily routine. Let's use your natural childlike imagination to help you face life's challenges and make decisions.

| Childlike Qs | Brief Description of Your Imaginary Scenario |
|---|---|
| 1. Feel the sense of adventure | 1. I can imagine that I am going on a canoe and riding down the Colorado River. |
| 2. Wanting to have fun | 2. |
| 3. Desire to play | 3. |
| 4. Need to be creative | 4. |
| 5. Longing to learn | 5. |
| 6. Urge to laugh and find humor | 6. |
| 7. Find joy of being spontaneous | 7. |
| 8. Being open and teachable | 8. |
| 9. Needing to be genuine | 9. |
| 10. Taking chances or risks | 10. |

## ACTIVITY #7: CREATIVITY

1. Q-doodling: This psychomotor activity allows your body to be distracted while your mind and spirit ponder. One approach is to reflect upon a specific life challenge. Find a pencil or crayons and paper, and simply begin to doodle. Just think about solutions and continue to just draw aimlessly. You may need to doodle for fifteen minutes to a half hour, but in the process, you will discover creative solutions to your problems. Another approach is to doodle while you ponder specific childlike Qs.

2. Q-painting: Do the same experience as Q-doodling, except use paint.

3. Q-modeling: Do the same experience as Q-doodling, except use clay.

4. Q-mask: As you ponder adopting childlike Qs, one way to express your vision of your childlike nature is by creating a mask. Ponder the Q you want and draw a mask that fits that Q. You may want to pretend as you wear the mask.

5. Q-collage: Pondering the childlike qualities you want may prompt you to make a collage. By cutting images from magazines, or

cutting and pasting images from computers, you can create a collage that reminds you to adopt the childlike qualities.

## GAMES

Many games are designed to mimic life situations. Therefore, games can be a way to use your childlike nature to work through real-life situations. Play your favorite games and think about how the simulations in the game may be applicable. Consider Beth's real-life story as told by one of my students:

> Beth's company decided to downsize during a recession, and she lost her job. She had no income for six months and had to sell her home. She was forced to return home and live in her parents' basement.

> Beth, who was thirty-two, had always loved to play Monopoly. Metaphorically, she felt like she were just starting over, as if beginning a new Monopoly game. One day, she decided to use a Monopoly board to map out her life strategy. Each property represented financial goals. To start the game, she needed some start-up money. All she really had was furniture from the home she used to own. In order to start her "game" with some cash, she studied the best ways to sell furniture on the Internet. After much study, she found an online company that she trusted. She put one item of furniture up for sale at a time. With each sale, she got cash, and soon she had about $1,500. With her start-up money in hand, she picked a player piece and put it on "Go." She started with the cheaper properties of Monopoly, which in her mind, meant more modest financial goals. As she brainstormed how to meet the financial goals, she reflected upon how successful she had been selling her furniture. She thought that she could buy other things cheap and sell higher. She took some of her money and went to a local secondhand clothes distribution center. As she rummaged through the clothing, she found nice clothes for seventy-five cents

to a couple of dollars. She tried selling them online. She sold them for four and six dollars. As she moved around the Monopoly board, the properties became electronics, musical instruments, and furniture. Soon she was buying $200 and $300 items, fixing them up, and selling them for $600 and $800. It didn't take long for Beth to move out of her parents' home and regain her financial independence.

While Beth used a board game, other games can help with life situations as well. Charades is a particularly good game for trying on different personality traits. If you feel that it is right to create a new identity as a more fun-loving person, a playful person, a curious person, or any of the other childlike traits, then you can begin to act that way, and you can become that new identity over time.

## CHILDLIKE QS WITH CURRENT CHALLENGES

Many times, we approach difficult financial, relationship, health, and other challenges with worry, sadness, and hopelessness. The child that is within you views life's challenges a different way. Insurmountable tasks or strained relationships are viewed from the childlike view as opportunities for creativity, adventure, and risk taking. Consider the following story.

I remember a time when I had to discipline my son, who was about eight years old at the time. He had been teasing and picking on his younger sister until she came to me in tears. The conversation I had was calm and collected in a moment of parental wisdom, and I suggested to him that he sit in a corner and think about better ways to play with his sister. He begrudgingly walked to the corner with his head down. He sat down with a long look on his face. I told him that I would be back in a few minutes and we would discuss better options for playing with his sister. I walked out of the room and tiptoed to a vantage point where I could watch him undetected. It seemed clear that this opportunity to reflect upon his wrongdoing was working for him, and I felt smug that my intervention exemplified ideal parenting. For about a minute, he sat there thinking about something. I got a smile on my face and anxiously awaited our opportunity to talk. I let him ponder for a few more minutes to make sure enough time had passed for the disciplining to have real meaning. As I peered from my hiding place, I noticed that he started to rub his fingers through the carpet. He found a little thread. He grabbed the thread between his thumb and finger and started moving it along the wall like a little worm. The wall was textured, so the worm had numerous passageways to explore. He then reached into his pocket and pulled out a little pebble he had picked up during his outdoor adventures earlier that day. Now the worm began to chase the pebble through the textured matrix on the wall. He started making noises for the characters in this adventure. My best read was that the thread was a snake, as evidenced by the hissing sound, and the little pebble was his sister, based upon the falsetto voice of the pebble. Occasionally the snake would catch her and scare her, and then she (the pebble), would escape through the matrix screaming. My moment as a parenting genius was dashed within four minutes as my son continued to pester his sister, even if it was just in his mind.

Difficult situations can be softened when you choose to approach challenges with your childlike nature. From the resiliency process described in Experience 1, you know that when life events happen, you will initially feel hurt, loss, guilt, or fear. But during the disruption, you can access your childlike sense of creativity, adventure, and hope. In the face of adult challenges, consider that childlike Qs can lead to insightful moments. Stories abound of people in difficult situations using their childlike qualities to survive.

Mike, after being married for twenty-five years, found himself divorced and alone in a two-bedroom apartment. He felt lonely and rejected, and he didn't think anyone would ever want to be with him again. He was fifty-four years old. After work, he would just go home, hide out in his shell, and feel sorry for himself. He finally realized that this was no life, staying in his disruption. He wanted to create a new life but didn't know how to do so at his age. He began to brainstorm and pondered, *What are some of the things I used to like to do in high school and college?* He recalled that he loved to dance. He liked hiking. He loved to go to the mountains and play games like Capture the Flag. He knew a couple of other men who were single and had lost their childlike natures. He attended a church singles gathering with his colleagues and met some people. Mike convinced everyone that life was too short to sit around and not have any fun. The group decided to go to Mike's house and get acquainted. Mike brought out games, and the whole group had a great time. The word spread, and soon around thirty people would come together to ski, play Capture the Flag in the mountains, and go on adventures. After a few months, one of the women that joined the group caught Mike's eye, and a friendship developed. After dating and falling in love, they married.

Mike's childlike longing to be happy and be childlike became the avenue for him to rediscover a happy married life.

## Q-TALKING YOUR ROLES WITH CHILDLIKE RESILIENCE

Most people act and behave in ways that are dictated by their roles. For instance, you may play the roles of parent, professional, church member, and neighbor; these roles may lead you to act differently from how you would really like to act. Many people are afraid to be genuine. The following exercise first asks you to make a list of roles that you have in life. Include anytime a given situation leads you to behave in a different way. That is a role. For example, your parenting role with a nine-month-old baby may be different from your role when parenting a seventeen-year-old teenager.

## ACTIVITY #8: ROLES

1. List as many roles as you can in the chart below (spouse, son or daughter, parent, worker, neighbor, church member, volunteer, friend, etc.).

2. Describe how the roles could be better if you were to incorporate some of your childlike Qs into those roles. For example, what if you were able to help people in your world laugh? How could you make your daily responsibilities more adventurous or fun? As you consider the roles in your life, use your imagination to embrace the childlike qualities that would make your roles better. In your mind, rehearse the experience of becoming more childlike and imagine how each role could be enriched with them. Describe how your roles evolve in the chart below following the example.

| The Role (Friend, Family Member, Professional, etc.) | How the Role Could Be Better with Childlike Qs |
|---|---|
| 1. As a friend to Jim who lost his wife a year ago to cancer | 1. Take him with me to explore the caves in the nearby mountains. |
| 2. | 2. |
| 3. | 3. |
| 4. | 4. |
| 5. | 5. |
| 6. | 6. |
| 7. | 7. |

## In Summary

- Remember that there are childlike diamonds buried within you that can help you cope with life challenges.
- You should be able to laugh when you mess up if there are no serious consequences.
- You should be able to tackle life experiences with a sense of adventure. You should feel driven to satisfy your childlike curiosity.
- Remember that being childlike is not the same as being childish!
- Each childlike action should be safely housed within your sense of character and morality.
- In your quest to fulfill your childlike nature, be sure that acting upon your quest for humor, play, and adventure does not come at the expense of someone else's self-esteem or dignity.

The next experience will help you discover more diamonds—the diamonds of noble resilience.

# EXPERIENCE 3

# NOBLE RESILIENCE

> *Noble resilience is the experience of feeling an increase in self-worth and esteem through the mechanism of service.*

The drive to be noble is imbedded deeply in the soul of every human being. Your human spirit is noble by nature. Your story in life is about your nobility. Nobility begins in childhood as you would plead with your parents "Watch me!" as you were trying to do something that would please them. The incubation of nobility within childhood fantasies evolves as we are pushed into real-world expectations and maturity. Your noble drive to feel valued, important, and competent in school, work, and play becomes a major longing in your life. You yearn to feel a sense of worth and self-esteem. You long to be confident, comfortable, and significant among your family, friends, and coworkers. In your later years, you hope to leave a positive legacy.

*Noble resilience* is the drive for purpose and meaning in life. It is the yearning to feel worthy, valued, and competent. The means to nobility is through personal victories and genuine altruism.

In this experience, you will be guided to discover or rediscover your purpose and meaning in life. You will learn to establish your own kingdom or queendom, which is a critical part of being happy and resilient.

> You will always feel empty, unfulfilled, or unsettled until you are on the path with your heart leading to the fulfillment of your nobility.

Again, as you reflect upon your childhood, you may have fantasized about being noble and courageous as you would make-believe being a hero. Depending upon the wonderful age of fantasy you enjoyed, you may have played Mulan, Superman, Wonder Woman, Robin Hood, Merida (*Brave*), Hercules, Mary Poppins, or Peter Pan. You may have imagined yourself as powerful beyond reality in your adventures to save the less fortunate. As Marianne Williamson emotionally appealed to adults in her book called *Return to Love*, she persuades us to recognize that there is still something bigger inside us.

> Our deepest fear is not that we are inadequate. Our deepest fear is that we are powerful beyond measure. It is our light, not our darkness, that frightens us. We ask ourselves, "Who am I to be brilliant, gorgeous, talented, and fabulous?" Actually, who are you not to be? You are a child of God. Your playing small doesn't serve the world. There's nothing enlightened about shrinking so that other people won't feel insecure around you. We were born to make manifest the glory of God that is within us. It's not just in some of us; it's in everyone. And as we let our own light shine, we unconsciously give other people permission to do the same. As we are liberated from our own fear, our presence automatically liberates others.

We will explore how you can "play big and let your light shine" as you create your kingdom and queendom. Your journey to become a king or queen is to discover the diamonds and gems of your nobility. Consider the garnished Sufi story told in a book called *Tales of the Dervishes* by Idries Shah, where we can discover the journey of nobility. Look for the primary themes of nobility in this story, including personal victory, purpose, venturing, and meaning.

> Once upon a time in a land far away, there lived a king and a queen. The magnificent kingdom was enchanting and rich with beautiful forests, rivers, and meadows. It was located near the pristine sea. The king and queen had a son who grew up playing in the forests where he learned to hunt and fish. He would wander down to the harbors where the sea captains taught him to sail. A noble wizard spent hours with the prince, teaching him magical powers that would help him heal, find peace, and touch the lives of others. In his nurturing environment, the prince fantasized of becoming a great warrior and king one day.
>
> As the prince grew and became a young man, he became restless and eager to prove himself. One day, the king and queen brought the young prince into the castle and informed him that it was time for him to inherit part of the kingdom. In order to do so, he would have to take on a rite of passage and be given a challenge. Upon completion of the challenge, he would begin to rule. The challenge was to sail away to a land across the sea. There he would find a vicious fire-breathing dragon that was in the care and keeping of two precious gems. The prince was to secure the two gems, and to do so, he would have to use all his skills and powers to defeat the dragon.
>
> The adventurous young prince set out with great enthusiasm. He navigated across the sea with great skill. He kept aligned with the stars, navigated with great

precision, and maximized the strength of the wind to hurry him along his journey. Even during the tempestuous storms, he held firmly to the helm and tenaciously held to his mission.

Upon his arrival in the land far away, he was greeted warmly by the people of the village. He was welcomed into their homes. But a strange thing happened to him as he ate their food. It seemed to put him into a kind of stupor, and he lost his memory of his mother and father. In his stupor, he could not remember his mission or the purpose of the journey. The villagers were friendly and concerned. One gave him a job, and he spent his days working in a shop and his evenings visiting with newly found friends. He settled into a new life that seemed to fit him well. Still, at night, he would ponder what his life was like before he had arrived in the village.

As time passed, the king and queen became concerned about the well-being of their son. They summoned a trusted messenger and told him of their concern. They asked the messenger to travel to the land far away, remind the prince of who he was, and reinforce the importance of accomplishing his mission.

The servant boarded a ship and sailed across the sea to the land far away. It did not take long for the messenger to locate the young prince in the closely knit village. He approached the prince and declared, "Prince, remember who you are. You are the son of a great king and queen. You have an important mission to accomplish!" Suddenly, the young prince woke from his stupor. His memory of his parents and his mission once again became vividly clear. He quickly donned his sword and princely attire. The villagers, eager to help the prince, described the path that led to the dragon. The young prince, with his resurgence of energy and power, stormed up the mountain to face his dragon.

He held tightly to his sword that hung securely within its scabbard and prepared himself to fight the toughest battle he had ever imagined. As he approached the cave, the dragon emerged with fire bellowing from both nostrils, and his razor-sharp teeth glistened as though ready to tear apart anything that threatened to take away the precious gems he was guarding. A jolt of fear shot through the prince's entire frame. His sweaty palms gripped the sword's pearl handle as he pulled it from the scabbard. His fear began to subside as he felt a peace come over him, and he began to ponder the words of the kindly wizard with whom he had spent so much time in his youth. "Use your magical powers, young prince."

Knowing that he was no match for the fiery dragon physically, he tried to feel the power of the magic that he learned. The powers were based upon loving everyone— even dragons. The prince looked the dragon square in his eyes. As he looked deeply in the eyes of the dragon, he could sense fear behind the dragon's fury. That enabled the young prince to feel compassion for the dragon that lived all alone in the mountain cave. Looking past the angry fire-breathing foe, he imagined that the dragon was much like the dog he would play with as a child. The prince's soft eyes perplexed the dragon, and the dragon slowly stopped breathing fire. The dragon cocked his head, obviously confused by the loving prince. Then the dragon softened. After a few moments, the dragon became tired, crawled back into his cave, and fell asleep. The young prince, humbled by the experience, walked reverently into the cave, secured the precious gems, and returned down the mountain to the seashore.

As he was bidding farewell to his new friends, he pulled one of the gems from his pouch and presented it to the appreciative people of the village. He sailed back across the seas to rejoin his parents amid great celebration. In a ceremony, the prince offered the remaining gem to help the poor in the kingdom. He was given part of the kingdom to rule in wisdom forever. As the prince rested from his adventure, he reflected not so much about his victory over the dragon but rather the joy of the people in the village and the happiness he gave the poor in his kingdom.

Within the story of the young prince's journey to nobility, you can superimpose your journey by considering personal victories in your life, feeling and sensing purpose, venturing to fulfill the purpose, and celebrating meaning of your life. Look at the list in the box of exemplary noble Qs you can harvest.

You are already familiar with the process of how to acquire these wonderful noble Qs as per the resiliency model (Experience 1). You can experience the infusion of these qualities with each disruption and change in your life, and then you can recover, during the resilient cycle, to feel the infusion Qs of a successful journey. Noble resilience is the product of personal victories, purpose, venturing, and meaning.

### Noble Qs

- Importance
- Values
- Competence
- Confidence
- Self-Worth
- Self-Esteem
- Purpose
- Meaning
- Fulfillment
- Freedom
- Independence
- Power
- Control

## PERSONAL VICTORIES

Early in his childhood, the young prince had a series of personal victories. He learned to hunt, to fish, to sail, to use a sword, and to use magical powers.

You have also learned many skills of survival in today's society. Early on as a child, you took your first baby steps and felt the initial Q-infusions of independence and competence. When you first learned to ride a bike, you were exuberant and felt accomplished. You had academic and social victories as you worked your way through elementary school. You may have graduated from high school or from college with victory celebrations of accomplishment, competence, and worth. You may have learned a new skill or a new activity in daily living and felt the joy of the victory and infusion of Qs. You have learned enough in life to be able to feed and clothe yourself and create a home. Each personal victory required a leap of faith into a new opportunity, with each resulting in some degree of disruption. Still, you have repeatedly resiliently reintegrated from those disruptions and emerged with more Qs.

## ACTIVITY #9: PERSONAL VICTORIES

Take a moment to reflect upon past or current personal victories. These will be moments when you felt the infusion of Qs from physical, mental, spiritual, social, or ecological personal victories. Your memories will reflect a time when you accomplished a task, met some challenge, or finished a goal. Consider what your personal victory was and list it in column 2. Then, in column 3, describe the noble Qs (from the preceding list) you felt when you triumphed in these situations. For example, in the Personal Victory column, you may put "I have been exercising regularly for over three months now." The Qs you might feel are *control* or *self-esteem*.

| Areas of Personal Victories | Your Personal Victory | Noble Qs You Felt |
|---|---|---|
| Physical Victories | | |
| Mental Victories | | |
| Spiritual Victories | | |
| Social Victories | | |
| Ecological Victories | | |

It is good to appreciate and celebrate your personal victories.

## DISCOVERING YOUR PURPOSE

> The prince's purpose in the Sufi story was to use the skills he had learned from his personal victories to venture into experiences that would allow him to harvest Qs of worth, respect from the people, and confidence to one day become the king.

Your purpose in life is to create and embrace experiences that will infuse your soul with qualities and virtues that you want (Qs) and that you need to progress throughout your life. As you experiment with new experiences in your personal life and in your ecosystem, you will feel the infusion of Qs in some situations. You will play fun games with friends and be enlivened with humor, love, and companionship. Other situations will drain the Qs from you. You may find yourself in a social setting where people are using offensive language, getting drunk, or telling embarrassing stories. In those character-violating situations, you will experience Q-bleeding or a loss of comfort, peace, and character.

> Your purpose in life is to dig deep into your soul, discern your resilient yearnings, then ponder in your heart and mind as to how you will fulfill these progressive yearnings and harvest Qs throughout your life progression.

When we think of nobility, we often think of royalty, kings, and queens as per our introductory Sufi story. You can become a king or queen when you have purpose that fulfills your pure resilient yearnings. In addition to personal victories, real purpose comes by serving others. A favorite series of movies and theater involved Camelot, ruled by King Arthur and the Knights of the Round Table. One version of Camelot was in the movie entitled *First Knight* (1995) where King Arthur was played by Sean Connery. In that movie, the Round Table had the inscription, "By serving each other, we become free." The formula to become "free" from low self-worth, free from disappointment, free from guilt, and free to fulfill your resilient yearnings is to serve others.

*Glenn E. Richardson, PhD*

## Activity #10: Purpose in Life

Describe your purpose in life by expressing what you want to do in life in order to harvest the Qs you really want. The chart below is a sampling of the Qs you may want.

| | | |
|---|---|---|
| Enlightenment | Fun | Discernment |
| Meaning | Adventure | Guidance |
| Purpose | Enjoyment | Love |
| Understanding | Fulfillment | Belonging |
| Hope | Spirituality | Self-Worth |
| Honesty | Happiness | Value |
| Comfort | Courage | Peace |
| Miracles | Confidence | Inspiration |
| Pleasure | Power | Character |
| Wisdom | Freedom | Energy |
| Morals | Strength | Connections |

An example of a purpose statement from one of my students is simply:

> My purpose is to create a path in life where I can discover worth and importance on a life journey filled with adventure and joy while connecting with and serving others, all inspired by a heavenly influence.

Write your purpose here:

_____

_____

_____

_____

_____

# VENTURING

> Purpose leads to *venturing*, which is to act to fulfill
> your resilient drives by means of personal victories, but
> more impressively through the mechanism of serving
> others.

The fullness of purpose is found in the yearning and mechanism of altruism—that is, to selflessly help other people. As mentioned in the introduction of this experience, you feel the yearning to serve, even as a child. You loved to help your mother or father in the kitchen or in the yard. It is by helping, touching hearts, listening, and caring that you have the opportunity to feel the infusion of noble Qs.

It is the awakening of your purpose in life that leads to the desire for altruism and service. Helping others is a natural prompt of your noble resilient yearnings. Venturing is acting upon that prompt.

We will not spend significant time on venturing at this point. Overcoming fears to take leaps of faith is the essence of the experience on venturing (Experience 10). Venturing will help you discover Qs of courage to be able to act upon your purpose in life. Venturing is what we have to do to experience the joy of meaning.

Many feel a purpose in life by discerning resilient yearnings. They formulate plans on how to fulfill their purpose but fall short by not venturing into the actions required to fulfill that purpose. They fall short of finding meaning by not acting upon their purpose and therefore not being able to celebrate the joy of meaning.

## SENSING MEANING

> The young prince found meaning following his venture
> to the land of the dragon. He felt Qs when giving back to
> the people of the village living at the base of the dragon's
> mountain and also to the poor upon returning home
> to his kingdom. The meaning came as the infusion of
> noble Qs were showered upon him for the rest of his life.
> His reflections of the journey with the accompanying
> validation by the people in the kingdom continually

infused his soul with self-worth, importance, and a magnificent legacy.

The meaning of the prince's journey became clear through his personal victories when sailing through storms and wooing the dragon. His yearning to serve others was fulfilled by gifting the precious gem to the villagers as well as to the people of his kingdom. His purpose was to serve others. The evidence of meaning came first by the celebration of his personal victory of completing his mission and wooing the dragon. The personal self-worth and value came upon reflection of what he had been able to do. But the more powerful meaning came from the people he had served. For the rest of his life, he felt the infusion of Qs from the people who shared their love and appreciation and celebrated his legacy.

> Meaning is the experience of resonating to a purpose, acting upon it, and sensing an infusion of Qs that witness and confirm the fulfillment of purpose.

Each time you venture into an activity to fulfill your purpose and are diligent in your pursuit, the action follows the resiliency process. The meaning comes with resilient reintegration at the end of the resilient journey celebrated with infusion of Qs. The infusion of Qs is the experience of meaning. The reality is that you can find meaning throughout the resilient journey, particularly at the Q-nexus, but the biggest infusion may come at the completion of the journey as shown in the next figure.

**Figure 16. Meaning in the Resilient Journey**

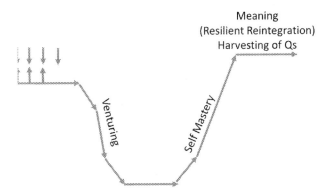

Meaning
(Resilient Reintegration)
Harvesting of Qs

Venturing

Self Mastery

For example:

- When we have personal victories, the Qs of satisfaction, self-worth, and confidence are the meaning.
- When we serve others, we feel the Q-infusions of feeling important, valued, and validated as meaning.
- When we listen and validate other people, their gratitude infuses our souls with meaning.

## EXPERIENCING JOY

Meaning may also be expressed as joy. The infusion of Qs, those wonderful feelings of peace, happiness, worth, and confidence, are felt as the emotion of joy. You can ponder the feeling of joy as an energy boost when you have had your personal victories or have felt the appreciation that comes from others when you have provided service.

## ACTIVITY #11: REFLECTION ON SERVICE AND MEANING

To personalize meaning, think about three different occasions when you had an opportunity to find meaning and felt the joy that comes from service. Complete the four columns of the chart as follows:

- Column 1: Describe an occasion when you provided a service to someone.
- Column 2: Reflect and list the Qs you felt during that experience.
- Column 3: What Qs do you think the recipient of your service gained?
- Column 4: Describe the meaning—in other words, how did your service contribute to your nobility and life mission?

| Service You Provided | Qs You Felt | Recipient's Qs or Benefits | Meaning of Your Service |
|---|---|---|---|
| 1. | | | |
| 2. | | | |
| 3. | | | |

## BUILDING YOUR KINGDOM/QUEENDOM

It is the awakening of your nobility that leads to the desire for altruism and service. Helping others is a natural prompt of the human spirit. The fullness of noble resilience is found in the yearning to be altruistic—that is, to selflessly help other people. As mentioned in the introduction of this experience, you felt the yearning to serve, even as a child. It is by helping, touching hearts, listening, and caring that you can exponentially feel the infusion of noble Qs.

Since nobility is the theme of this experience, let's revisit one of the most glamorized kingdoms in history or myth, which was Camelot. In 1967, Richard Harris starred as a caring King Arthur in the movie musical *Camelot*. The concluding strain of each verse of the title song was, "In short, there's simply not a more congenial spot for happily-ever-aftering than here in Camelot."

Your purpose in life is to create a Camelot within yourself that will naturally extend to creating a Camelot at home, at work, in worship settings, and with friends. Your Camelot within you is to find "happily-ever-aftering" with your own soul. You are able to find that purpose to fulfill your childlike and noble yearnings and find meaning when you feel infusions within your own soul as you have ventured with your purpose. What does your queendom or kingdom look like? Describe your "Camelot."

## ACTIVITY #12: YOUR "CAMELOT"

Describe the imagination of your Camelot life.

| |
|---|
| Your Camelot home: |
| Your Camelot family: |
| Your Camelot friendships: |
| Other Camelots (work, church, social groups): |

Activity #13 will help you build your Camelot queendom or kingdom. The first step will be to reflect upon the kingdoms to which you belong. Then you will follow the role model's example to build your own.

## ACTIVITY #13: HOW YOU BUILD YOUR KINGDOM OR QUEENDOM

**Part 1:**

Reflect for a moment upon your childhood. Childhood can mean any time growing up when you had some positive memories of associating with people. Answer the following questions:

- Was there someone in your life who helped you, loved you, guided you, or listened to you? This may have been a parent, grandparent, teacher, Scout leader, or any other person that nurtured you through the early years. Write the name of the person who helped you through your younger years.

_____

_____

- What did this person do or say to help you? Listened? Helped? Believed in you? Gave you time?

_____

_____

- How did you feel when you were with him or her?

_____

_____

- If a situation emerged and this person asked you for help (even though he or she may have already passed away), how quickly would you have responded?

_____

_____

In all likelihood, the person you identified believed in you. This person made you feel loved, important, and valued. This person guided you and was compassionate, kind, and caring. If that person were to ever ask you for a favor, in all probability, you would respond enthusiastically. Your response to serve this person is a loving power that he or she has over you. This is not manipulative but a product of unconditional nobility.

You are part of this person's kingdom or queendom.

This person's power over you is soft. It is because of love, appreciation, and respect. It is because he or she was humble. You want to be part of his or her kingdom. An important part of that power is that his or her rule is not manipulative or self-centered. It is because of the loving influence you have felt.

**Part 2:**

Reverse the situation and now you can build your own kingdom. You do it the same way that the person you identified created his or her kingdom. You can start building your kingdom or queendom today.

1. You can help others find Qs today.
2. You can look for opportunities to help someone feel important today.
3. You can give someone unconditional love today.
4. You can have character and humility around someone today.
5. You can show someone you care by listening today.
6. You can validate someone's feelings today.
7. You can perform some act of kindness today.

Take a moment to ponder your life situation. Envision the whole day and think about where you can serve, validate, and help someone feel good about himself or herself. Feel your nobility as you look for opportunities to serve.

## ACTIVITY #14: NOBLE Q-IMAGERY

In your mind, experience the entire day—at home, at work or school, among friends, in stores, and with other people. Look to serve. Describe below how you will experience your nobility that whole day. Imagine your noble actions coupled with character and humility. Write a paragraph of how you can begin to build your kingdom/queendom.

_____

_____

_____

_____

# In Summary

- Noble resilience is the yearning and drive to feel important and valued. It is to feel self-worth and self-esteem.
- Nobility is to feel more self-worth, self-esteem, and sense of importance throughout your lifetime through the mechanism of altruism. The noble journey embraces personal victories, purpose, venturing, and meaning within the boundaries of character.
- Personal victories bring confidence and skills in readiness for purpose.
- *Purpose* is the experience of discovering ways to fulfill resilient yearnings.
- *Venturing* is taking action to fulfill your purpose.
- *Meaning* is the joy (infusion of Qs) you feel upon, during, or upon completion of your purpose.
- The full magnitude and power of your human spirit is manifested through your nobility. Deep within your innermost self, by nature, is a strong desire to feel enough personal strength and energy to be in a position to touch the hearts of other people. The power of your nobility is a major force in resiliently reintegrating from your life disruptions.

# CHARACTER RESILIENCE

> *Character resilience is the experience of conserving energy and feeling free from guilt through the mechanism of designing and living with a chosen character framework.*

In the experience on noble resilience, the story of the young prince can again be considered. Remember:

> The young prince journeyed to the land of the dragon by crossing the sea. He navigated the journey by using the constants of the stars and a compass.

The constants of the stars are the constants of character resilience. For happiness and progression, your resilient journey in life needs to be guided by your sense of honesty, integrity, and honor. The constants of character exist in every culture, religion, and society on the earth.

**Character Qs**

- Honesty
- Integrity
- Honor
- Fairness
- Loyalty
- Appreciation
- Fidelity
- Kindness
- Morality
- Courage

> *Character resilience* is the yearning and drive to feel the peace of living within a chosen moral framework.

Character qualities are evident across cultures and include some of those listed in the box to the right. As you ponder each of the qualities, you should feel a resonating sense of rightness with each. Think how honesty, integrity, and honor feel in your heart.

Metaphorically, the stars that accompanied the prince on his journey represent the character virtues. Sailing life's journey by thinking, feeling, and living within these character constants will keep you on course. If you violate these basic virtues of character, it is like dark clouds looming in the sky, and your journey and purpose can be compromised.

One of the amazing feelings is the feeling of joy that you have from receiving noble Q-infusions. There is a delicate balance between the peaceful or powerful feelings from the infusion of noble Qs and the energy drain that occurs when your Qs are lost through compromising your character code.

Nobility is enhanced when you follow the path of honesty, integrity, honor, loyalty, and morality. Conversely, outcomes of compromising one's character include guilt, dishonor, and shame that bleed the soul of Qs.

> Nobility is to feel the joy of Q-infusions. Violating character causes Q-bleeding.

The foundation upon which to solidify and ground your nobility is through your character resilience and by listening to your innate yearnings to be kind, honest, loyal, and to live with integrity.

To this point, you have been building upon the vitality of your childlike nature, coupled with the purpose and meaning of nobility, which will lead to progression and harmonious living. Living a life that is congruent with your own sense of character channels your energies into pursuing a resilient life of progression. When you violate your own personal code of conduct, energy is diverted to remedy the violation.

## ACTIVITY #15: REFLECT UPON Q-BLEEDING

For a moment, consider times when you may have felt Q-bleeding from life situations. Just by thinking of this time, you will feel the energy drain.

- Feel the energy spent in trying to cover a lie?
- Remember a time when you said you would do something and didn't do it? How much energy was diverted from good causes?
- How draining is the guilt you may have felt from thinking or doing something outside of your sense of character?
- How nobility draining is it when you are aware that some people feel you cannot be trusted to be honest or relied upon to do what you say you will do?

You can write your feelings about Q-bleeding here.

_____

_____

_____

The other consideration of nobility is how ineffective you are in touching the lives of others if you are pompous, proud, and arrogant. People will turn away from braggarts and boasters. Optimal nobility is manifest not only in accomplishment but coupled with character qualities of humility, honesty, and integrity.

In the 1967 version of the movie *Camelot*, the motivating creed to the knights was "Might for Right." Those knights thought that the sword as the "might" was the essence of protecting freedoms and dreams. In this day and age when enforcement by swords is inappropriate, the creed might have been better stated as "Might *by* Right," suggesting that power comes from living right. You will have power to engage in your purpose in life when you live within your character code, coupled with humility.

## ACTIVITY #16: CHARACTER RESILIENCE

Draw your own character coat of arms. As per the knights of old, symbols on the shield represented the qualities of character. Do one of two things. If you have an artistic flair, draw some of the most important character and noble qualities in the chambers of the shield. For example, you may represent courage as a lion or honor as stars. If you do not feel that you want to draw, simply write the most important qualities to which you aspire in each of the six chambers on the shield.

**Figure 17. Personal Character Coat of Arms**

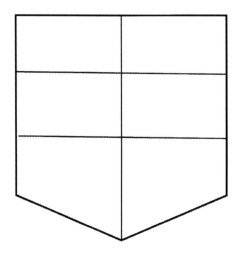

You may want to post a bigger version of this on a mirror or other noticeable place to remind you of your character code. As you reflect upon your coat of arms, perhaps you can do some character commitment by feeling the Qs of character affirmations.

1. I will follow my convictions.
2. I will walk and talk within my character code.
3. I will be honorable.
4. I will be loyal and faithful.
5. I will be honest.
6. I will do what I say I will do.
7. I will appreciate what life has given me.
8. I will be fair and kind.
9. I will live within my moral framework.
10. I will live by the Golden Rule (treat others like I want to be treated).

A great example of someone fulfilling a sense of character by being kind and living the Golden Rule was demonstrated by a neighbor who had heard that I had been hit by a car and was in a coma at the university hospital. Consider the story of Laurie's character and nobility.

> It was Christmas Eve, and my situation had taken a bad turn, and I began to slip into a deeper and deeper coma for no apparent reason. My wife had spent the entire day with me at the hospital and left to go home to get some rest. Driving home with a heavy heart, the realities of four children at home expecting a traditional Christmas celebration began to weigh on her. My mother was home watching the children, but still, the weight of Christmas seemed overwhelming to my wife. Both my wife and mother were exhausted and emotionally drained. As she had done during the previous four days, with Mother's help, my wife found an inner strength to continue to carry everyone through this ordeal. It was dark when she arrived home, and the children would be hungry. As she drove in the driveway, there was a dear neighbor that lived three houses away approaching the front door. Laurie was holding a large covered tray with a complete dinner inside for the whole family. As my wife got out of the car and approached this kind soul, a warm greeting and smile melted her heart. My wife said, "Why are you doing this on Christmas Eve? Shouldn't you be home with your own children?"

> With a spirit of love in her voice, Laurie responded softly and compassionately, "What do you think Christmas is all about?"

> I can rarely reflect upon this experience without becoming very emotional and teary. Why did Laurie, with a household of children of her own, give up part of her family celebration to prepare and deliver a Christmas

meal for a family that was struggling? Here is a saint who listened to her noble heart and gave in the season of giving. For one act of service many years ago, I am still a subject in Laurie's queendom and continue to celebrate her legacy.

The next experience will help you to find the Qs of energy and peace from the world around you.

# In Summary

- Living within your chosen character resilience is the means to conserving energy and avoiding guilt.
- Telling the truth frees you from having to cover your tracks and remember what lies you've told.
- Integrity allows to your do what you say you will do, which lays down a foundation of trust.
- Fidelity and loyalty labels free you from guilt.
- Acts of kindness fulfill both your sense of character resilience and your noble resilience.

## EXPERIENCE 5

# ECOLOGICAL RESILIENCE

> *Ecological resilience is the experience of feeling an infusion of peace and energy from one's ecosystem, including colors, natural settings, music, smells, pets, and home environments.*

I f your heart is open to it, it only takes stepping outdoors and smelling flowers and trees to feel infusions of peace and comfort. When listening to a favorite musical piece, your mood can be heightened. When watching a motivational movie, you will feel the stirring of Qs in your soul. When you feel the touch of someone dear to you, the precious spark of love fills your soul. When you eat fresh-baked bread or cookies from the oven, the taste may inspire fond memories of childhood. Your magnificent senses of smelling, hearing, seeing, touching, and tasting are like radars scanning your world for triggers that will enliven your life situation.

> *Ecological resilience* is the yearning to access the Qs of peace, inspiration, motivation, and energy that emanate from the world around you.

This experience will highlight the environmental processes and sources that can enrich your life as you become aware of the Qs in the world around you. You will also learn that you can be the architect of an ecosystem that will enrich your body, mind, and spirit.

## THE PROCESS

Everything in your world sends out vibrations—some good vibrations and others not so good. You are walking through the vibrations every minute of every day. You can choose which vibrations you are aware of to some degree. The formula that explains the process of receiving good vibrations is scientific and in one sense simple.

### Figure 18. Vibrations Affect Body

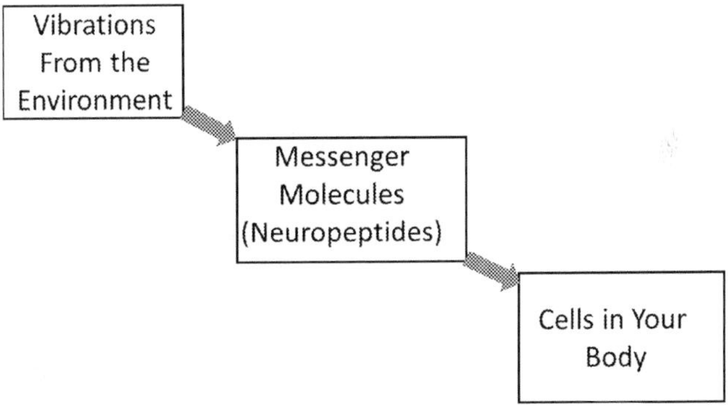

```
┌─────────────┐
│ Vibrations  │
│ From the    │
│ Environment │──┐
└─────────────┘  ▼
          ┌──────────────┐
          │  Messenger   │
          │  Molecules   │
          │(Neuropeptides)│──┐
          └──────────────┘   ▼
                    ┌──────────────┐
                    │ Cells in Your │
                    │     Body      │
                    └──────────────┘
```

Perhaps one of the best descriptions of how we harvest Qs from the world around us is described in the work from the late scientist Candace Pert. Published in 1999, Dr. Pert wrote a fascinating book entitled *Molecules of Emotion: The Science between Mind-Body Medicine* in which she describes how we are connected to our environment. The science behind the process of nature's messages of peace and the complicated process of connecting thoughts, hormones, chemicals, and the nervous system is beyond the scope of this book. But let me just highlight this very intricate yet logical process. For greater detail, her book is a fascinating read.

First, it is important that you are open and receptive to soft vibrations. If you are steeped in worry and fear and preoccupied with life challenges, then you may miss these softer vibrations. The vibrations come to you through your senses. You can feel them if you are mindful and open to them.

1. From nature, from smells, from sounds, from sights, and the other senses, Dr. Pert describes soft vibrations that touch our bodies.

2.  Throughout our bodies are numerous messenger molecules called *neuropeptides*. If we are open and soft, the neuropeptides begin to vibrate at the same frequency as the soft vibrations they are receiving from the external stimuli in nature.
3.  The soft, vibrating messenger molecules find cells within our bodies that have receptor sites and attach to them.
4.  The cells then begin to vibrate at the same soft, healing, and Q-infusion frequency.

The vibrations that come from nature are soft (7.8 hertz) and touch our bodies, stimulating soft neuropeptides at a frequency that is similar to the alpha frequency in our brains. The alpha state is a relaxed, peaceful, and optimal state for inspiration and learning. As you walk in nature and your mind is not cluttered with worries and distractions, you will feel the soft vibrations. You can feel the infusion of natural vibrations in the form of the desired Qs of peace and inspiration. It will also put you in a state to learn and make decisions at your optimal level.

The Beach Boys were right when they sang of "good vibrations." They may have been singing about being around an attractive woman, but the good vibrations also apply to the good vibrations from calming smells, soft sounds, and beautiful sights.

The amazing connection between you and your environment not only affects your mood but can also affect the optimal function of organs and systems in your body. As you are exposed to positive environments and are mindful of the experience, it can positively affect your mind and spirit to be enriched and sparked.

> A feeling sparked in your mind will translate as a peptide being released somewhere [in your body]. Peptides regulate every aspect of your body, from whether you're going to digest your food properly to whether you're going to destroy a tumor cell.
>
> —Candace Pert

Dr. Pert's book *Molecules of Emotion* also explains the science of resonation as one of the postulates or truths of the Q-nexus. You can resonate to the source of many vibrations and be positively enriched and Q-infused.

## THE SOURCES OF ECOLOGICAL QS

This experience will highlight a few ecological sources of Qs. Bookstores and libraries are full of books written about sources of ecological resilience. For example, Dr. Esther Sternberg (2010) has written a powerful book entitled *Healing Spaces: The Science of Place and Well-Being*, which goes into great detail into the power of an enriching environment. Ecological sources of strength can come from music, nature, historical sites, plants, pets, aromas, art, movies, and other people, among many. Each person is unique and will resonate to one or more of these ecological sources to try to enrich his or her world.

You long for energy beyond yourself. Remember that UEUs also come from your environment and ecosystem. You will feel enlivened when you sense the infusion of needed Qs. We will use the term *quickening* from the introduction of this book to describe the process when the vibrations from your environment influence the neuropeptides in your body. These vibrations can positively affect your whole soul if you will let them. We described quickening in the introduction as follows:

> When we are infused with Qs, such as love or courage, *quickening* provides a renewed sense of energy that brings us to life. This experience is likened to the first indications of life from a baby in a mother's womb—an experience known as *quickening*. Therefore, the revitalizing experience of receiving an infusion of Qs is also called *quickening*.

## ACTIVITY #17: MUSIC QUICKENING

You likely have experienced mood changes based upon the vibrations that come from music. With lively music, you feel energized. With patriotic music, you may feel honor and loyalty. With sacred music, you may feel reverent. With romantic music, you may feel loving. It is difficult to walk into a dance and resist moving when your favorite music is playing. As you review the list of qualities you really want in life, you can find music that will send vibrations to you that will stimulate that feeling. See the box for examples of the desired Qs that can be sensed by listening to customized music.

| | | |
|---|---|---|
| Enlightenment | Fun | Discernment |
| Meaning | Adventure | Guidance |
| Purpose | Enjoyment | Love |
| Hope | Fulfillment | Self-Worth |
| Honesty | Spirituality | Value |
| Comfort | Happiness | Peace |
| Pleasure | Courage | Inspiration |
| Wisdom | Confidence | Energy |
| Moral Strength | Power | Healing |
| | Freedom | Inspiration |
| | Strength | |

As you listen to a variety of your favorite music, write down the Qs that you feel when listening to it.

1. _____
2. _____
3. _____
4. _____
5. _____

## ACTIVITY #18: CHANGING MOOD WITH MUSIC

Consider the mood that you want to have in a day. Is there a time to be loving? Is there a time to be engaging? Is there a time to be spiritual? As you think through the events of your day and consider the moods you want, plan a time when you can listen to music (driving, walking, etc.). Identify music that will create the best mood or ability to harvest Qs for you in each occasion. Complete the chart below. One example is provided for you.

| Situation | Music | Outcome |
|---|---|---|
| 1. Change from work to being home with children | Theme from Sesame Street | Mood changes to be more childlike |
| 2. | | |
| 3. | | |
| 4. | | |
| 5. | | |

## WATER QUICKENING

Water is an amazing source of Qs ranging from invigoration by jumping into a swimming pool to relaxing in a hot bath. You can laugh and play, evoking childlike Qs by getting into a water fight with hoses, running through sprinklers, getting into a squirt gun war, or finding yourself launching water balloons. You can bond and connect with others chatting in the relaxing environment of a hot tub. You can ponder meaning and purpose sitting with your feet dangling in a lake or stream or sitting on a beach overlooking the ocean. Sometimes the magic of a shower can help you ponder solutions to life's challenges.

## ACTIVITY #19: WATER IN YOUR DAY

In your pursuit of Qs, ponder for a moment how you might be able to feel peace, relaxation, spirituality, or enhanced connections from a form of water quickening.

_____

_____

_____

_____

## MOVIE QUICKENING

Most of us like to go to movies. Sometimes we go to comedies and identify with the humor and fun the actors are exemplifying. Sometimes we go to adventure movies that quicken the spirit of adventure and courage within us. Sometimes we go to romantic movies that quicken the lover in us. Sometimes we go to meaningful dramas that may trigger the spiritual nature within us.

When you are feeling down and need an infusion of Qs to your soul, it is always good to have an inspiring movie or even a television show available. Sometimes it may take seeing the entire movie again and sometimes it only takes a four- to five-minute clip of the impactful parts of the movie. Many key clips are available on electronic sites on the Internet.

It may be important to update your arsenal of movie clips. We often become desensitized to a scene and need something new. As you go to new movies, you can make a note to yourself that when the movie becomes available, it would be a good purchase for desired Qs.

## ACTIVITY #20: MOVIE QUICKENING

You may want to purchase selected movies or identify a website where clips are stored. For each of the movie clips, describe the moment that best infuses the desired Qs you are seeking. You will want to have it available for when you need the quickening experience. One example is shown in the chart. You can complete the rest of the chart and identify other mood needs as well.

| Desired Qs | Movie | Specific Scene |
|------------|-------|----------------|
| Honor and Unity | Remember the Titans | When Coach Herman Boone, as played by Denzel Washington, is talking about honor and unity in bringing the football team together in the graveyard at Gettysburg |

| | | |
|---|---|---|
| | | |
| | | |

## Nature Quickening

It is human nature to enjoy natural settings. We cited earlier the simplistic version of how vibrations can quicken your soul. Vibrations from nature are the soft vibrations that will gently bring you peace and comfort. When you are mindful of the experiences, using plants and trees in your yard, plants in your home, or when you are in parks, you will be able to quicken your soul with peace, comfort, and spirituality. Mindful means that you dismiss extraneous thoughts and focus on the natural source and what is happening to you as you find yourself in these locations. When you are in the mountains, you feel enlivened and refreshed. When you are in a park, you feel better. Even in your own home, it is likely that you have plants around you and you will be able to sense their vibrations as well. Sometimes a fresh breeze will touch your soul. Even the seasons may enrich you. The first fallen snow or the invigoration of rain can initially be quickening for you. The more you are mindful of your natural surroundings, the better you will feel because these sources are authentic, pure, and unadulterated vibrations and, if you are receptive, have potential for nature quickening.

## Activity #21: Mindfulness in Nature

Take the opportunity to feel the vibrations coming to your messenger molecules and affecting the cells of your body. Go to a place that has trees, flowers, shrubs, grass, rocks, or other natural elements. While you are there, try the following imagery strategy:

1.  Get comfortable in your natural setting and try to be free of distractions.
2.  Close your eyes and visualize the natural elements in your situation.

3. Imagine the healing, peaceful, and inspiring vibrations that come from the elements. See the vibrations coming into your imagination.
4. See the vibrations touch your skin as they surround you.
5. Imagine the vibrations igniting little cells that are the messenger molecules to vibrate at the same frequency.
6. See the vibrating messenger molecules going to cells in your body as the cells begin to vibrate.
7. Feel the infusion of peace and other desired Qs that come from the vibrations.

## HISTORICAL QUICKENING

One of the most inspiring, reflective, and appreciative experiences is to visit sites where significant historical events have taken place. Prior to visiting the site, it is best to review the story about the people, their courage, and their nobility as they made selected sites special and therefore ready to quicken your soul.

> When I was a twelve-year-old boy, my family took a cross-country vacation from San Diego to Maine to visit my father's roots. Although we visited many places along the way, one of the most impressionable stops was our visit to Gettysburg, Pennsylvania. The park ranger described the great Civil War battle that occurred at the site and shared with great detail the thousands of soldiers that died that day for their cause. I was in awe. I stood at the top of Cemetery Ridge and heard the ranger describe the Confederate charge. "During the afternoon of July 3, 1863, the Confederate infantry attacked the Union center on Cemetery Ridge. Pickett's Charge momentarily pierced the Union line, but the infantry was driven back with severe casualties. The next few days saw General Lee retreat and his train of wounded stretched more than fourteen miles."

I was struck with the spirit of the ground I was walking on. I tried to imagine the bravery and loyalty on both sides of the Civil War. What feelings and thoughts were in the minds of these brave soldiers who walked in Napoleonic combat lines, shoulder to shoulder, into a hail of rifle, cannon fire, and residual smoke? Even as a child, the powerful Qs of honor, commitment, and sacrifice for a cause resonated to my soul.

## ACTIVITY #22: HISTORICAL QUICKENING

Take the opportunity to think about opportunities that you have had to visit historical sites. Perhaps you have visited historic government buildings, religious settings, military battlegrounds, 9/11 monuments, Mount Rushmore, pioneer trails, or numerous other places. You may have discovered histories of ancestors and have felt the resonation of genealogy. You may have felt the quickening by reading about historical events. Reflect upon at least three different experiences in the box.

| Historical Site or Reading | Key Event | Qs You Felt |
|---|---|---|
| 1. | | |
| 2. | | |
| 3. | | |

## ANIMAL QUICKENING

I have always been amazed at pets. When I was growing up, we always had a dog. In a short amount of time, they become loyal and protective. If people don't abuse them, they are loyal to whatever type of people take them into their homes. They are loyal to seniors, children, all genders, all races, and all languages. They can be trained to do tasks or tricks. Cat people will argue that cats are the most loyal and loveable. Cats can bring the same infusion of love.

Other animals can also be as loyal as dogs and cats. The benefits of pet therapy are well documented. Animals have simple lives in comparison to humans. Most pets are loving, accepting, and loyal. You may resonate to different types of animals. If you live on a farm or ranch, you can experience the connection to a wider variety of animals, such as horses, cows, sheep, or pigs. If you live in town, then you may be restricted by city ordinances to fish, birds, hamsters, cats, or dogs. The literature is full of examples of how pets have been shown to diminish emotional and physical pain, reduce boredom and anxiety, and provide the Q-infusion of love, loyalty, and happiness. You can be quickened by your pet's unconditional love and loyalty. Think of a time, either current or in the past, where you received warmth, comfort, fun, or other Qs from a pet. Complete the box below as you reflect upon a couple of times when you felt the good feelings from a pet.

| Describe a Time When You Received Qs from a Pet | Qs You Felt |
| --- | --- |
| 1. | |
| 2. | |

## AROMA QUICKENING

Oftentimes we are not aware of the smells around us. Researchers have shown some benefits of different smells and oils that seem to be therapeutic (Cooke and Ernst 2000). *Aromatherapy* Therapy is the practice of using natural oils extracted from flowers, bark, stems, leaves, roots, or other parts of a plant to enhance psychological and physical well-being. Aromatherapy is gaining momentum. It is used for a variety of applications, including pain relief, mood enhancement, and increased cognitive function.

The most popular sources of aromas to deal with depression, anxiety, and increased energy include:

- eucalyptus
- lavender
- cinnamon
- peppermint
- jasmine
- sandalwood
- orange
- lemon

You can explore the claimed benefits of these aromas that are available through a number of commercial outlets. A noncommercial perspective is to simply associate smells with positive Qs in your life. For example:

- If you want to feel romantic, perhaps a particular cologne or perfume will enliven your romantic feelings.
- If you want to be energized to exercise, perhaps the smell of a gym or fresh-cut grass on a playing field will do that.
- If you need to feel noble and professional, perhaps the smell of a business suit will trigger that quality.
- If you need to feel connected with family, perhaps the smell of food in the kitchen will promote feelings of love.
- If you want to remember the messages and Qs you received from a particular movie, perhaps all you will have to do is pop some popcorn and the aromas may trigger excitement.

The list could go on, but the effect depends upon you and to what you resonate. You do the associations.

## ACTIVITY #23: AROMA QUICKENING

List a Q that you want, and then think about some smells that may trigger the emergence of that quality.

| Desired Quality or Mood | Aroma |
|---|---|
| 1. | |
| 2. | |
| 3. | |

## ART QUICKENING

Some of us enter art galleries and are amazed at the masterpieces that we see. We look online and see amazing photographs and images. Depending upon the nature of the art, we will feel many of the desired Qs we want. Whether the artwork is sculpture, paintings, or photography, we can stand in awe of great works as we feel the infusion of Qs of appreciation and, depending upon the work of art, other resilient qualities. Think of a time when you had the opportunity to gaze upon a work of art and felt Qs.

| What Were the Works of Art? | Qs You Felt |
|---|---|
| 1. | |
| 2. | |

## OTHER PEOPLE

Not much will be described about other people and the energy that they can provide you in this book. This book is about you, your drives, your resources, and your resilient journey. There is little question that we are influenced and can harvest Qs from trusted family and friends. It is also true that others can drain Qs from your life. You can feel the vibrations of love, trust, acceptance, and worth. You can share your noble, childlike, and character drives with others to multiply the Qs you can harvest. There is much to be said when two people come together with their resilient journeys and resilient needs. You will want to consider other people to help you on your resilient journey, for you know the great feelings you can get when you are with people you love. Consider them a source of Qs if you mindfully focus on their love for you. This volume will focus on you. I only mention this now because it is obvious that other people send out vibrations; the good vibrations will enrich your life, and the bad vibrations may drain you. They are integral to your world.

## DESIGNING YOUR ECOSYSTEM

If ecological resilience is the yearning to access the peace, inspiration, motivation, and energy that emanate from the world around you, then it seems wise to design an enriching environment at your home, work, play, and with your transportation. Consider the things that you can do.

- You can visit places that are enriching.

- You can design your home and office with pictures, plants, aromas, and music.
- You can have a yard that has flowers, plants, and trees.

Professionals can also help you design a home that feels warm and peaceful. You can study the practice of feng shui, which is a Chinese system of harmonizing everyone with his or her surrounding environment.

Write your thoughts here about how you can enrich your ecosystem or go to places that are enriching.

 

An excerpt from my journal describing my feeling following my accident and demonstrates how one musical piece meant so much to me during my rehabilitation.

> It was with some difficulty that my wife and children helped me into our family minivan and put the wheelchair into the back as I ventured to attend church for the first time since the accident. We drove the three blocks to the church, and the ritual repeated itself as they helped me out of the car and into my wheelchair. I rolled into church and was greeted by loving friends who all knew of my accident and welcomed me back to our congregation. I felt a little awkward being the center of so much attention, but I also basked in their warmth and love. I had not been to church for a couple of months. To me, much of the spirit of church comes from the music and messages included in the lyrics from the hymns. I love the powerful, moving pieces as well as the reverent, reflective melodies. After I settled in with my wheelchair alongside the pew where my family was sitting, the opening hymn was announced from the pulpit. As the introductory organ music touched my ears, I was shocked by my reaction. The music re-created in my mind and heart the wonderful peace I had felt during

my coma, and I suddenly felt the magnificence of those endearing memories of warmth and love. The message of the familiar hymn touched my soul. "The Spirit of God Like a Fire Is Burning" filled my whole being as though it were on fire. I began to weep uncontrollably. I tried to stop crying, but the powerful music kept playing. I'm sure I embarrassed my family, but I could not hold it back. The music inspired me and lifted my spirits!

The next experience will focus on the origin of that spirit I felt—universal resilience.

# In Summary

- You can feel the Q-nexus when you live in a Q-enriching world.
- You can control your moods through careful listening to various types of music.
- You can refresh or relax by immersing yourself in cool or warm water.
- Being in nature helps you experience peace.
- You can acquire the Qs of great people by visiting historical sites.
- Animals, art, aromas, and other people can also help you acquire Qs.

## EXPERIENCE 6

# UNIVERSAL RESILIENCE

> *Universal resilience is the experience of connecting to a source of wisdom, energy, and strength beyond normal consciousness.*

In your life story, there are times when challenges are overwhelming and the hope of overcoming the seemingly insurmountable adversity seems far beyond possibility. These moments can bring despair and discouragement. But you may have experienced special moments when in the hopeless troughs of discouragement you discovered glimmers of hope and insight that triggered some kind of renewed energy and sparks of courage. With that hope, coupled with persistence, you marveled that you ended up celebrating a victory over the obstacle. It is as though a force pushed you and lifted you to greater heights.

> *Universal resilience* is the yearning and drive to access and connect to a force, energy, or power beyond normal capacity—to feel the infusion of universal Qs.

This experience will help you be aware that there is a source of energy, power, and inspiration that is all around you and within you. Whether you look at theories of psychology or the mysteries of theoretical physics, all suggest that our cognitive minds are extremely limited, but our innate capacity allows us to access greater strengths and abilities. This experience will review several of the perspectives from different academic disciplines that validate the experience of accessing a strength beyond normal—your universal resilience.

> Despair melts into hope when you realize that you are sailing life's voyage in a sea of enlightenment, peace, and miracles that lie just beyond the bandwidth of the human conscious mind.

We see numerous examples of heroes all around us who have overcome the odds and left legacies of great accomplishment. People report feeling power and energy to deal with life crises in a way they had never experienced previously. We see the energy of fear transformed into the power of courage. We see where initial stressors and changes were used as springboards for growth. We see confusion at a time of important decision making evolve into keen discernment and enduring confidence. It is important to be aware of this force around you. It will help you discover jewels of hope in the mire of depression. If you are concerned about what is right or wrong, universal forces will confirm the truth.

We see heroes and heroines in sports, business, service, relationships, and in history that have benefited from universal resilience. Historians tell the story of the Continental Army in the beginning weeks of the Revolutionary War where, were it not for universal and ecological interventions, the Americans may have lost that war.

> In the first few days of the American Revolution, George Washington's poorly trained Continental Army of about nine thousand was facing the British army, the most powerful military force in the world at that time. Washington's soldiers found themselves trapped at the end of Long Island with the East River at their backs and thirty thousand disciplined and trained British soldiers at their front. The British had formed a half circle around the Continental Army, which offered no escape. While the two army encampments prepared for battle, the British

commander, William Howe, for some reason chose not to attack for two days. Instead, the British soldiers lay in siege even though a victory was imminent and the American Revolution would have been smothered in the first days of the war. Washington's army tried to prepare for the likely suicidal resistance. As the British prepared to attack the next day, a storm arose, which again delayed the assault on the Continentals. Washington and his officers saw this as a chance to escape. During the storm, the Continental Army made a daring plan to flee. They secured as many small boats as possible. In the dark of night, they secretly began to transport troops across the expansive mile-wide river in order to escape the impending tragedy. All through the night, the boats crossed again and again, evacuating the army across the restless waters of the East River. As the sun rose the next morning, many troops were still on the island, and it became clear that the army needed at least another three hours before the escape would be complete. As destiny or divine province would have it, the Continental Army's escape was protected by a dense fog. Major Ben Tallmadge wrote in his journal, "At this time a very dense fog began to rise, and it seemed to settle in a peculiar manner over both encampments. I recollect this peculiar providential occurrence perfectly well; and so very dense was the atmosphere that I could scarcely discern a man at six yards' distance. … we tarried until the sun had risen, but the fog remained as dense as ever."

The army was given enough time by the fog to escape and regroup away from enemy lines and later were reinforced to fight the great American Revolution. The United States would not have won the war by all accounts had it not been for the "miracle" of the protective fog. Upon receiving great praise for his leadership in the war, General George Washington wrote, "I was but the humble agent of favoring Heaven, whose benign influence was so often manifested in our behalf, and to whom alone the praise of victory is due."

Whether the Continental Army's escape was the intervention from God, a spiritual source, providence, or fortunate timing of weather conditions, still the dramatic outcome occurred because of a strength or intervention beyond what the army could create by itself.

Humans throughout history and across cultures have consistently longed for a power beyond their normal capacity. They have longed to be part of something bigger than themselves. Quiet moments looking at the stars or gazing at a sunset can awaken the awareness of universal and ecological Qs and the yearning to receive them.

This experience will help you recognize that across the disciplines, there is a common understanding about the tiny bits of energy that produce the universal and ecological Qs you really want in life. There are many names for these bits of energy, depending upon the field of study, but for the purposes of this book, we have called them *universal energy units*, or *UEUs*. UEUs are the source of all the Qs we really want in life. Whether it be to receive help in escaping impending disasters, as per the Continental Army, or to know where to live when moving to a new community, subtle insights and strengths come through the UEUs. Relying upon the perspective of the many academic disciplines, you will learn of the remarkable nature of UEUs. You will also learn the mechanism of how the UEUs touch our beings so we feel the infusions of the magnificent universal Qs.

## DIVERSELY CONGRUENT VIEW OF UEUS

There are many names and views of the boundless energizing life force that

### Universal Energy Unit Synonyms

- Qi or chi
- Quark or quanta
- Human essence
- Strings
- Unified force
- Vitality
- Life force
- Human spirit
- Subtle energy
- Prana
- Vital energy
- Kun long
- Light
- Glory

enlivens us to feel, perform, and think better than we do normally. It is almost humorous to witness people disagreeing about the origin and nature of strength beyond normal when they are speaking of the same energy source. People who believe in God (theists) say that they can find peace and hope through God's Spirit. Some academics are excited about the possibilities of receiving energy from strings or quanta from the field of energy described in theoretical physics. Some people embrace the principles of the Eastern philosophies and speak of the free flow of energy that is within us and all around us known as *qi* or *chi*. Some psychologists hunger for the greater wisdom of the ages that is housed in the sanctuaries of our own collective unconscious minds. Though the names change with belief systems and academic perspectives, the function of the UEUs is the same. In the box is a list of labels or names that people use to describe UEUs. As the UEUs touch your being, your whole soul can be enlivened with desired Qs. You will feel the wonderful infusions of universal Qs, such as the following:

- healing
- peace
- energy
- joy
- comfort
- understanding
- wisdom
- guidance
- enlightenment or inspiration
- love
- truths confirmed
- happiness

> UEUs (universal energy units) infuse your soul and are manifest by or experienced as strength, courage, inspiration, meaning, wisdom, or other enlivening Qs you need.

## THE MIND-SET OF BELIEF

One of the prerequisites for receiving the infusion of UEUs with the resulting Qs is for you to have hope, belief, or faith that UEUs exist and understand the nature of their amazing power. I hope that as you continue reading you will realize that their existence is supported and described by several disciplines. Hopefully the evidence presented will ignite or confirm the requisite belief that these UEUs are the essence of a sea of energy and wisdom in which you live. Belief or faith is an important element or postulate for accessing the UEUs. In psychology, the belief that you will experience positive Qs is called *self-efficacy*. In religion, it is called *faith*. In the self-help literature, it is called *intention*. We will explore a couple of disciplines that talk about UEUs using their terms and hopefully confirm your belief in a force or strength beyond your normal capacity. We will first consider the nature of the world around us and the omnipresence of UEUs. Secondly, we look at belief systems and theories that describe the source of wisdom beyond normal consciousness. Lastly, we will explore the nature and power of the UEUs.

## OMNIPRESENT UEUS

Science and theology suggest that the UEUs are everywhere. We are living in a world full of UEUs. They are all around us and within us. For support of this concept, let's take a casual look at theoretical physics, Eastern philosophy, molecular theory, and theism.

## THEORETICAL PHYSICS

UEUs may be described in terms of a universal energy that is within us and all around us. Theoretical physics' most daring argument is that the basis of all life is a one-dimensional energy unit called a *string*, among other name variations. Strings are a billion, billion times smaller than an atom. With today's technology, strings cannot be seen, but mathematically, they do seem to exist. This is the fulfillment of Einstein's dream of uniting all the forces of the universe into one force. The force of gravity (attraction of two masses), electromagnetism (electricity and lightning), the strong nuclear force (neutrons and protons held together in atoms), and the weak nuclear force (beta decay turning neutrons into protons) are elementary forces if we accept string theory. It explains how big things move (general relativity), as well as how little things function (quantum mechanics).

The tiny bits of energy activate everything in the universe and control the order in all things. Perhaps this is best understood when we see the fictitious character Yoda in the *Star Wars* movies moving objects using the Force. The common little energy packets are part of us and around us and are the vitalizing force in everything. It is nicknamed the Theory of Everything (Greene 1999). Strings energize all the Qs within us and are connected to the strings in the universe in which we live. Everything in the universe is formed by the way these strings vibrate. It would be amazing for us to be able to access this energy source or UEUs that will improve our moods and activate our resilient drives.

> In essence, we can say, "We are walking, living, and breathing in a universe full of infinitely small vibrating energy packets (strings) that define and energize everything. The infusion of strings into our souls results in feeling desired Qs."

## EASTERN PHILOSOPHIES

The Eastern philosophies teach about a life force or life energy. It is the active force that is the principle energy of any living thing. It is the vitalizing force within people, animals, the air, and the earth. In traditional Chinese culture and Taoist philosophy, qi is literally translated as *breath, air,* or *gas.* Qi is experienced as vibrations in nature and the universe, sustaining the flow that connects and moves everything at the molecular, atomic, and subatomic levels. Taoists practice skills to feel the qi, which promotes healing, peace, and other Qs, throughout their bodies. In Japan, it is called *ki,* and in India, *prana* or *Shakti.* The ancient Egyptians referred to it as *ka,* and the ancient Greeks as *pneuma.* For Native Americans, it is the *Great Spirit* and for Christians, the *Holy Spirit.* In Africa, it's known as *ashe,* and in Hawaii as *ha* or *mana.* There are similar concepts across the Eastern cultures. It is truly amazing that so many cultures believe in the common phenomenon of being in a world full of UEUs, yet it cannot be seen. Again, the same concepts exist.

> In essence, we can say, "We are walking, living, breathing in a universe full of infinitely small vibrating energy packets (qi, ki, prana, or chi) that define and energize everything. The infusion of Qi into our souls results in feeling desired Qs."

## MOLECULAR THEORY

Molecular theory is the foundation of ecological resilience as mentioned earlier in the work of Candace Pert. To be more specific, vibrations that come from nature are soft (7.8 hertz) and touch our bodies, stimulating the messenger molecules to affect receptors in the cells in our bodies. The frequency of the vibrations is comparable to the alpha frequency in our brains. The alpha state is a relaxed peaceful and optimal state for inspiration and learning. As you walk in nature and your mind is not cluttered with worries and distractions, you will feel the soft vibrations. You can feel the infusion of natural vibrations of peace, comfort, and inspiration. It will put you in a state to learn and make decisions at your optimal level.

> In essence, we can say, "We are walking, living, breathing in a universe full of infinitely small vibrating energy packets (molecules from nature) that define and energize everything. The infusion of soft vibrations into our souls results in feeling the desired Qs."

## THEISM AND SPIRITUALITY

According to a 2013 Harris Poll, 74 percent of Americans believe in some form of God or gods. The perceptions of God vary from a being in a glorious human form to an omnipresent awareness to a type of fiery source of light and truth. Most people recognize that God has powers and benevolence beyond human capacity. Many speak of God's Spirit as a divine grace or power that proceeds from God to fill the immensity of space or what many call the Holy Spirit. When people feel the spirit, it is like a positive vibration in the chest, a sense of peace, a feeling of devotion or the infusion of a warm truth. God's Spirit results in the desired Qs we need. Those that believe in God(s) generally believe that

125

they also have a human spirit within themselves and that connections and infusions of strength, wisdom, peace, and power can be made with God's Spirit. Prayer and meditation are the rituals of attempting to align one's spirit with God's so that "His will, will be done." In cases of deep spirituality, prayer, meditation, and service become a way of being and living life in alignment (harmony) with God's will and wisdom. Answers to prayer come when God's Spirit vibrates truth to our souls via spiritual vibrations.

> In essence, we can say, "We are walking, living, breathing in a universe full of infinitely small vibrating energy packets (God's Spirit) that define and energize everything. The infusion of God's Spirit into our souls results in feeling desired Qs."

## ACTIVITY #24: WALKING IN THE SEA OF UEUS

I want you to imagine for a moment that you are walking outside on an invigorating yet comfortable night in a natural setting. Imagine the natural trees and flowers are all around you, and a gentle stream babbles a distance away. As you look upward toward the clear and glorious sky, you see the heavens peppered with stars. You ponder the awe and wonder of this beautiful night. You consider your connection with the great and mysterious. Picture in your mind that the stars begin to shower tiny bits of light, and you watch them gently descend down to earth. You can sense their touch as they gently rain upon you. As you walk through these little specks of light, you can feel the wonderful infusions of energy as they gently alight on you. With each speck of light that touches you, you feel bursts of the Qs you want. Imagine that some of the particles of light fall on you, and you feel bits of peace come over you. Other specks of light make you feel more and more courageous. Still others make you feel more hope and optimism. As you inhale, the specks of light fill your lungs and then your soul with love of yourself and then of others. Imagine breathing in and feeling desired Qs that fill your entire being.

# BELIEF SYSTEMS AND THEORIES OF WISDOM BEYOND CONSCIOUSNESS

We have confirmed from a few disciplines that UEUs are all around us and within us. The reason we can't see them is that our conscious thinking capacities are extremely limited in their functionality and bandwidth. You have so much more wisdom and insight that you can imagine as will be described throughout this experience. The famous psychologist Carl Jung described our conscious thinking as the tip of the iceberg. Beyond our conscious thinking is a vast reservoir of thought and wisdom housed within our unconscious and collective unconscious minds. Considering recent understandings of the enormity of our minds' and spirits' capacity, the percentage of our conscious minds that we actually use is likely very small. In your life, you can only see, for example, within a bandwidth of 400 to 1,400 nanometers. Beyond your sight, at bandwidths that are slower and faster than you can see, wonderful things are occurring. For example, softer than the 400 nanometers, a beam of light at 380 nanometers projected on a partially destroyed cell will restore the cell to 100 percent within twenty-four hours (McTaggart 2008). The soft healing wave is just outside of our bandwidth. The amazing vibrations and energy that are available in our ecosystem and the universe are communicated generally beyond our normal range of awareness. We have to be soft and open in order to experience the positives of the energy field in which we live.

Still we can enjoy the infusion of UEUs and the resulting Qs by recognizing that there is much we can do to access the Qs from within ourselves. It is important to recognize that you have a tremendous reservoir of energy within you. Several disciplines have suggested that you have more potential within you than you can imagine.

## COLLECTIVE UNCONSCIOUS

The famous Swedish psychologist Carl Jung introduced a concept called the *collective unconscious*. He suggested that each person has a part of his or her brain that is a collection of the wisdom and experiences of all humankind but that is beyond conscious thinking. Whether the Qs accumulate from generation to generation or the more universal perspective of the UEUs bumping into each other and exchanging and gathering information over time, the result is that you have a reservoir of wisdom (Qs) that is the combined wisdom of all the humans that have ever lived. This is a vast reservoir of wisdom that is most difficult for us to access unless we are aware of it and use skills to access that wisdom.

With integrative health techniques, such as meditation, imagery, or music enrichment, you can discover some of that wisdom. As you reflect upon your family history and ponder the writings of your ancestors, you can feel a resonating part of you that connects with their spirit of adventure, their altruism, and their wisdom. You can read about heroes in history who represent the courage and hope you wish you had and then feel that it is inside you. You may read the stories of heroes, wisdom and guidance from the Bible, the Qur'an, the *Tao Te Ching*, the Vedas, the Talmud, or the Book of Mormon, among many spiritual writings, and feel the joy of resonating to the teachings. You have within you the same qualities as those heroes. The wisdom they have can be communicated to you through soft vibrations (dreams, meditation, and music) that represent the best of all humankind. Jung spoke of *archetypes*, or characters that lie within us, and we have the potential to access the wisdom of those characters of the ages. We can be influenced and seek the wisdom of everyone who has ever lived.

> Sheltered within us and around us are transcendent champions, heroes, and exemplars that are keepers of the treasuries of the universal energy units, sparking wisdom, courage, inspiration, and all the other Qs we desire.

## ACTIVITY #25: JOURNEY TO THE COLLECTIVE UNCONSCIOUS

Reflect upon a decision or challenge you have at the moment. It may be a choice, or you may be struggling with the courage to do what you need to do. With the situation in the back of your mind, think about the people in your history or the history of humankind that may have encountered similar problems. You can review their capacities to respond to challenges and learn how they exemplified powerful Qs you wish you had. Perhaps it is a religious person, such as Buddha, Jesus, or Jehovah. Perhaps it is a courageous and persistent hero, such as Eleanor Roosevelt, Rosa Parks, or Mahatma Gandhi. Perhaps you are thinking of a person of wisdom and compassion and Abraham Lincoln or Mother Teresa comes to mind. Perhaps it is one of your ancestors. Pick one or two people.

Now, in your imagination, I want you to take a journey into your collective unconscious mind. Fantasize that you have become very tiny and will enter your brain, which appears to be a vast auditorium. There is a path that winds through the great auditorium of your mind. Imagine that you are walking along the endless path and there are branches along the way that lead to different people. You will see the people at the end of the branching paths as you might imagine them. As you walk along the path, you decide to visit one of the people in your ancestry or a famous person in history. Pick a person from whom you would like to seek counsel. Imagine yourself walking up the path and meeting the person you have sought for counsel and as an exemplar of the Qs you are seeking. As you arrive at his or her location, imagine what the situation is and how he or she might look. Imagine that the hero embraces you, and you sit down to talk. You can feel the Qs that you desire from this hero. Imagine the conversation you might have. What wisdom will be given to you? Feel the Qs the person exemplifies radiating toward you, and feel yourself becoming like your hero. You feel his or her character and goodness as you assume his or her strengths. Rehearse in your mind how you might engage your challenge or decision with the acquired Qs. Enjoy the conversation for a few moments. As you end the imagery, keep the power of the Qs within you.

## WESTERN PHILOSOPHIES

Many Western philosophers speak of receiving Qs from strength within themselves but are connected to an external power using a variety of identifiers. Joseph Campbell stated, "Follow your bliss and the universe will open doors where there were only walls." Ram Dass said, "The spiritual journey is individual, highly personal. It can't be organized or regulated. It isn't true that everyone should follow one path. Listen to your own truth."

> Your soul is guided by a personal navigator charged
> with enlightening and prompting your mind to embark
> on adventurous voyages. En route to the discovery of

meaningful Q-treasures, your navigator speaks to you with soft yearnings and coded drives as to how to thrive, enjoy, find meaning, and live with integrity.

## NEAR-DEATH EXPERIENCES (NDES)

Many people have experienced "near-death" or "life-after-life" experiences. Some of the time, people will report the experience, and other times they choose not to out of reverence and an inability to even describe what happened. Most often, these NDEs occurred at a time when someone's life was slipping away, and, in most cases, the heart had stopped beating. Those who share their experience describe feelings of love, peace, and happiness in a feeling like none other in their lives. The experience of dying, for most, is an amazing transcendent experience. Some people who have had these experiences became irritated when they were brought back to life because the connection to a source of love and light was so wonderful. Thousands have reported experiences in such books as *Life after Life* by Raymond Moody and *Evidence of the Afterlife* by Jeffrey Long. In NDEs, people report encounters with loved ones that have passed on. People describe a world of joy and rapture far beyond human comprehension.

In addition to NDEs, there have been reports of apparitions and visions from angels and other spiritual or physical beings revealed to individuals, providing guidance and insight. There are many books suggesting that some people have a gift or can acquire a psychospiritual state that visitations can happen. Often these angelic visits are life changing.

Whether this is a real phenomenon or brain chemistry adjustments during difficult times, still the experience is far too common to ignore. From a practical perspective, you can imagine that you receive personal enlightenment from a source beyond normal consciousness. As you look for strength beyond normal capacity or universal resilience, you can sense the drive to connect with a power beyond normal. Many have testified of such a force during an NDE.

There may be some support for the concept of encountering influences or beings just beyond the human bandwidth. When you add the concept of parallel universes from theoretical physics into the formula, it becomes clearer. Theoretical physicists suggest that at a frequency that humans cannot normally discern, beings may be living right next to us in another dimension. As people become closer to death, they may be able to communicate with the parallel and coinciding universe.

## THEISM AND PRAYER

In the hearts and minds of many people, personal insights, inspiration, and revelation come directly from God. In Christianity, in particular, many pray to a Heavenly Father or Mother Mary or God through Jesus Christ. Some pray directly to Jesus Christ or saints to receive inspiration and strength beyond their own perceived abilities. Prayers for God vary based upon beliefs, but God may include Jehovah, Elohim (Judaism), Tara (Buddhism), Allah (Islam), Brahman (Hinduism), and Baha (Baha'i), among many others. Religious literature of all denominations and philosophies cites stories of visitations by spiritual beings that give answers to prayers. The range of answers comes through visitations from heavenly beings to feeling prompts of rightness in choices or synchronicity. Consider the following exercise.

## ACTIVITY #26: DOODLING YOUR SOURCE OF SPIRITUAL STRENGTH

Find a blank piece of paper and a pencil. Take a few moments to consider what you truly believe exists as your source of spiritual strength. Is it a form of God, a personal guide, a source of light, truth, and energy, your collective unconscious, or perhaps guidance from another dimension of life? Try to clear your mind of other thoughts and just focus on your source of spiritual strength. Begin to doodle. Initially, this may be difficult, but give yourself several minutes to get into a flow state or trance. Holding the pencil, let it draw what it will draw. Get more paper if you need to. The exercise is not for the pictures to be pretty or artistic; it is to let your mind explore what you believe.

Note: An alternative approach is to write words or thoughts on the piece of paper as you ponder the nature of your source of spiritual strength.

## Amazing Nature of UEUs

We have talked about the belief that we are living in a sea of universal energy units as supported by a number of disciplines. We have also described how academics, philosophers, and theologians speak of a strength beyond normal capacity using a variety of terms yet with common functions. The nature of the UEUs is also fascinating as each of the disciplines attempts to describe the power and benefits of the UEUs. UEUs have a number of properties and characteristics that comply with natural laws but in some cases defy normal laws of Newtonian physics. Here are some highlights from three different authors (Greene 2003, Pert 1997, and McTaggart 2008).

1. UEUs carry information: As UEUs collide with each other, they exchange information. The information that one UEU contains is transmitted to the other so that both UEUs depart enriched. Since the beginning of time, these UEUs have collided and collected information until they have reached our time. They truly carry the wisdom and knowledge of the world. The amount of information that these tiny UEUs contain is enormous. It has been speculated that if everything that had ever been written since the beginning of time, including every book in every library in the world, could be put on UEUs that together would only amount to a library about the size of a sugar cube. You are living in a world of tiny particles of information.

2. UEUs have a primary drive to connect and influence: One of the fascinating qualities of the UEUs is their magnetic attraction for other UEUs. As the UEUs attach to each other, they form patterns. They ultimately become the energy fields that serve as a blueprint for rocks, animals, plants, and human beings. The connections are evident in animal and human behavior as groups, packs, families, and religions naturally form. The postulate of resonation is the experience of knowing what to do and how to do what you need to do and the rightness that comes through the resonation of UEUs.

3. UEUs can heal: When UEUs enter the body, the tiny information-laden energy packets result in the human experience

of Q-infusions. People feel hope and optimism that they can overcome whatever obstacle is in their path. There is significant evidence that demonstrates that placebos (hope, optimism) help people feel better and even help them heal themselves. A placebo is a healing effect attributable to a pill, procedure, or potion but not to its pharmacodynamic properties. People believing that a pill is a healing pill will report the reduction of symptoms and speedy recovery from illnesses. The pill may only be a sugar pill with no drugs at all. In essence, a placebo gives the mind permission to heal itself. Depending upon the illness, placebos have been reported to "cure" a third of all illnesses. UEUs infuse the body, which produces positive Q-feelings, and in many cases, the Qs will help the body heal itself. We have also seen where faith healing and prayer have resulted in miraculous healing. At a soft frequency (380 nanometers) that emanates from UEUs, cells that may have been partially destroyed can be restored to full function. Humility and reverent positive thoughts and feelings seem to be healing.

4. UEUs have limitless capacity: The more UEUs you have, the greater your capacity to absorb UEUs. This comes from theoretical physics string theory, which is part of quantum mechanics. This phenomenon opposes what we traditionally think in physics. Let me explain. With traditional thinking, we can think of air being pumped into a container, such as a tire. If we pump air into the tire long enough, the pressure will become so high that we can no longer put any more air into the tire or the tire will explode. But if we are talking about the infusion of UEUs being pumped into a container, the more you put into the container, the more capacity there is and the space becomes greater to absorb even more UEUs. The more UEUs we have, the greater our capacity to absorb more UEUs. Succinctly stated, we can make the following postulate:

The more UEUs you seek, are open to, and absorb, the greater your Q capacity. The greater your Q capacity, the greater your understanding of truth and wisdom.

## ACTIVITY #27: LIMITLESS CAPACITY

Reflect again upon the Qs you really want in life. Write the Qs, which may include some of those listed at the beginning of this experience, as a list. You should have several on your list, such as *peace, courage, happiness, energy, understanding,* or *enlightenment.* Ask yourself the following question for each of your desired Qs: Can I ever have too much of that Q?

For example, "Can I ever have too much love?"

_____

_____

_____

_____

_____

_____

5.  UEUs are everlasting and common to all living things: UEUs are not created; they have always existed and will always exist. They cannot be destroyed but only change form. A UEU is like ice in one form that can be transformed into water or, with increased heat, can be transformed into steam. UEUs are the common substance in all forms of matter, life, thoughts, and feelings. This means that our bones, blood, organs, and thoughts and feelings are made up of the same basic energy or life force. There is a free exchange and interdependence of UEUs within every part of our bodies. UEUs are the basic substances in everything that is physical, mental, and spiritual. UEUs become the communication medium between all living things. They are interchangeable and interdependent with all UEUs that are throughout your body and the bodies of others. There is nonverbal communication between people, animals, and plant life at the foundational level of UEUs. They are the nexuses that bonds humans to humans. UEUs connect humans to animals, nature, and the earth. They are in everything and are also in the world around us. UEUs are the connecting substances that come from us, journey through our ecological mediums of UEUs, and subsequently can connect with a receptive living thing that also is made up of these infinitely small energy units.

UEUs are the connections within ourselves. They are the means whereby we can explore the far reaches of our collective unconscious minds, our spiritual origins, and our innate purpose and meaning in life. UEUs function as connecting substances between an individual's body, mind, and human spirit.

To try to feel the UEUs, try sitting in a comfortable chair. After relaxing for a few moments and taking a few cleansing breaths, lift your hands so they are chest high and about two feet apart. Rotate your hands so that the palms are facing each other. Now slowly, so slowly, begin to move your hands toward each other. At some point, you will begin to feel a gentle and almost undetectable resistance. It will feel almost like squeezing a cotton ball except you cannot feel the cotton. That resistance is the energy field created by the UEUs. Feeling the UEUs between your hands may take some practice.

This exercise is also interesting to do with someone else. As you stand about four feet apart with palms facing each other, begin to move your hands forward until you feel the energy between you. You can check the accuracy of the sensation by doing it with your partner closing his or her eyes and determining if the distance between the two of you is about the same as when the partner feels it.

The purpose of this experience is to help you become aware of the vast reservoir of UEUs in the world around you. Because the world of strings, qi, or spirit is beyond the limited bandwidth of sight, many people doubt that there is such a great reservoir in their world. But as we have discussed, the concept that there is a world of energy, wisdom, and light all around us is validated by many academic disciplines. Most people and academics think there is this reserve. Sometimes we can experience the wonderful feelings that are available.

# In Summary

- Universal resilience describes the yearning that comes from within you to discover strength beyond normal capacity.
- Universal resilience is about the desire to connect with a source of power and wisdom that is beyond your normal intellectual capacity.
- Labels as to the nature of universal energy units vary depending upon the science, philosophy, or theology. *Strings*, *qi*, *collective unconscious*, *molecules of emotion*, or *spirit* are, in function, synonymous.
- In essence, we can say, "We are walking, living, breathing in a universe full of infinitely small vibrating energy packets that define and energize everything."

The next experience is on essential resilience. We will learn how our bodies communicate with us to optimize our physical health.

# ESSENTIAL RESILIENCE AND THE SOUL

*Essential resilience is the experience of listening to the messages that come from your body, enabling optimal physical functioning.*

E ssential resilience, in its most basic form, is the drive to survive and thrive. It is the will to live. It is yearning to move freely, to feel refreshed after a good sleep, and have energy to fulfill other feelings-based resilient drives.

> *Essential resilience* is the drive to live and function at an optimal physical state without pain. It is the capacity to listen to body messages that wisely prompt the mind as to when, what, and how to rest, eat, and move.

You have been blessed with a magnificent physical body complete with vivid senses to help you to thrive and enjoy your world. Your senses will create stimulating images for you to enjoy while you witness beautiful sunsets, smell wonderful fragrances, taste tantalizing foods, enjoy the tender touch from those you love, and listen to your favorite music. Your physical senses can trigger great joy or pain. Your physical body will tell you, sometimes loudly and sometimes softly, how to take care of your physical self and assure that you function optimally. Your amazing body automatically prepares you to optimize your physical capacities in the presence of danger.

The dynamic interplay of dimensions of your body, mind, and spirit creates an interdependent system to infuse energy into all facets of your life. Your physical self is designed to optimize its potential and continually sends messages to your mind as to how to feel good. By acting upon these sometimes subtle essential messages, you can not only respond to the physical needs of your body but, at the same time, enrich your mind and your human spirit.

It is important to note that the human entity is one interdependent system, and the whole system is affected when any one dimension of that system is quickened or energized.

- When you exercise, mood-elevating hormones are activated and improve your intellectual capacities as well as your spiritual well-being.
- When you get adequate sleep, you have sufficiently allowed your mind and spirit to rest, and you wake refreshed and ready to perform optimally.
- When you eat healthy foods, your mind functions better, and you have more energy as opposed to mood swings and lethargy from eating high-sugar and fatty foods.

What your mind is thinking will affect your essential resilience, meaning your physical energy. Your essential resilience can also be enlivened by the Q-infusions that are generated from your childlike, character, noble, ecological, and universal yearnings. This experience will focus on two main interdependent concepts.

1. Listening and acting upon resilient yearnings for physical health is the first concept. The concept suggests that that by listening and attempting to fulfill the yearnings and drives of your innate childlike, noble, character, ecological, and universal resilience, you will naturally enrich your physical body.

2. The art of essential listening is the second concept and will focus on the mindful and resonate messages that emerge from your essential self—your physical body. By acting upon those messages, you will know how to function optimally. Both mindful essential listening and resonate essential listening will be experienced through the activities.

> **Note: Before you engage in any new exercise or nutritional program, it is important to confer with your health care provider to assure that the activities are safe and beneficial for you.**

Before we get into those sections, let me describe what this experience is *not*. Recognize that this is *not* an experience on how to exercise, eat well, and sleep better. Educational programs and popular media have kept you aware of good physical practices throughout your life. You already know most of the information that will help you to optimize physical functioning. You have been bombarded with information from television, magazines, and social media about how to improve your physical health. You have seen commercials for aerobic equipment, aerobic dance, Zumba, yoga, and dozens of other unique ways to get your body in shape. Aerobic exercise, flexibility, and strengthening muscles are important to do on a regular basis, but still only half of the people in the United States exercise at least three days a week (WebMD 2010).

You have also been exposed to nutritional approaches to health with supporting strategies about how to lose weight. Too many of these programs just focus on a variety of diets or a wide variety of pills that promote weight loss. You know you should follow government nutritional guidelines, which is to eat 2½–6½ cups of fruits and vegetables per day along with whole grains and lean proteins, but still almost half of Americans eat poorly and are overweight or obese. Figure 19 shows optimal portions from the USDA's Food Plate (http://www.choosemyplate.gov).

**Figure 19. Food Plate**

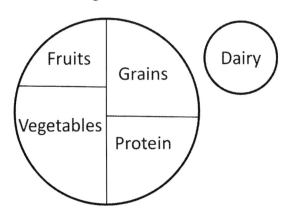

You are exposed to the sales campaigns from pharmaceutical and nutrition companies that push supplements and pills that help you sleep, wake up, lose weight, lower your cholesterol, and elevate your mood. You know you should sleep seven to eight hours a night depending upon which amount helps you wake refreshed, yet only a third of Americans say that they get adequate sleep according to a *US News & World Report.*

It is important to recognize that your resilient journey in life is fortified when your body is functioning optimally. You can optimize your physical health by listening and responding to the messages that come from not only your resilient spiritual yearnings but also that come from your physical body. We will first review what your resilient yearnings and drives are telling you to do in order to fulfill your essential resilient needs for optimal physical health.

## CONCEPT 1: LISTENING AND ACTING UPON RESILIENT YEARNINGS FOR PHYSICAL HEALTH

The best essential or physical health program for you is not to do what someone else tells you to do but rather to listen to the messages that come from both your resilient yearnings and from your innate essential resilience to tell you what to do. Concept 1 will focus on your resilient yearnings and drives and how acting upon them will help you to feel better. You will do this by pairing the resilient drives with important physical activities, such as getting enough sleep, being active, and eating nutritiously.

# CHILDLIKE AND ESSENTIAL RESILIENCE

You recognized your childlike nature in Experience 2, and you may have determined that it is important to tap into your adventuresome, creative, and playful childlike nature to optimize your health. When you act on your adventuresome spirit, it is likely that the fulfillment of the sense of adventure will result in moving. When you are playful, you are moving. When you are laughing, you experience physical responses to relieve tension, boost your immune system, decrease your stress hormones, increase your immune cells (infection-fighting antibodies), and trigger the release of endorphins (your body's natural feel-good chemicals).

## ACTIVITY #28: CHILDLIKE RESILIENCE

To apply these important principles of listening to your childlike yearnings and being active, ponder the pairings in the matrix below. Begin the matrix by pairing a potential essential activity on the top with the childlike drive on the left side. Ponder each of the squares in the matrix below and think of ways your childlike drives match or pair with the optimal physical health recommendations. For example, when you pair *adventure* with *healthy eating*, an image can come to mind about the adventure of trying new healthy foods. Perhaps you may adventure into experimenting with food by combining vegetables into a type of stew or soup that you haven't eaten previously. With adventure and aerobic activity, you may imagine yourself hiking and exploring nature. You can continue to do such pairing throughout the boxes in this forced matrix.

| Childlike Resilience | Healthy Eating | Aerobic Activity | Weight Control | Getting Good Sleep |
|---|---|---|---|---|
| Adventure | | | | |
| Play/fun/laugh | | | | |
| Spontaneous | | | | |
| Creative | | | | |
| Curious/risks | | | | |

Your love of play and fun is an obvious adventure to fulfill the yearnings of the body to move, be strong, and to be in shape. It is fun to go to parks and see adults playing games of softball, football, or tag. One of the best all-around exercise programs would be to follow a child around on a playground for thirty minutes to an hour. Think about it. You would be running from the slides to the swings and to the monkey bars. In the process, you would build your upper-body and leg strength, your aerobic capacity, and your flexibility. Your childlike nature, if you listen to it, will prompt you to move.

Young children have the ability to go to sleep when their bodies tells them they need to rest. I remember a humorous event when my granddaughter fell asleep in her car seat with a half-eaten cracker hanging out of her mouth. Children will sleep when it is time, whether a cracker is eaten or not. Adults have the same abilities to sleep when their bodies tell them to, except that their minds are preoccupied with schedules, tasks to be performed, worries, or the need to watch their favorite TV show late at night. You still have the same abilities to fall asleep if you recharge the magic of your childlike nature.

Perhaps the greatest gift of childlike resilience is your ability to fantasize and escape reality. You might try an imagery strategy—something like the following to facilitate sleep:

> After doing all the chores and preparations you need to do before you go to bed, assure that where you sleep is comfortable (lights, sounds, and surroundings). As you lie down to sleep, begin by breathing diaphragmatically (with your stomach moving, not your chest). Imagine refreshing air going into your lungs, and with each exhalation, you feel yourself becoming more relaxed. The incoming air carries with it a sleep potion that makes you drowsy. Each inhalation makes the potion stronger, and as you exhale, you feel the effects as you become more and more relaxed. The potion helps you magically go back to any age you would like to go. In your imagination, go to a time in your youth that was a good time for you. Perhaps you can imagine being held and rocked by one of your parents/

guardians. Drift into watching yourself as a child at your favorite age doing the things you enjoyed doing. In the back of your mind, you continue to feel yourself becoming sleepier and sleepier.

Imagery strategies like the previous scenario should be tailored to the most relaxing scenes for you. You may want to imagine your favorite childhood story that takes you away from present situations and leads you into a fantasyland where you will drift off to sleep.

### a) Noble Yearnings and Essential Resilience

Remember that your noble yearnings are to feel valued, to feel important, and have self-esteem. You want to feel good about yourself. If you are able to move, feel rested, and are eating well, you feel that nobility. Sometimes your perception of your physical state of health challenges your sense of noble worth.

Remember that the mechanism to feel good about yourself is through the action of service. It is about building your kingdom or queendom by helping, listening, and nurturing with movement and physical activity. Service is enhanced when you can become a role model for friends and loved ones. When you help a receptive family member to eat better and be more active, it enriches the relationship and fulfills your noble resilient drives.

## ACTIVITY #29: NOBLE RESILIENCE

For this activity, I want you to complete another matrix below. For each of the categories you can ponder how your need to feel worth, have order, to serve, and to create a kingdom or queendom can be enhanced by helping others to eat better, be active, or control weight. For example, you may have some of the following ideas for associating the qualities of noble resilience with essential enrichment activities:

- Self-worth and self-esteem: As you reflect upon living a healthier lifestyle, you will enhance your sense of worth and accomplishment.

- Autonomy/independence/order/control: You can begin a new chapter in your life by controlling your priorities. If essential health is important to you, then you can show how you can avoid entertainment or food addictions, eat what is good, and be active instead of being sedentary.
- Altruism/service: Look for opportunities to help others to eat healthfully be active, control unhealthy weight, or get good sleep; chart them. Helping others to do chores or projects may involve physical movement, which fulfills the drive to be noble but also increases strength and burns calories.

Create your kingdom/queendom: You can be engaged in the cause of helping yourself eat better, move better, and sleep better by touching multiple lives and modeling healthy eating and movement. If handled in a gentle, supportive mode, you will create your own kingdom/queendom.

Consider each of the squares of the matrix and write down those activities that will enrich your physical health by embracing your noble yearnings and drives. In the table, write how your need for self-worth can be enhanced if you engage in the physical activities. Complete the chart here.

| Noble Resilience | Healthy Eating | Aerobic Activity | Weight Control | Good Sleep |
|---|---|---|---|---|
| Self-Worth/ Self-Esteem | | | | |
| Autonomy/ independence order/control | | | | |
| Altruism/ service | | | | |
| Create your kingdom | | | | |

b)   **Character Yearnings and Essential Resilience**

When you think about your essential thoughts and behaviors, it is important that you be true to yourself. If you live with the Qs of character resilience, you will have more energy to accomplish the essential behaviors in the chart.

## ACTIVITY #30: PAIRING CHARACTER WITH ESSENTIAL RESILIENCE

Consider how character resilience can provide energy to accomplish the essential drives in the chart. You may have considered some of the following ideas:

- Integrity: Commit to yourself to do some of the essential behaviors you have identified and do what you say you will do.
- Honesty: When you are trying to practice some of the essential behaviors, be honest with yourself in your behaviors—or with someone else if you are doing some of the activities together.
- Freedom: As you practice essential behaviors, it is important to feel the freedom of being guiltless rather than the guilt of not doing them.

| Character Resilience | Healthy Eating | Aerobic Activity | Weight Control | Good Sleep |
|---|---|---|---|---|
| Integrity | | | | |
| Honesty | | | | |
| Freedom | | | | |

c)   **Ecological/Universal Resilience and Essential Resilience**

With your drive to be connected with a strength beyond yourself, consider how you might be able to use the sources of strength from your ecosystem to help you in your quest to practice essential health behaviors.

## ACTIVITY #31: PAIRING ECOLOGICAL RESILIENCE WITH ESSENTIAL HEALTH

To provide some prompts to help you complete the chart, consider some of the following bulleted thoughts and ideas. These can kick-start you into thinking about how to access strength beyond your normal capacity to promote essential health.

- Nature: Focusing on the beauty of nature in parks, mountains, beaches, and lakes will prompt wandering or movement.
- Smells: The right smells may prompt healthy eating.
- Pets: Some pets need to be walked and thereby will prompt movement.
- Music/sounds: Carefully selected music can prompt movement, sleep, or strength to overcome addictions.

Strength from universal sources: As per Experience 6, consider your source of spiritual strength, and practice meditation, prayer, or imagery to access that additional energy to move, sleep, or eat better. Consider each of the boxes in the chart below.

| Ecological Universal Resilience | Healthy Eating | Aerobic Activity | Weight Control | Good Sleep |
|---|---|---|---|---|
| Nature | | | | |
| Smells | | | | |
| Pets | | | | |
| Music/sounds | | | | |
| Strength from universal sources | | | | |

## PICK ONE BEHAVIOR

The previous examples help you look at the connections between resilient drives and essential health behaviors, but it may be more manageable for you to choose one behavior. You are being exposed to a number of guidelines that can help you, but they may seem overwhelming. You may want to do just one thing. In selecting the one activity, you will want to use your ability to resonate. As you consider the ideas, which of the activities feels right for you? It is much like being in an ice cream shop offering multiple flavors. You are best off selecting one flavor rather than trying to have them all on one cone. You will want to work on one goal at a time. Activity #32 will guide you through the pairing process to help you select one behavior.

## ACTIVITY #32: PAIRING DRIVES WITH ESSENTIAL GOALS

In the chart below, pick one behavior, such as becoming more physically active, and then describe your physical activity in light of your resilient nature. On the left side of the matrix is a listing of the resilient yearnings and drives that come from the human spirit. For each pairing between drive and goal, you can write some ideas to promote essential health.

I have written some ideas for how you can use the chart. As there is not enough room in the chart to describe your ideas, the important thing is to look at the sample and make your own chart and write down your ideas.

| DRIVE | GOAL |
|---|---|
| C = Childlike<br>N = Noble<br>Ch = Character<br>E = Ecological<br>U = Universal | **My goal is to become more physically active.** |
| C: Adventure | Describe several activities that you would like to do or would do that are adventurous. Explore nature, hike, take road trips, learn a new dance, get acquainted with a neighborhood, etc. Take the opportunity to try one of the activities each day and feel the fulfillment of your adventurous drives. At the same time, recognize that you are more active. |

| | |
|---|---|
| C: Play/fun/laugh | Describe the things you liked to do as a kid, such as playing games or playing with others. You may enjoy following some children around on a playground playing Follow the Leader with the child as the leader. |
| C: Spontaneous | Set a timer for ninety minutes. When the timer goes off, do some crazy and spontaneous movements for just a few minutes—act like a prize fighter, become a ballerina, pretend you are jumping rope, or go on a treasure hunt for trash in your location. Repeat. |
| C: Creative | Think wildly and crazily to discover different ways to have fun and be active. There are no limitations. After you have several ideas, refine them and make them feasible. |
| C: Curious/risks | With all the different types of movement programs out there, satisfy your curiosity to learn and try aerobic dance, Pilates, Zumba. Find out if you would enjoy swimming, jogging, etc. |
| Ch: Freedom | Enjoy the freedom of being away from all the stressors of the day by going out and moving. |
| Ch: Honesty | Be honest with yourself: Are you as fit as you want to be? Are there excuses that are not valid? Listen to the promptings to move, be childlike, to serve, and be honest with those feelings. |
| Ch: Integrity | Make a commitment to yourself (a lifestyle contract) and feel the integrity by doing what you say you will do. |
| N: Value/esteem | Think about what a good role model you will be for your family and friends as you regularly engage in movement and activity. |
| N: Autonomy/independence | Discover your independence as you engage in movement activities on your own—go out and enjoy being alone or take a movement class with people you don't know so you can celebrate independence and activity. |

| N: Control | Put together a schedule for a day and include four ten-minute intervals when you will do some exercise—climb stairs, walk around, and jump in place. Keep to the schedule. |
|---|---|
| N: Altruism/ create kingdom | See how many people you can help with some physical chore each day—at work, school, home, or in the community. Become known as the helping king/queen. |
| E: Nature/plants | Be active in natural settings with plants, trees, etc. Feel the peace and wisdom that comes from being in nature. |
| E: Music/sounds | Select several music themes that prompt you to move. Listen and move for several minutes each day. |
| E: Smells | Select a scented candle, essential oil, spice, fragrance, tree smell, or food that, when you smell it, will prompt you to move. |
| E: Pets | If you have a dog, enjoy the companionship as you take the dog for a walk or run. |
| U: Strength beyond | Pray, meditate, and ponder the importance of moving, and seek strength from your source of spiritual strength to be motivated to be active. |
| U: Practices | While you are being active, ponder the nature of your universal source of strength. Use the distraction of the body doing repetitive movements to ponder |

As you complete the chart, it is important that the ideas be yours. You will want to create a matrix for each of the essential resilient activities that are important over time, but for now, resonate and choose one activity.

Reflecting again upon my introductory story, being hit by a car, I remember a moment in my rehabilitation when I resonated to my childlike nature and took off on an adventurous experience. Upon reflection, I'm not too sure how safe it was, but it was exhilarating. The spontaneity in the experience was enlivening.

I returned to work at the university in early March after three months of rehabilitating at home. I was still in a wheelchair, and the eight pins were still in my lower legs. My administrative assistant, Lu Jean, had been very concerned with the ordeal I had been through. Many people at work had donated blood on my behalf. Everyone became very motherly in the office. My childlike sense of adventure and play was boiling inside of me, yet I was still trapped in a wheelchair. I tried to get back to my normal routine and started working on projects. When writing an article, I knew that I would need some references for the project. The excitement of going to the library by myself seemed freeing and fun. I wheeled past Lu Jean, simply saying, "I'm going to the library," and sped out the door as quickly as I could without hearing her response. My office was located at the top of a sidewalk that had downhill grade of some five hundred yards. At the bottom of the grade was the library. The fresh air seemed to ignite my soul. I started rolling down the hill as Lu Jean came flying out of the office, yelling, "Dr. Richardson! Dr. Richardson! I'll get your references. You shouldn't do this!" Too late; I was rollin'. I accelerated and began to go faster and faster until the wheelchair started to shimmy and shake. The thrill of letting loose filled my soul, and I was exuberant. Even the fear of potentially crashing felt good for a while until I realized that wheelchairs were not meant to go as fast as mine was moving. With my whole body vibrating, I tried to slow the wheelchair down with my bare hands on the wheels, with little effect. While rolling down the hill, I waved to students as they jumped out of the way. As I went flying by, they just giggled to see the runaway professor in the wheelchair. I finally got to the bottom of the hill without crashing. What a rush! It felt so good to do something crazy and fun because it had been bottled up inside me for months. It was great to be free from the mothering. Upon reflection, I realized that I took a serious risk, and I could have hurt myself and others, but oh, it was energizing. After doing my research in the library, the wheeling up the hill was more laborious. I had forgotten how out of shape I was. I would push the wheels for about one hundred feet and then have to rest. Then I would push for another one hundred feet. Students were gracious in offering to help, but I would simply respond that I was doing my aerobics. I was exhausted by the time I reached my office. I realized that now I had a new identity: I was a wheelchair-bound warrior.

## CONCEPT 2: THE ART OF ESSENTIAL LISTENING

In addition to listening to your childlike, noble, ecological, and universal prompts to nurture your essential needs and drives, you also can develop skills of listening to the wise messages that emerge from your body (essential resilience). Essential listening consists of two primary skills: essential mindful listening and essential resonate listening.

The art of essential mindful listening is being cognitively aware of what your body is doing, feeling, and needing. Essential mindfulness is primarily a cognitive function or something that you think about and can control. It is sensing what is good for you and what is not good for you.

Essential resonation, on the other hand, stems from the subtle messages of your subconscious mind. It is the sensing and becoming aware of needs and messages your body is sending in the process we often call *intuition* or *gut feelings*. Essential resonate messages will tell you what you should do and when you should do it in order to maximize your physical health. Both approaches can be developed to guide you as to how to optimize your energy and enjoyment of your physical health.

## ESSENTIAL MINDFUL LISTENING

Mindfulness is a classic stress management skill that is traditionally practiced to help you relax and focus on the present. By focusing on the present, you do not feel guilt or sadness from past events, and you do not need to feel anxiety and worry about future events. A common mindfulness practice is to focus on and imagine your breathing as the air goes into and out of your lungs. The focus on the breathing distracts you from life's worries. Another traditional mindful practice is to focus on your food as you savor the smell, taste, and pleasure of what you are eating. Essential mindful practices help you monitor the amount of exercise, food, and sleep you need.

*Essential mindful physical activity* is to celebrate and enjoy the ability to move and perform physical functions. Activity or exercise is any physical movement using your large muscles that results in an energy expenditure above a resting level. After you exercise, be mindful of some of the following positive feelings or indicators (check those that apply):

o   My mood improves.
o   I feel improved circulation to my muscles.
o   I breathe deeper and more efficiently.
o   I feel like I have better endurance.
o   I sense that I have more energy.

Mindful exercise is to know when to exercise. You can be aware of when you become sluggish with low energy—you know then that it is time to move or stretch. You will know how much to exercise because fatigue is a message.

Essential mindfulness heightens experiences as you walk, do aerobic exercise, or engage in activities that promote flexibility. Activity #33 includes some mindful guidelines to help you amplify your appreciation of movement.

## ACTIVITY #33: ESSENTIAL MINDFULNESS

Try some of the following experiences to help you appreciate and heighten your movement activities:

1.   Throughout your normal day, think about what movements you are making. As you move by walking, driving, or doing chores, ponder how amazingly your physical body functions. As you do go through your regular routines of bathing, brushing your teeth, cooking food, or other activities, look in awe at how your fingers, arms, and legs work. Then take a moment to appreciate the amazing machine in which you live. Those of you that may

have lost a limb or have other physical challenges, focus on those functions that you do have.

2. Begin or continue an exercise program that is suitable for your health condition. Any movement—whether walking, dancing, or rolling in a wheelchair—offer opportunities for exercise. Whatever you do to increase your heart rate, celebrate and focus on the ability of your body to respond to the demand. Imagine your muscles using the oxygen you are breathing and burning it as fuel to have more energy. Each time you work your muscles, you can appreciate what they are doing.

3. When exercising, remember the resiliency process as it pertains to movement. As you use and exhaust your muscles in exercise, be mindful that they are in the bottom of the resiliency trough, and with time they will rebuild stronger. Be mindful of the building journey as it applies to your mucles and your lungs.

Describe here how you will be able to use these mindful skills in your daily life.

_____

_____

*Essential mindful eating* will help you be aware of when to eat, how to eat, how much to eat, and what to eat. For most of us, this may be difficult in light of schedules and availability of food when we should be eating. Here are some guidelines.

- When to eat: As time passes without eating, hunger messages are sent to your brain indicating a need for food energy. As you mindfully listen to and feel your hunger messages, you will know that it is time to eat. It does not mean that you have to have a full meal. In all likelihood, you will be eating more than three meals a day this way, but mindful eating suggests that you respond to the hunger messages. Regular eating will keep blood sugar levels more constant.

- How to eat: Part of the amazing features of your body are the taste buds that send messages to your conscious thinking. The foods you eat with accompanying tastes of sour, bitter, sweet, or salty can make eating a wonderful mindful experience. If, while you are eating, you are thinking of other things or are more involved in conversation than being aware of your eating, you will not only miss enjoying the variety of tastes but also it is likely you will overeat.

- How much to eat: If you are eating mindfully, paying attention to the eating experience, then you are eating slowly as you savor each bit of food. At the point of satiety, you will want to stop. As you mindfully listen and eat slowly, your body will tell you that you have reached a level of satiety or satisfaction, which is the message to stop eating. Eating socially often interrupts the messages of reaching satisfaction. The conversation and social engagements are wonderful but do not allow for mindful eating because of the distractions.

- What to eat: Mindful eating is the experience of smelling the food first, tasting it, enjoying the stimulation of the taste buds, and savoring it as you chew it slowly. It is to be aware of what you are eating. Because you have been educated as to what is healthy and what is not as healthy to eat, you are in a position to experience the taste and sense how beneficial foods are or how unhealthy they are. You will make choices and celebrate the healthy food choices and consequentially feel better.

## ACTIVITY #34: ESSENTIAL MINDFUL EATING

The next time you eat a food that may not be considered healthy, such as a french fry, try the following:

Let's assume that you have made the choice to quit eating so many french fries. Before you place the fry into your mouth, smell it. Can you smell the grease and odor of the deep-fat fryer? Put the fry in your mouth and taste the salt. Rather than chewing the fry, let it stay in your mouth for a while. After some time, you will feel the potato portion dissolve, and you will just have the remaining greasy slime in your mouth. Think of what you know about nutrition and what the fat might do. You can try the same activity with other foods, such as doughnuts. Another approach is to do the same activity with fruits and vegetables and notice the fiber and freshness of the food as you eat it mindfully. Describe here how you feel about the foods you mindfully ate.

_____

_____

*Essential mindful sleep* is being aware of when you are sleepy and tired. Your body sends sleep messages, and if you are mindful of them, you will know when you should sleep. Many people force themselves to stay awake to watch the nightly news or a favorite television show. Many people would benefit from a twenty-minute nap in the middle of the afternoon but instead drink their favorite source of caffeine. Most people are subject to start and end times for sleep depending upon home responsibilities, work hours, and demands of others. Still, the communication from your body is usually clear, and when possible, we ought to listen to the messages.

Circadian biorhythms describe your natural energy highs and lows during a twenty-four-hour day. You can know when to sleep by being aware of your circadian rhythms. Some people are morning people, while others are night people. Lifestyle factors will try to force you to modify the natural rhythms, and in a few cases, it can be done. Circadian rhythms are important in determining human sleep patterns. Your body has a master clock (called the *suprachiasmatic nucleus*, or SCN) that controls sleep by producing melatonin, a hormone that makes you sleepy. When there is less light—like at night—the SCN tells the brain to make more melatonin so you get drowsy. To fight the circadian rhythms is to fight physiology. Your body is trying to help you get enough rest by sending messages to you through drowsiness. By fighting your natural circadian rhythms, it may result in a variety of sleep disorders.

Unfortunately, people who are night people often struggle with an 8:00 a.m.–5:00 p.m. working day because they have trouble getting adequate sleep. Staying up late and getting up early shortchanges the reenergizing nature of sleep. That said, a good mindful activity is to determine what your natural cycles are and try to live within those rhythms. Exercise will boost your body with energy when you need it. If you have trouble waking up in the morning, perhaps twenty minutes of aerobic activity will help wake you up. If you have trouble sleeping at night, an early evening aerobic experience may exhaust you enough that you are able to rest. Although aerobic exercise generates energizing hormones for a couple of hours, you will be able to sleep better being somewhat fatigued from the activity.

## ACTIVITY #35: MINDFUL SLEEP

When you do go to bed, your thinking should be free of worries. Beforehand, do what you have to do to be prepared for the next day. As you feel your eyes begin to respond to the early messages of sleep that come from the melatonin hormone, capitalize on that experience.

Imagine and feel the first indicators of sleep. It may come as heaviness to your eyes or drowsiness. As you focus on the feeling, you can see it, feel it growing and becoming stronger. Your resonation is to connect to the vibrations that are coming from your heavy eyelids. Feel yourself becoming sleepier and sleepier. Soon you will drift off if you avoid other thoughts.

## ESSENTIAL RESONANT LISTENING

Reflecting upon the prevaling concept of resonation that has been evident throughout this book, it is important to be active, eat, and sleep according to guidance of your universal and essential wisdom. As you use your intellectual resilience to study things out in your mind, you will resonate to the best decisions in life and, in this case, how to be active, eat, and sleep.

## ESSENTIAL RESONANT PHYSICAL ACTIVITY

You will know when you should do physical activity if you are being mindful, but the ability to enjoy the exercise is a function of resonate listening. You will feel a good feeling inside as you ponder various forms of movement. You may like the feelings associated with jogging, swimming, doing calisthenics, biking, jumping rope, dancing, walking briskly, or playing Follow the Leader with children at a playground. You may want to create your own way to move your large muscles, such as playing a game of running up and down stairs in your home. Maybe you will try to meet new friends by walking through your neighborhood. You might want to jump on a backyard trampoline. You should do that to which you resonate. Even if you are in a wheelchair, you will enjoy the invigoration of movement.

## ACTIVITY #36: RESONANT PHYSICAL ACTIVITY

When you have a moment to relax, find a place where you will not be distracted and where you will be comfortable. Take a moment to close your eyes or daydream and think about the movement activities to which you resonate. There are hundreds of activities you can imagine, but here are some examples. As you ponder these, imagine yourself doing them and feeling either the good or the negative vibrations of resonation.

- Walking in a neighborhood
- Doing a form of dance—Zumba, aerobic dance, etc.
- Swimming
- Playing competitive sports (raquetball, tennis, etc.)
- Weight lifting
- Practing Eastern arts (tai chi, yoga, etc.)
- Others

*Essential resonate eating* is knowing what to eat, which is a more challenging skill than just being mindful. Resonate eating can be mastered better after you have learned basic information about nutrition. After you have learned about the importance of eating fruits, vegetables, whole grains, and low-fat sources of protein, you can ponder the information and seek resonating feelings. As you consider options within those food categories, you will resonate to or feel good about several types of these foods that your body may need. A sample activity for experiencing resonate eating is to try the following (the underlying assumption is that you are trying to eat a healthier diet):

## ACTIVITY #37: RESONANT EATING

In a state of openness and humility coupled with your sense of adventure from your childlike nature, go to a grocery store. Do not have the intent of buying anything until the end of the activity. Wander through the store with what you have learned about nutrition in the back of your head. As you wander through the produce section, stop and focus on one fruit and vegetable at a time. As you look at the fruit or vegetable, try to sense a resonating feeling. Does the thought of smelling, tasting, or eating that particular fruit or vegetable feel good? Does it feel right? Continue through the store and ponder meats and other groceries. Are there foods that give you bad feelings? As you stand in front of sugared cereals or processed packages, ponder what might be in those boxes. How do you feel?

The more challenging skill is to resonate to food because your body needs that food. If you are low on iron, then you may crave liver, broccoli, squash, or a sirloin steak. This skill generally requires that you eat prudently for a few weeks so that your sugar and caffeine addictions are no longer evident. Then ponder foods you would like to eat, and you will see that your diet will improve, as will your energy, because you will be eating those food items that your body needs.

Resonant eating is challenging if you have sugar and fat addictions. What you may be sensing is a craving for a candy bar or a doughnut, and the vegetables and fruits don't appeal to you. In that case, it may be best to do this exercise when you have satisfied your need to eat.

## ESSENTIAL RESONANT SLEEP

If you have difficulty falling to sleep when it is time to sleep, try the two techniques described below. It has already been suggested that, through mindful awareness of the fatigue in the eyes, you should focus on and enhance those prompts for sleep. From a resonation approach to sleep, you will want to 1) study it out and resonate, and 2) sense prompts to go to your sleepy place. To study it out and resonate, you will want to review the many strategies available to you that will guide you through sleep experiences. The strategies may range from self-hypnosis to nutritional ideas. There are dozens of effective approaches, and you may resonate to a favorite one.

You may, for example, resonate to the idea of creating a mantra, symbol, or phrase for sleep. As you lie in a sleeping position, you can focus on the image of a religious symbol, a star, a mountain, or a waterfall. You may want to use a traditional mantra and repeat the word *Om*. You may try self-hypnotic words in your mind, like "I am sleepy" or "I feel warm and heavy." Just by reading this example, you may feel that it is a good idea and you will want to try it. Others will think it will not work for them, so they do not resonate. Study and try several approaches, and one will likely feel right for you.

The second approach is to sense the prompts to go to your universal source of Qs or a favorite place. Activity #38 will guide you through a sample experience.

## ACTIVITY #38: RESONANT SLEEP

When you are a comfortable sleeping situation, close your eyes and mindfully focus on your breathing. Think about the Qs you need to be able to sleep. You will think of peace, comfort, and bliss. Imagine the universal source of these Qs (from qi, strings, God's Spirit, etc.). As you breathe in, imagine that the Qs of peace are entering your soul and calming your mind, body, and spirit. As you breathe out, imagine the tensions and stressors of life are leaving. Continue to do so and let yourself drift off into sleep as you resonate to the peace of your universal source of strength.

## MINDFUL WEIGHT MANAGEMENT

To this point, we have not discussed weight management. A healthy weight will result if you listen to your body's messages. If you listen to your resilient nature, you do not need to follow a diet. If you focus too much on weight control, you will have a difficult time with weight. One of the unhealthiest weight management–related activities that you can do is go through the "lose weight–gain it back–lose weight–gain it back" cycle.

The best way to deal with weight control is to be mindful of your eating, movement, and sleep. Resonate to your drives and fulfill your childlike, noble, character, ecological, and universal drives, and you will discover as a secondary benefit that you will feel better physically. This short section on weight control is to confirm that it is more important to engage in life, fulfill drives, and listen to your body. When we do that, the weight will take care of itself.

You can look at your essential life more simply by considering the figure below. You have the opportunity to mindfully listen and resonate to thoughts and actions that will optimize your physical functioning.

## Figure 20. Mindful Listening

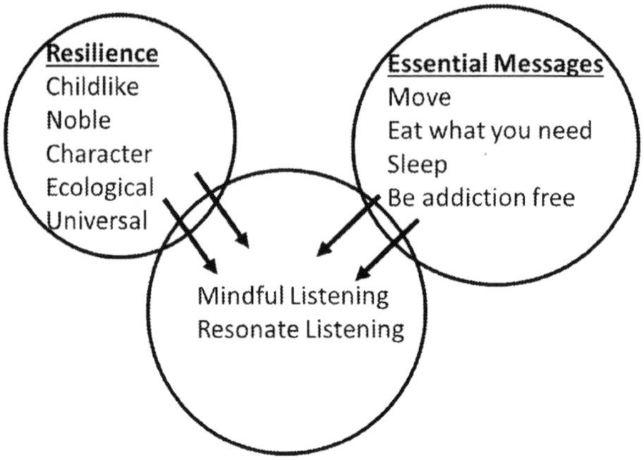

*Resonant essential resilience*, then, is the ability to feel the yearnings and drives to be physically healthy by sensing and listening to your childlike, noble, character, ecological, and universal drives. *Mindful listening* is the ability to be present and be aware of what you are doing to feed, move, and rest your body. Resonate listening will help you to know what to eat when your body is craving certain nutritious foods. Resonate listening will also allow you to know your best form of exercise. Try completing the following reflective activity.

## ACTIVITY #39: RESONANT ESSENTIAL LISTENING

Consider information you have received on mindful and resonant listening in this experience. Sit in a comfortable chair and close your eyes. Ponder the model of resonant listening to your resilient drives. What is your adventurous and playful, childlike nature telling you to do? How much energy do you have from living within your moral framework? What are your feelings about serving others, and how will that help you move? Have you felt the peace of moving in nature? What is your spiritual source of strength telling you about movement, rest, and eating? As you continue to relax, become mindful of what your body is telling you about food, activity, sleep, and any addictions you may have. When you complete the exercise, write down your ideas on how you can improve your essential physical health.

# In Summary

- It is clear that your essential self (your physical body) is constantly sending messages to you as to how, when, and what to eat; to be physically active; and when and how to sleep.
- Remember that the art of essential mindful listening is being cognitively aware of what your body is doing, feeling, and needing.
- Essential mindfulness is primarily a cognitive function or something that you think about and can control.
- Being intuitive and harvesting the wisdom of your collective unconscious mind is essential resonance.
- What a comforting experience it is to sense what you should do and when you should do it in order to maximize your physical health.

Experience 8 will focus on your mind, which is your resilience control center.

## EXPERIENCE 8

# INTELLECTUAL RESILIENCE AND THE SOUL

> *Intellectual resilience is the experience of discerning, choosing, and planning ways to fulfill innate resilient yearnings and drives.*

You have reflected upon the subtle yearnings that come from your innate resilience, or in other words, your spiritual yearnings and drives. You have also considered the messages that are being sent to your mind from your essential prompts, instructing you how to optimize your physical functioning. The resilient drives of your human spirit (childlike, character, noble, ecological, and universal resilience) and the messages from your essential resilience are all positive, designed to help you feel good. Even painful messages, such as spraining an ankle or experiencing disappointment, are positive messages because they inform your mind that you need to fix the problem. Intellectual resilience allows you to make sense of these directional and optimizing yearnings and to discover avenues to effectively fulfill these resilient drives within your challenging world. Intellectual resilience is the drive that you can control. You embrace the postulate of agency. You can make the choice to listen or not to listen to resilient yearnings and drives—this is your conscious thinking.

> *Intellectual resilience* is the drive to harvest intellectual qualities and virtues of conscious thought, including knowledge, understanding, agency, meaning, control, and discernment to know what to do and how to do it.

The uniqueness of intellectual resilience is that you have more control over what you are thinking. You can choose to listen to your essential and spiritual drives, or you can choose not to. Intellectual resilience is the essence of your conscious mind and allows you to control and make decisions. It is the part of you that is obvious as you are reading this experience—you are thinking. Intellectual resilience is the drive to be in control, and your mind is the control center. With your mind in control, if you want to quit reading this book, you will stop. If you want to go for a walk, you will go for the walk. If you want to call someone, you have the control to make that call. If you want to understand something, you can learn about it. Intellectual resilience is the drive to plan and organize. It is the drive to create and learn.

In previous experiences, we have discussed the subtle resilient messages that often go unnoticed by your conscious mind; but by listening to the messages, you will be able to optimize your life. Again, you can choose to listen or not to listen to them. As described in the previous experience, resilient listening is the intellectual skill of escaping the distractions of daily living and mindfully listening to the prompts that come from your human soul (integrated mind, body, and spirit). The intellectual resilient skills of (1) resilient Q-listening, (2) understanding, and (3) visioning are described in the sections that follow.

## RESILIENT Q-LISTENING (POSTULATE OF INNATENESS)

Your spirit and your body are constantly sending messages to your mind. In the previous experience, the mindfulness focused on essential prompts where this experience will help you to become more mindful of spiritual drives. Most people have difficulty listening to the greater wisdom because they let life challenges dictate their thoughts. They do not allow themselves the time to escape the problems of life and create peaceful mind-sets that foster conditions for insights and answers to life challenges. So many people are so concerned with job expectations, financial problems, or dealing with relationship issues that they don't take the time or feel the inclination to listen to softer positive directional prompts.

> Resilient listening is the art of assuming an open mind-set preparatory to mindfully resonating to soft, enriching, and wise spiritual messages.

In addition to listening to the subtle messages that come from your body to move, eat, and sleep, use your agency and mind to listen to your resilient yearnings and drives.

## ACTIVITY #40: RESILIENT LISTENING EXERCISE

As with the essential resilience experience, block about thirty minutes in your day when you can dedicate some time to resilient listening. Again, write down all your busy, distracting thoughts, such as tasks that need to be done, problems, and other externally demanding distractions. Identify a time when you will address these issues. In your mind, set those tasks on a shelf to be dealt with later. Remember that you have energy sources that come from your resilient drives. Resilient listening exercises allow you to listen to those drives to help you find the qualities and virtues you need. The exercise below will help you consider each of the drives, or sources of Qs you want or need. This exercise should require significant time if done correctly, and you may want to do several sessions of the resilient listening exercise with a different drive. I would suggest that you listen to one resilient drive at a time. Even though you may not be aware of it, your mind at this moment is receiving multiple messages from each of your resilient drives. Each of the Qs associated with each drive is worth spending a few minutes to ponder. First, do the preparatory exercise followed by listening to your greater resilient wisdom.

## PREPARATION:

1. Find a comfortable place to sit or lie down.
2. In a comfortable position, focus first on your breathing—try to breathe with your stomach (diaphragmatically).

## RESILIENTLY LISTEN:

1. Childlike Q-listening: As you inhale, feel each of the following childlike Qs. Sense the infusions and feelings of the Qs. As you exhale, imagine images or circumstances where you can fulfill those Qs. For example, as you breathe in the Q of adventure, feel the energy that it creates, and as you exhale, imagine a scene like climbing in the mountains that will fulfill that Q. With each exhalation, mindfully focus on each of the childlike Qs and how it applies to your life.

   - the Q of adventure
   - the Qs of fun and play
   - the Qs of humor and laughter
   - the Q of being genuine
   - the Q of curiosity
   - the Q of taking risks

When you are done breathing in each of the Qs, write your feelings about your childlike yearnings and how they could enrich your life.

Continue the exercise with the other resilient drives. Focus your thoughts and feelings on the character, noble, ecological, universal, and essential resilient drives. Again, with each inhalation, feel the Q, and with each exhalation, see how it might better your life.

2. **Focus on the Qs of Character Resilience**

   - the Q of honesty
   - the Q of integrity
   - the Qs of loyalty and fidelity
   - the Q of kindness

Again, write down your thoughts and feelings. How could you enrich your life as you listen to your character Qs?

3. **Focus on the Qs of Noble Resilience**

- the Qs of feeling important/valued and of worth
- the Q of freedom
- the Q of competency
- the Q of purpose
- the Qs of service and altruism
- the Q of meaning
- the Q of legacy

Again, write down your thoughts and feelings. How could you enrich your life as you listen to your noble Qs?

4. **Focus on the Qs of ecological resilience as you imagine yourself in an enriching environment (music, nature, art, etc.).**

- the Q of peace
- the Q of inspiration

Again, write down your thoughts and feelings. How could you enrich your life as you listen to your ecological Qs?

5. **Qs of Universal Resilience**

As you try to Q-listen to your source of universal resilience, you can be mindful of the infusion of Qs. As you sit comfortably, imagine your source of universal resilience. Ponder the world of energy, enlightenment, and wisdom that is all around you as per your belief system of either qi, strings, or God's Spirit. You may choose to visit the source of wisdom and strength that is housed within you (collective unconscious). As you visit the sources, consider the Qs you can harvest.

- the Qs of healing and miracles
- the Qs of peace
- the Qs of courage
- the Qs of hope

- the Qs of wisdom
- the Qs of guidance
- the Qs of enlightenment and inspiration
- the Qs of feeling love from beyond yourself

Write down your thoughts and feelings. How could you enrich your life as you listen to your universal Q?

## UNDERSTANDING

When you sense or resonate to messages from your essential or spiritual resilient sources, you feel some degree of urgency to respond. Understanding embraces the three experiences of discernment, knowledge, and meaning. Understanding will help you to know if what you are about to do is truly for your best good and will allow you to progress. Embracing discernment, knowledge, and meaning will help you know whether the messages you are receiving are simply quick fix messages with limited or negative long-term outcomes or whether the messages are progressive Q-enriching choices.

## DISCERNMENT

Discernment is the art of listening to innate spiritual and essential prompts that will infuse your soul with Qs. It is deciphering the greater wisdom of the prompts that will help you progress throughout your lifetime. The challenge of discernment is to sift through the prompts and feelings that come to your mind to determine whether the prompt is from a wise source or a short-term pleasure or quick fix source. Spiritual prompts are the soft resonations that will suggest ways to fulfill your childlike, character, noble, ecological, and universal resilient drives without violating any of them. These soft messages of rightness are contrasted to quick fix messages that are damaging and Q-draining in the long term.

For example, if you ever feel your nobility threatened, such as when someone belittles you, you will hear messages of anger that are louder than Q-messages. It requires a moment to discern the origin of the anger message to hear the softer message of peace in a relationship. The anger message is a shadow message that, if delivered, will result in a shortsighted retaliation effort to demean the offending source. The reactive anger approach will result in an escalation of negative emotions and damaged relationships. Your wiser and softer self will feel compassion. You will know that the person who offended you is suffering from a lack of nobility or worth. Acting upon the Qs of nobility and character will prompt you to listen and validate feelings.

It is important to learn the skill of discerning between essential messages that are wise versus those that are short-term fixes. You may have already formed addictions to sugar, knowing that excessive amounts are not healthy. You may have formed a habit of using tobacco, again knowing that it is not healthy. You may overuse prescription drugs, knowing that this is not a healthy habit. Because of the messages that your mind and your body are sending you, you will likely feel guilty in the aftermath of consuming those substances. When you are consumed in the mind about these choices, it is tougher to hear the soft, gentle messages of the greater wisdom inside you where you will find the energy of restraint and seek a healthier source of energy. The art of discernment is to know the difference between a short-term pleasure fix and a long-term directional prompt to progress.

It is an important skill to be able to feel a long-lasting positive prompt to do progressive actions. Whether it be to eat certain foods, reach out to help someone, or study a particular source of spiritual literature, all Q-progressing prompts rely upon the postulate of resonation. A truth will come to you through a vibrational message of peace and rightness. You will have a vision of the truth affecting you positively for the long term and should be part of your dream in life.

## KNOWLEDGE

Your intellectual resilience is a strong desire to learn and gather knowledge. You were like a sponge as a child as you learned from children's books, television, and daily instruction at school. Today, children are exposed to more information and knowledge through the Internet. The more people know, the better equipped they are to make quality decisions.

Knowledge and discernment go hand in hand. As you gain more and more knowledge, your ability to discern is enhanced. The more you learn about nutrition, exercise, and sleep, the more options become available to you to discern or resonate to what is best for you. If you understand the nutrition labels on foods, you progress in knowledge. You will resonate to foods that provide vitamins, minerals, and fiber. With that knowledge, you will be more mindful of what you are eating, how often you are moving, and how much sleep you are getting.

- With knowledge, you will be able to better discover and renew your spiritual resilient drives.
- With knowledge, you will learn about the great people in history, and by understanding them, you can aspire to new resilient qualities.
- With knowledge, you will learn some of the philosophies and theologies of cultures and religions across the globe and be able to discover those that have principles and beliefs to which you will resonate.
- With more knowledge, you will enliven your character resilience as you learn from history and see examples of great role models that demonstrated integrity, honesty, and honor.

## MEANING

As you discern through knowledge, you will be able to celebrate meaning. You will feel the impact of your thoughts and feelings on yourself as well as the Qs that come from serving others.

Meaning completes understanding.

The selection of the knowledge that will help you progress is confirmed with the resonating comfort of meaning. When you know something is right because you have learned from reliable sources and it resonates through your entire soul, you enjoy the progressive infusion of the Qs of confidence and courage. Meaning is to feel the sense of progression that enhances the Qs within your integrated soul.

## VISIONING (POSTULATE OF AGENCY)

Armed with (1) listening to your spiritual and essential resilient prompts, (2) knowledge, (3) discernment of Q-enriching options, and (4) a sense of meaning and fulfillment, you will be able to create a natural vision of what your life should be. That vision will appear in your intellectual resilient mind. You will receive impressions of changes or new identities that will enrich your life with Qs and promote progression. Intellectual resilience is the drive to respond to the resilient messages by identifying the means to fulfill the needs. We will explore in later experiences the details of becoming the identity you need to become to fulfill resilient prompts. This experience is merely an introduction to the function of your control center—your intellectual resilience as the drive to understand and make good choices that have lasting potential. For a practical application of understanding, consider the following experience from my life:

> Several years ago when I was a professor at Texas A&M University, I felt an urge to look farther west for job opportunities in order to be closer to family. I was very happy in Texas, but the twenty-one-hour drive to visit family in Utah was difficult to do very frequently. I began to review job announcements as they surfaced, but my eye caught an opening at the University of Colorado in Boulder. Boulder is a beautiful city, and the university would be a great place to work. The idea of going to Boulder seemed like a great idea and would reduce the driving distance to be with family. I applied for the position and was invited to visit the campus for an interview. The experience was wonderful. The faculty were friendly and supportive. They were interested in my area of study (resiliency). Before I left, I was offered the position. I was thrilled and honored. As I was traveling home, I began to fantasize about living in Boulder and what it would be like at the University of Colorado. For some reason, it just didn't click. I struggled to sense what my feelings were. I began to sense an uneasy feeling that came over me. It was an emptiness that replaced the jubilation I had felt when I left campus. I had talked to my wife earlier about how excited I was and how wonderful it would be to live in Boulder.
>
> When we spoke again as I arrived home, the empty feeling prevailed. She addressed me and said, "We're not going to Boulder, are we?"

I responded, "No, but I have no idea why."

I turned down the job.

For a year, I wondered why I had the mixed feelings, but I returned to my job and remained content at Texas A&M. Several months later and much to my surprise, I read in a university newsletter that the University of Colorado had cut the very program of which I was to be a part. Several untenured professors had lost their jobs. A couple of months after reading that, I received a call from the University of Utah, inviting me to apply for the position of department chair of the Health Science Department (now Health Promotion and Education), which was just eighty-five miles from my folks' house. I came out one week for an interview and ten days later had to return for my father's funeral. I have been grateful that I have been close enough to my widowed mother to help her cope. What would have happened if I had taken the Colorado job?

With this experience, we can examine the postulates and intellectual resilient drives. Consider the following:

1.  Love: I had a yearning to be reconnected with my family who lived in Utah—a comfortable and beautiful eight-hour drive versus a twenty-one-hour drive. I wanted to connect to nature and the beautiful Rocky Mountains and fulfill my ecological resilient drives.

2.  Knowledge: I had been at Texas A&M for some time and felt that a new job would increase my skills. I studied the responsibilities of the new position and read the publications of the professors there. I knew it would be an opportunity to learn, make new friends, and progress professionally.

3.  Innateness: I knew I had the potential to be able to learn and progress if I moved to Boulder. The faculty members had skills

and experiences from which I could learn. I felt innately that I would progress.

4. Discernment: After I had gathered all the knowledge and information I needed for the job, including the campus interview, I did not resonate to the job. I felt unfulfilled and frustrated.

5. Faith/belief: In this case, there was no faith or belief that I should take the job. Without resonation, I did not feel the belief that it was a good thing.

6. Agency (understanding and visioning): Without resonation, there was no vision, and I lacked understanding as to why I shouldn't accept the job. I just knew that I shouldn't take the job. I had the agency to choose not to accept the position because of the lack of confirming rightness.

The magic formula to make all the right decisions in life is quite simple. Acquire understanding by acquiring knowledge (studying it out in your mind), resiliently listening to sources of greater wisdom, discerning short-versus long-term benefits, and choose the options to which you resonate.

## REMINISCENCE

As you reflect upon past experiences and how you have learned or progressed, you will find meaning in your ventures. You have in your mind impressions of past successes that can provide courage to engage in a new vision with current challenges. You can reflect upon past resiliency processes and recognize that you have an arsenal of skills gleaned from past successes that you have used in previous challenges and the sense of how you might use them in current challenges. You can benefit by remembering the times when you spontaneously took a family member on an adventure, fulfilling your childlike resilience. You can remember the motivation, attitude, and skills you developed when you were negotiating a deal or interviewing for a job. You can remember when you were romantic, used wisdom, were humorous, were clever, and demonstrated persistence. You can reminisce about the nature of your successes and the skill or identity you had at the time.

# In Summary

- It should be clear that you have within you a vast reservoir of wisdom, motivation, and strength to guide you to a happy life.
- The figure below represents a summary of the forces and yearnings discussed in Experiences 4–8.
- Figure 21 is a map of your human soul. Your body (essential resilience), mind (intellectual resilience), and spirit (spiritual resilience) are all interdependent and connected.
- Each dimension affects the others.

**Figure 21. Summary of Innate Yearnings—Body, Mind, and Spirit**

As discussed in Experience 3 on noble resilience, your purpose in life is for your intellectual resilience to determine the means and methods to be able to fulfill your spiritual, intellectual, and essential resilient drives. Experience 9 will focus on who you are and where you are going.

# PART 4

# VENTURING

Part 4 is about your dream and taking action to fulfill
it. It is your vision of your life each day and throughout
your lifetime. The dream prompts your intention to
plan, act, and pursue a path with heart. When the
vision is prompted and maintained with resonance and
quickening, you can call it your Q-path.

An example of a Q-path that drove someone throughout his lifetime
was that of the famous civil rights leader Dr. Martin Luther King
Jr. The elements of his powerful Q-path to eliminate racism are
important to consider. Some highlights of the "I Have a Dream" speech
of August 28, 1963, follow.

I say to you today, my friends, though, even though we
face the difficulties of today and tomorrow, I still have
a dream. It is a dream deeply rooted in the American
dream. I have a dream that one day this nation will rise
up and live out the true meaning of its creed: "We hold
these truths to be self-evident: that all men are created
equal." I have a dream that one day on the red hills of
Georgia the sons of former slaves and the sons of former
slave owners will be able to sit down together at the table
of brotherhood ... I have a dream that my four little
children will one day live in a nation where they will not

be judged by the color of their skin but by the content of their character. I have a dream today ... I have a dream that one day ... little black boys and black girls will be able to join hands with little white boys and white girls as sisters and brothers. I have a dream today. I have a dream that one day every valley shall be exalted, every hill and mountain shall be made low, the rough places will be made plain, and the crooked places will be made straight, and the glory of the Lord shall be revealed, and all flesh shall see it together.

We should all have our own dream that projects a life path to happiness. Dr. King's dream was big and broad, and yours can be as well. Your Q-path is a vision of the energy field that is created by your innate resilient drives in harmony with the guidance and direction that comes from your universal sources of strength. Experience 9 will summarize your human condition, which will allow you to maximize the capacity of your soul. Experience 9 will help you formulate your dream in life.

# VISIONING AND YOUR INNATE DREAM

> *Visioning is the experience of creating a dream that represents the fulfillment of resilient drives to which you will resonate throughout a lifetime.*

How many times have you thought, *Am I on the right path in life?* Sometimes it takes a major life experience to jolt us into finding the right path in life. The story of my accident on campus changed my professional life from pursuing administrative positions in universities to realizing that my life should be in the classroom and in the community, talking about resilience and resiliency. Wake-up calls can come in much easier formats, such as hearing a motivational speaker, resulting in a quickening moment for you. It is important to reassess periodically to feel the resonation and quickening to know where you are really going.

The Q-path is your intrinsically guided progressive journey in life that allows you to harvest qualities and virtues (Qs) throughout your lifetime.

The common term we use in conversation is *dream* to suggest where we want to go in life. More often than not, goals are stated as dreams: "My dream is to have a beautiful home." But let's start with the term *dream* and try to understand what it really means. Your dream is the avenue or direction in your life that will fulfill your childlike, noble, character, ecological, universal, essential, and intellectual drives. Living your dream is the experience of feeling fulfilled with peace.

A dream creates a self-fulfilling prophecy that, if you think it will happen and believe it with all your being and work toward it, will happen. Once you have formulated your dream and are passionate about it, the self-fulfilling prophecy happens because it is supposed to happen. Your resilient drives are guiding you on a path that will best fulfill your potential, and your innate wisdom will assure you will become what you want to become and experience what you want to experience.

We will introduce the concept of a Q-path at the end of the experience. This more accurately describes the direction you are going. Q-path obviously means that in your life journey you are maximizing experiences to harvest Qs throughout your normal day.

The dream is a big picture of your life progression and provides direction as to how to fulfill your resilient yearnings. In the beginning, the dream may feel like you are standing at the bottom of a huge mountain, and the hike to the peak may appear impossible with pitfalls and hardships.

> Life is like climbing a mountain. From afar, you can see the majestic peak. You can imagine the views you will have when you reach the summit. The trail will be long and challenging, so keep the image of the peak in your mind, because it will motivate you to keep climbing. Remember, it is a step at a time, but with each step, you come closer to the peak, accomplishing your dream. Along the way, there will be barriers. You may have to cross streams, fallen trees, and large rocks. Each obstacle will make you stronger and get you closer to your dream. Life is about taking one step at a time—one foot in front of the other. Life is about overcoming the obstacles, knowing that you will be closer to fulfillment. Keep the peak or dream in mind, and then set immediate goals. When you reach it, set another goal.

Experience #9 will describe four concepts and skills that will help you progress and harvest Qs throughout your life. There is a unique optimal path that will allow you to maximize your life experience. We will discuss the answers to four main questions in this experience.

1. How do you formulate a dream that will endure throughout your life?
2. What is the nature of goals that will help you live your dream?
3. How does the "Lisa Experience" (described later in this chapter) help you to live the dream moment by moment?
4. How do you follow the Q-path?

## HOW TO FORMULATE A DREAM

The essence of your dream will be the same throughout your lifetime. You will always want to fulfill your resilient yearnings and drives, even into your senior years. Goals will change depending upon your life circumstances, but the dream will be the same. Let me guide you through two exercises that should help to formulate your dream. The first approach will be to reflect upon your resilient yearnings and see what kind of an image or statement emerges. The second will be the "rocking chair" reflection.

## ACTIVITY #41: REFLECTION UPON RESILIENT YEARNINGS

We have already discussed your yearnings and the driving forces in your life. Your dream is a journey to fulfill those yearnings over your lifetime. Ask yourself the following questions about your dream:

1. What is your childlike dream? How will you ensure that your life is filled with adventure, fun, humor, and curiosity?
2. What is your character dream? How will you enjoy the freedom from guilt by living with honor, integrity, honesty, and appreciation?
3. What is your noble dream? What will you do to feel good about yourself as you engage much of your energy touching lives and being in the service of others?

4. What is your ecological dream? What kind of environment will you create to enrich your life?

5. What is your universal dream? How will you ensure that you are able to receive guidance and comfort from sources beyond normal thinking?

As you reflect upon your answers, write a statement below about your dream. If you are artistic and would rather write a poem, draw a picture, or compose music to make up your dream, then that might be even more impactful. The important thing is that the dream is the outcome or infusion of Qs from the process and accomplishment of goals—it is a picture of resilient fulfillment throughout your lifetime. Here is a simple yet inclusive example of a dream statement that was written by one of my graduate students.

> My dream is to feel enough inner peace and strength so that I may be in a position to help other people live their dreams.

The simple dream is truly full of meaning. "To feel inner peace" would suggest living a life of fulfillment of all the resilient drives. The dream of strength would hint of gaining confidence, courage, and other Qs from universal sources of Qs. To be "in a position" hints of ecological resilience and nobility, and "help other people to live their dream" is a strong statement of nobility.

What is your dream?

_____

_____

_____

_____

_____

_____

## ACTIVITY #42: ROCKING CHAIR REFLECTION

A second way to think about your dream is to imagine yourself sitting in a rocking chair in your senior years and reflecting upon your life. As you imagine yourself rocking and reflecting upon your life, what are the things you did to fulfill each of the drives?

- What did you do to feel childlike?
- How did you live within your character framework?
- How are you feeling about yourself in light of the service you were able to render?
- How do you enrich your life with music, art, sounds, and your environment?
- How has your relationship with your universal/spiritual source of strength evolved over your lifetime?

Based upon this exercise, how do you want to enrich your dream statement?

_____

_____

_____

_____

_____

_____

## THE THREE CREATIONS OF YOUR DREAM

Three creations formulate your dream. You have already completed the first creation with your dream statement. It comes from your innate resilience—it feels right. It is the fulfillment of the your childlike, noble, character, ecological, and universal natures. It also needs to be adventuresome, fun, and comforting and provide learning and growth experiences to fulfill the childlike nature in you. Your noble nature has a strong yearning to touch the lives of others. The dream obviously needs to be within your character framework, or guilt will destroy the dream. Your universal nature tells you which lives you are best fit to touch. There is love and a peaceful feeling that comes when imagining living that dream. For example, perhaps your heart tells you that no matter where you are, you are going to make colleagues in the work site, family members at home, neighbors, and other people in the community feel better and happier because they came into contact with you during a day.

The second creation is in your intellectual resilience. Your mind figures out a way to live the dream. You make goals to strive toward the dream. You make decisions, develop personality characteristics, make plans, receive training, get educated, and develop social skills. When the first and second creations of the dream are made, then all friends, circumstances, and experiences are viewed as contributing to the dream or taking away from it.

The third creation is the action and implementation of the goals that will lead toward the dream. The body now responds to the mind and heart as it talks, acts, and does in accordance with the internal plans you have made. Your entire soul (body, mind, and spirit) should begin to follow a path with hope, heart, and direction.

## GOALS THAT HELP YOU LIVE YOUR DREAM

You form your goals based upon the needs, drives, and yearnings of your heart. Before we work on your goals, let's make sure you understand the difference between a dream and a goal. Dreams are constant throughout your life. Goals are short term or long term, but they will change as they are accomplished. If, in your dream statement, you included anything that was tangible, that was a goal. To find the dream in the goal, you ask yourself the question, "Why do I want this?" For example, if your dream was to own a house, I would say that is a goal. Why do you want a house? The answers are Qs. You want the house to feel safe (essential resilience), feel good about your situation (noble resilience), to provide for your family (noble resilience), and so on. Part of your dream, then, is to feel safe, feel good about where you live, and be able to help those you love.

Goals can be set for the short or long term, but all goals are designed to fulfill yearnings and drives and contribute toward the dream.

## ACTIVITY #43: RESILIENT DRIVES GOAL SETTING

This chart of goals is a way to encourage you to think. There will not be enough room in the chart to put all your goals. For example, with essential goals, you may set a short-term goal of beginning an exercise program. The long-term goal might be to reach your optimal weight.

| Innate Resilience | Short-Term Goals | Long-Term Goals |
|---|---|---|
| Childlike | | |
| Noble | | |
| Character | | |
| Ecological | | |
| Universal | | |
| Essential | | |
| Intellectual | | |

## ACTIVITY #44: BABY STEPS OR TRANSFORMATIONS

The most common and accepted protocol for accomplishing goals is the "one step at a time" approach as you climb the mountain. Your essential goal may be "I'm going to have a healthy breakfast and walk twenty minutes." Each day, then, you increase the time you walk and at the same time try one day to eat a healthy breakfast. Then, as you continue to walk on subsequent days, try eating a healthy breakfast for two days of the week. Progress from there on subsequent days. Your noble goal may be to help someone at least once a week and then increase the frequency for service. You may want to do your goal planning that way.

Other professionals have endorsed a total life-transformation approach. When you receive a vision from a quickening experience, you rearrange your life and just begin to live it. You are starting to eat well, exercise, play every day, touch lives every day, enjoy music every day, and be in touch with a source of spiritual strength every day. Write your approach to accomplishing your goals—baby steps or transformations.

| Baby Steps | Transformations |
|---|---|
| | |
| | |
| | |
| | |
| | |

## THE LISA EXPERIENCE

An important metaphor for the Q-path is the journey. Let me tell you the true story of Lisa. She taught me an important lesson over twenty years ago.

> I was teaching a personal resiliency class at the university. As usual, I spoke of the core human spirit, and then I began to talk about the dream. I talked about life as climbing a mountain peak. The class assignment was for the students to write their dreams and their goals. After the students turned in their papers, I took them home to relax in my recliner and read them. As I was reading the papers with dreams, I came across Lisa's. Lisa started her paper by saying, "Writing a dream is difficult for me because I really only have about four months to live. I have leukemia and after so many treatments for so many years, I have decided to let my life just go as long as it will go." I felt my heart breaking as I continued to read her touching paper. My emotions began to run all over the spectrum as I continued to read. "But here is my dream. My dream is to live—I want to live!!" Now a feeling of fear came over me as I reflected upon the mountain peak metaphor I had used in class. What could her peak look like? Lisa continued, "I want to live. I want to live each moment of every day and thank God for it. I want to celebrate whatever I learn now. I love each living step in my walks in my neighborhood. I relish each musical selection I hear knowing it could be my last. I embrace each moment with another human being. I cherish the touch when I pet my dog. My dream is to live—to live each moment for the rest of my life—no matter how long I live." I gently cried as I read her dream and realized that she was on a path with heart. Lisa and I had some wonderful conversations during that class, and I encouraged her to speak out more. Consequently, in a class discussion of resilient relationships versus unproductive relationships,

Lisa spoke up. She essentially scolded everyone in the class when they were complaining about the little things that their significant others were doing. She said, "You people don't get it! Don't you realize what a blessing it is to be with someone you care about? You don't have time to waste in judging, blaming, and denying. Love them now—love this moment." She ultimately divulged her secret about a short life. The spirit of the class changed that day.

Now what is amazing about this story is the follow-up. Lisa lived through to the end of the class and then, unfortunately, I lost track of her. I assumed that she had quietly passed away. About four years after the class was over, I was teaching another class on stress management at the university, and Lisa showed up on the first day as a student. I was shocked and in disbelief. She just grinned at me, and I went over to her and, with a twinkle in my eye, said, "Lisa, what are you doing here? You were supposed to be dead."

We both laughed, and she said, "It was a miracle—I just felt grateful to wake up every day and celebrated everything and kept living." When she checked with her doctors a few weeks after the class had ended, they were amazed as well—she was in full remission.

Lisa's story is meaningful and teaches us a great lesson. Your dream can be lived and experienced every day. She celebrated all the wonderful experiences in life and harvested the Qs of love, happiness, appreciation, and accomplishment throughout every day. There is substantial literature to support the healing power and peace that comes when you mindfully celebrate each day of living.

So rather than the dream being a mountain peak, the dream becomes the entire journey. Yes, we can celebrate when we reach the top, but we can live the dream every day, in every moment.

- Can you enjoy being childlike every day—laugh, have fun, or participate in an adventure?
- Can you be guilt-free every day by living with your sense of character every day?

- Can you feel an infusion of Qs by helping someone or providing a service every day?
- Can you do some ritual to be close to your universal/spiritual source of strength every day?

The other part of living the dream every day is to have "Lisa Experiences" every day. You can celebrate and feel an infusion of Qs by just being aware of all that is positive and good around you.

- You can enjoy the air you breathe during the everyday climb.
- You can appreciate the experience of working hard to make progress or overcome an obstacle.
- You can enjoy the scenery along the trail.
- You can celebrate the gift of being able to see, hear, taste, or touch.
- When you are upset or discouraged, you can appreciate the lows knowing that with time you will resiliently reintegrate.

You can truly respect obstacles and challenges. You can enjoy the good things that happen. Just look at what you have. There is much good all around you.

## THE Q-PATH

Let's build upon the dream idea and discuss the Q-path. You have been consciously thinking about your dream. You are trying to be sensitive to the resilient drives that come from your soul. One important skill is to discern the messages that come from the drives, but the other is to listen to the resonating feelings or rightness and peace that come from being on the right path. Your life is about following the Q-path, which is a resonating energy field. Your blueprint in life is a spiritual blueprint that will guide you to fulfill your potential and lead you through an ideal life. Your unique blend of mental, physical, and spiritual genetics has customized your nature for a particular path of progression to make a noble contribution in life. This blueprint for your life is the Q-path.

Harold S. Burr was a professor of anatomy at Yale School of Medicine. Back in 1937, Professor Burr began a series of experiments that demonstrated that salamander embryos as well as frog embryos had energy fields in the form of adult salamanders and frogs. Your blueprint for physical, mental, and spiritual growth is patterned as a progressive energy field of Qs that you can harvest in daily living. Your Q-path is housed within your soul, projecting a resonating optimal journey to fulfill your potential. Your life can be guided daily by resonating energy fields around you.

James Hillman, in his book *The Soul's Code*, suggests that we are like acorns. Housed within us is a full-grown and magnificent oak tree. If we continue with the metaphor, we can see that for the oak tree to flourish, it needs sunlight and water. We too need sunlight and water—the guidance and wisdom of universal and ecological forces to fulfill our potentials. You can wake up every day and imagine the energy field, or the field of Qs that you can harvest every day, to help grow and progress into your physical, mental, and spiritual ideal.

## THE NATURE OF YOUR DREAM AND Q-PATH

The Q-path that is now projecting out from you will last a lifetime. It will evolve, be modified, and grow larger, but it will be the same path because it comes from your soul. Your Q-path allows the spiritual gifts that you have been given to touch the hearts of others.

You can now know what is important and what is unimportant. If something contributes to your dream and is on the Q-path, it is important. If it does not, then it is not important. In all likelihood, you can eliminate some roles and distractions in life with this simple formula.

# In Summary

- Your vision or dream for a happy life is based upon your understanding of your innate drives of your body, mind, and spirit.
- You answer the age-old questions "Who am I?" and "Where am I going?" by understanding these drives—and when you do, you can formulate a vision of where you really want to go in life.
- Your vision remains constant throughout your lifetime.
- Goals that you set to support your dream and are flexible (as well as measurable and accomplishable).

The book to this point has been a journey of introspection to help you know who you are and where you want to go in life. Although there have been many opportunities to act upon the ideas and insights, the next experience will discuss venturing. On the resiliency model, it is the leap of faith.

# VENTURING: TAKING THE LEAP OF FAITH

> *Venturing is the experience of turning fear into courage and acting upon resilient prompts to fulfill dreams and goals.*

To this point in the book, we have inferred but really not examined any kind of action topics. When we consider where we are on the resiliency model, we are still at the beginning—the comfort zone. You have considered the road map of resiliency to know the nature of your journey of progression. You have explored your vast reservoir of resilient yearnings and drives that provide direction and energy to thrive in the resiliency process. You have pondered who you are and where you want to go in life. To continue, you need to take the leap of faith and act upon your dreams and goals.

> You can dream, set goals, plan, and imagine forever from the comfort of your recliner, but at some point, sooner rather than later, you need to lace up your hiking boots, grab your compass, and start blazing new trails.

Perhaps the best demonstration of a leap of faith was shown in the classic *Indiana Jones* series of movies.

In the 1989 movie *Indiana Jones and the Last Crusade*, we watch Indiana Jones in a desperate situation to try to help his father. The Holy Grail, which would heal his father, was on the other side of a vast chasm. The process of venturing is demonstrated perfectly in the leap of faith scene. First, Indiana Jones studied an ancient manuscript that demonstrated how to cross the chasm. He had to study it out in his mind and figure out what to do. He knows he must step out to what appears to be certain death because all he can see is a thousand-foot drop-off. But his study lets him know that if he takes the leap of faith, he will be able to get to the other side of the chasm. With faith and belief, he steps out and begins to fall, only to be supported by a camouflaged bridge that takes him to the Holy Grail.

Although a fantasy, the process is precisely what we need to do to progress and begin our resilient journeys. We study it out, resonate, and act. We will first consider turning fear into courage, and the next experience examines specific skills to ready yourself for the Q-nexus.

If you have embraced and applied the previous experiences, you now have a sense of your resilient journey, of where you want to go in life, and how to access your innate energy to succeed in your journey. If that is the case, it is now time to actually venture. *Venturing* is to take action by leaving your comfort zone (homeostasis) and engaging in new experiences that accomplish goals that contribute to your Q-path. As we referred to earlier, there are at least three general ways to venture.

1. Optimally, you can choose to venture and engage in planned challenges and adventures that will fulfill resilient drives. This is your leap of faith.
2. You can be forced to venture by being blindsided by a life event.
3. You can make poor life choices that differ from your sense of character and suffer in the trough of guilt.

On your life journey, you are starting to move through the disruptive reintegrative process by first venturing. Reflect again upon the resiliency model below with *venturing* circled.

**Figure 22. Venturing**

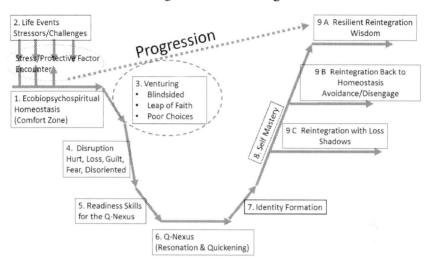

To take the leap of faith, you'll have to activate your innate courage to overcome fear. The essence of overcoming fear is to tip the scales toward courage. You do that by disarming fear and building courage, as shown in the figure. Your view of life begins to focus on the successes you have had, the strengths you have, and that the glass is actually half-full.

**Figure 23. Tipping the Scales**

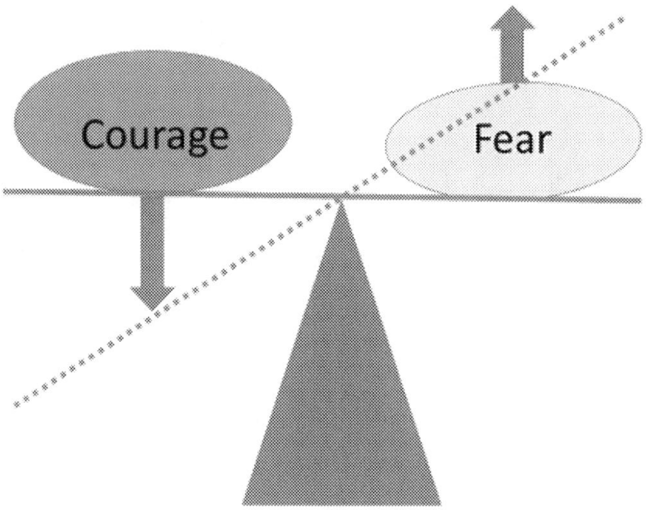

191

A great metaphor for increasing courage and reducing fear is much like eaglets finding the courage to fly.

> The awkward young eaglet is programmed to fly and to survive on its own. The first flight from the nest is a combination of restlessness from being restricted in the nest combined with the innate aspiration to become a flying eagle. The young eaglet will practice flapping her wings while standing in the safety of the comfortable nest. The eaglet dreams of fulfilling her potential with the goal of flying. She learns to feel the power of her wings to sense their readiness to carry her weight. At a magical moment after preparation, the drive to fly and fulfill the eaglet's potential outweighs the comfort of the nest. The young eagle finds courage to take the leap of faith and jumps from the nest for the first time. This is the natural order of progression for the eaglet.

We, too, can find ourselves afraid of flying. Leaving home for college, getting married, or taking a new job are all "leaving the nest" experiences. Some of us are like the eaglets that require being pushed out of the nest by their mothers in order to fly. It may be of interest to look up "eaglets leaving the nest" on the Internet to watch the magical moment when courage tips the scales and is stronger than fear for these eaglets. Our lives are like that as well. We have our resilient yearnings bubbling inside us that will help fill the voids in our lives if we will just venture out past our physical, mental, spiritual, and ecological comfort zones.

It seems in life that if you are engaged in venturing, learning, and growing on your own, there is less nudging from outside forces. Sitting around waiting for good things to happen results in weakness and vulnerability of body, mind, and spirit. Looking forward to venturing into a progressive experience enlivens the soul, where stagnation is generally filled with frustration and regret. If you are not venturing, it seems that more things happen in your life that are not progressive. You need to take control and venture on your own. People who live in fear and do not take leaps of faith into new challenges seem to have more issues in life than those who are adventurers.

Let's look at disarming fear and the essence of turning fear into courage by heightening the rewards and excitement of venturing. We'll first look at the nature of fear. Then we will consider how to disarm it.

## THE NATURE OF FEAR

> It is not uncommon for people to spend their whole life waiting to start living.
>
> —Eckhart Tolle

To some degree, fear is a good thing. Fear breeds caution, which keeps you from doing things that have extremely high levels of risk. Fear is not good when you are reluctant to try new things for fear of failure, loss of self-esteem, or emotional pain. I recognize that fear and anxiety can be very serious and may require therapy. Extreme fear-based conditions include the following, among others:

- Panic disorders: Recurrent unexpected extreme fear for no apparent reason.
- Obsessive-compulsive disorder: Urgent, frequent actions to deal with fear, such as frequent handwashing.
- Post-traumatic stress disorder: Reliving frightening memories of past traumatic experiences.
- Social phobias: Extreme fear of being judged by others in social settings.
- Specific phobias: Intense fear of something that may or may not pose real risk.

In severe cases of fear that disrupt your life, it is important to seek a qualified professional to help you. Most of us experience milder forms of these conditions in our normal lives. Experience 10 is for those of us who need more courage to do some of the things that would enrich our lives and fulfill our resilient yearnings.

## Disarming Fear

Disarming fear is a function of understanding, desensitization, and momentary catastrophizing that will be described below. We will focus on disarming the fear of taking leaps of faith into new adventures, but the same principles apply to overcoming social and specific phobias mentioned earlier.

## Understanding

Venturing is about seeking and taking opportunities to improve your situation. Even though it is for your own good, still you may have fear. The fear of venturing into experiences that will increase your capacity and allow you to harvest Qs generally stems from a lack of detailed understanding. With every new venture, whether it be to begin to exercise, to be more assertive, to deal with a problem, or making any kind of change, the important first step is to understand it—study it out. You may ask yourselves some questions that will guide your study of the venture and help you study it out.

1. What is the nature of the fear of the new experience? What is involved with each step?
2. Why do I have fear of leaving my comfort zone?
3. Why do I have fear of taking this leap of faith?
4. What are all the components of this fear?
5. How can I better understand the factors that make the leap of faith frightening?
6. What is the origin of the fear?

For example, let's assume that you have an okay job but perhaps it is not fulfilling your resilient drives. Let's say that one of your friends tells you of a job that would be more fulfilling and would increase your income, but it would require you to learn new skills and compel you to move. Numerous fears emerge as you ponder the new position. You interview and receive a job offer. The fearful person would begin to worry. *What if I can't learn the new required skills? What if I don't like the people I work with? How will I find a new place to live? Will I like it there? How will this affect my family?*

To lessen fear, you must increase understanding. To gain understanding, you must find the answers to these questions. If you find yourself having fear about the new skills, then *study it out*! Find out what the new skills are and what kind of effort it will take to learn them. If you find yourself asking, *What if I don't like the people I work with?* then *study it out*! Find out who the people are and learn about their likes and dislikes, and have phone conversations with them. If you ask yourself the question, *How will I find a new place to live?* then *study it out*! Get online and learn about housing options and neighborhoods. Check your credit standing with loan institutions and investigate what housing is available. If you ask yourself the question, *Will I like it there?* then *study it out*! If you ask yourself the question, *How will this affect my family?* then *study it out*! You should have heart-to-heart conversations with all family members that might be affected. Your intellectual resilience will help disarm the fears by helping you understand what it will be like.

## DESENSITIZATION

When working to overcome a fear of heights, water, spiders, or other things, the therapeutic strategy is often systematic desensitization. In other words, you expose yourself to the object of fear a little bit at a time. With fear of water, you might stand on the sandy shore of a lake and just enjoy it. Then you would put your feet in the water and pair it with some relaxing thoughts. Step out a little farther, up to your midcalf, and again embrace relaxing thoughts. The steps continue until you are in the water.

The same process of desensitization can occur when venturing into new activities. The more you are exposed to a situation that triggers fear, the more familiar you become with it. If you need to update your understanding of the latest technology with its inherent fear of being overwhelmed, just exercise your childlike curiosity and dabble with it. Try to do one thing, celebrate doing that, and then try another. If, for example, you want to begin an exercise program at a gym, the first time, simply go over and observe the activities that other people are doing. The second time you may watch and in your mind mimic the activities you observe. You could practice some at home. Finally, you may become more comfortable, do a couple of activities, and feel your courage and confidence grow.

## MOMENTARY CATASTROPHIZING

Helpful in disarming a fear is to do momentary catastrophizing. You imagine the worst possible outcome of the event that is causing you to fear and then determine if you could cope with it. If the worst possible outcome is injury or death, then caution and safety is advised. But if the catastrophic outcome is embarrassment, then weigh that outcome with the possible benefits.

As you take some time to do momentary catastrophizing, it will allow you to have an exit plan for any negative outcomes. If you have that coping strategy in your mind, then again, you are disarming fear. Consider the following story about disarming fear.

> Cheri was a member of a predominant faith throughout her childhood. When she married, she continued to be affiliated with the faith. Now, in her middle years, Cheri found herself divorced and began to question God and traditional religions. She continued to attend family religious functions because it was expected and everyone in her family belonged to that faith. In her personal life, however, Cheri didn't want anything to do with any religion, but still she often pondered the existence of God. In her questioning, she prayed one day, and in her words, she asked, "God, are you really there? Do you really answer my prayers? Can I really have a personal relationship with you?" She felt a stirring in her heart to find something greater than herself. She wanted a God to guide her and give her love, peace, and joy. Amazingly, later in the afternoon on the same day at work, a couple of coworkers were talking about faith. One reported that she had joined a new faith that described God as personal. Cheri was surprised to hear that discussion in light of her prayer that morning, and she joined in the conversation. Cheri committed to attend worship service with the coworker and continued to do so for several weeks. Cheri felt a sense of peace and guidance as to how to have effective prayers. The church leaders asked if Cheri wanted to be baptized

Proactive and Applied Resilience

and join the faith. Cheri felt a sudden fear race through her soul. *What would my family think if I left the family faith and joined this new faith?* she pondered. *This new faith feels so good—it gives me hope and makes me happy—but I know my family would shun me. Would I be happier in the new faith without my family, or should I stay in the old faith with my family?*

Cheri felt a deep fear about venturing into the new faith due to possible reprisals from her family, but she followed the suggestions in this experience. She studied it out. She read all the reading materials that the church offered her. She went to the church meetings and began to understand the rituals and practices. She met many of the people of the church, and they welcomed her as part of their church family.

Her biggest fear was facing her family and letting them know that she was leaving their traditional faith. In studying out this leap of faith, Cheri not only needed to understand the new faith but she needed to understand the fear of ridicule she would face from her family if she should join. She needed to imagine if she would be happy even if her family shunned her.

Before Cheri committed to the new faith, she decided to understand the potential fear of ridicule and rejection from the family. She started with her sister, with whom she was extremely close. She asked her, "Our family has always been of this particular faith—are you really into it?" The question opened an engaging conversation, and the sister admitted that she belonged just because it was tradition. She really hadn't thought about the beliefs. Cheri had similar conversations with her other three siblings. Later, she renewed conversations and asked, "What do you think Mom and Dad would say if one of us would join another faith?" The conversation led to disclosing some of Cheri's thoughts about changing faiths. She was surprised at the openness of the family, but like Cheri, they weren't sure what the parents would think. Buoyed by the openness from her siblings, she followed the same questioning with her parents. She shared her thoughts accompanied with expressions of love and was also open with them about the fear she had to talk with them about changing faiths. She said, "Family is so important to me, and I love you, but I am not feeling fulfilled in our current faith. Would you still love and accept me if I looked for other ways to believe?" Mom was fine and expressed her unconditional love. Dad, on the other hand, was disappointed and felt somewhat betrayed. But this introduction was the first in many conversations about what everyone really believed beyond tradition. Cheri ultimately joined the new church. Over time, even Dad accepted Cheri's choice.

Cheri's fear was disarmed by understanding what the family really thought about her changing faiths. She had momentarily catastrophized to be able to ponder if she could be happy being in the new faith and living with the ridicule and rejection of her family. She understood enough about venturing into the new religion that the fear of venturing became a nonissue.

## BUILDING COURAGE

It is vital to build your courage to be stronger, more powerful, and sufficiently energized to tip the scales of balance to the courage side of the scale. The following sections talk about how to have enough courage to overcome fear, enabling the ability to venture.

## COURAGE THROUGH SELF-EFFICACY AND FAITH

Self-efficacy and faith are critical and powerful Qs requisite for venturing. Albert Bandura (1994) described self-efficacy as "the belief in one's capabilities to organize and execute the courses of action required to manage prospective situations." In other words, self-efficacy is a person's belief in his or her ability to venture into an opportunistic situations and progress through the experience. Faith is also a belief that you can venture into a new experience, but the belief is fortified and enlivened through the help of one's spiritual sources of strength—universal resilience. Faith embraces one's perception of his or her abilities to accomplish something, but also includes sensing a spiritual comfort, peace, and assurance that he or she can make things happen.

Self-efficacy is fostered through progressive resilient reintegration. Each time you resiliently reintegrate as per resiliency mapping, you gain more self-efficacy. As you review past experiences, think about the state of homeostasis and when you felt an urge to learn or do something. You can think about the process of resiliency mapping. You may remember moments of doubt or hesitation, but you can also remember the moment of venturing. You may have struggled, but in the end, you resiliently reintegrated.

## ACTIVITY #45: REMEMBERING LEAPS OF FAITH

Something as simple as riding a bike is an example. When was the moment you first tried to ride a bike? You were afraid and likely needed help from an experienced person. You felt fear, but the excitement of learning tipped the scales to venturing. You can likely think of several times in the past when you overcame a fear to learn or grow. Write some of those here.

1. _____
2. _____
3. _____

In the introductory experience of this text, we spoke of the postulate of faith. Faith relies heavily upon the postulate of resonation described earlier.

The art of faith is initiated with resonation, which confirms rightness of the venture. In addition, faith is the expectation and confidence that during the leap of faith, quickening will occur. The quickening is a feeling of strength, power, comfort, and assurance that infuses your soul from a perceived universal resilience source.

> If faith can move a mountain, you will need to start digging and believe that a magical force will pitch in to give you a helping hand to haul the dirt.

Faith is also enlarged by having repeated experiences that help you progress. You had faith before, so you have some experience to know that progression will happen again. Self-efficacy is your belief that you can venture by your own will and persistence. Faith is your conviction that you can venture with a universal strength that will help you through repeated resilient reintegration. With each disruption, you gain more belief that you can accomplish more—more self-efficacy. With faith, you have accomplished something in the past and have felt the resonating energy from your universal resilience, and then you have more confidence with each experience.

## ACTIVITY #46: YOUR LEAP-OF-FAITH EXPERIENCE

Describe your reflection of faith. Remember a time in your past when you needed to venture into something, sought your source of universal resilience, and then took the leap of faith. Write that experience here.

_____

_____

_____

_____

_____

## COURAGE THROUGH STORIES AND HERO MODELING

Since you were a child, you have had heroes. You had cartoon heroes, children's book heroes, Disney heroes, and numerous television heroes. Bolstering courage to venture can be facilitated by hero modeling. As a child, you may have imagined your life like Snow White or as Jack and the Beanstalk. As you got older, you may have wanted to be "cool" like characters in popular television shows. You may have fantasized about adopting Qs from heroes in classic literature, such as King Arthur or Jane Eyre. More than likely, you have identified with heroes and heroines in popular movies, such as *Indiana Jones*, *Fried Green Tomatoes*, *Steel Magnolias*, *Star Wars*, *Back to the Future*, *Independence Day*, and many others. You may have sports heroes, political heroes, and performing heroes.

In your mind, you can imagine yourself acting like one of your heroes as you venture into college, sports, marriage, or a career. How would he or she do it? Can you find that identity within your soul? You can watch carefully as the hero exemplifies the successful venturing journey. You will be able to increase your faith that you can do the same.

## ACTIVITY #47: IMAGERY TO BECOME YOUR HERO

In a current life venture, do some imagery. Imagine that your hero is doing what you are wanting to do. Imagine in detail. Then imagine yourself doing the same thing. Describe the experience here.

_____

_____

_____

_____

_____

## COURAGE BUILDING THROUGH CREATIVITY

Some people increase their faith or self-efficacy if they feel they are using a unique approach to the venture. Thinking creatively gives you ownership and excitement about your unique approach to venturing. Again, courage requires energy, and you need to generate more positive energy than fear energy (which thwarts your intentions).

**Thinking Wild and Crazy:** It is helpful to brainstorm creative ideas on how to increase your courage by first thinking "wild and crazy." When you have several out-of-the-box ideas, then you can see if something practical results to give you a new approach to your venturing. Brainstorming is a way that lets you think outside of the box. For example, your ideas should be unrestricted:

Time is not a factor.
Time travel is a possibility.
You can create a clone of yourself.
You can shrink yourself or make yourself huge.
Money is no object.
You can beam yourself anywhere.
Reality is not a factor.

When you are done brainstorming, think about how some of the ideas, when brought back to reality, could be implemented.

> MaryAnn, who was very timid and reserved, worked as a cashier at a department store. In her leisure time, MaryAnn would read decorating magazines, and she would sometimes imagine how her store could be so much more appealing if they were to move some of the more appealing displays to the front and add some color and images to the walls. In staff meetings, she was so shy that she failed to ever say anything. After some guidance about brainstorming in a wild and crazy fashion, she took the opportunity on one of her walks to think outside of the box and let her bosses know what she was thinking. She was afraid to approach them. She didn't have a degree in decorating or interior design, but still she had what she thought were good ideas. In her wild and crazy thinking, she imagined that if she could make herself invisible and be in the room where the bosses were making decisions, she could cast a spell on them to seek her out as a decorating consultant. As she pondered how to make herself invisible and still influence the bosses, she had a quickening moment. She could not be there, but her influence could be. She took a photo of part of the store that she felt needed the most aesthetic help. She enlarged the photo and placed it on half of a poster. On the other half of the poster, she created an ideal design for the room and put her name on the bottom of the poster. She checked with the administrative assistant to determine where and when the next meeting would occur. Just before the meeting, MaryAnn placed the poster, with the optimal design, in the meeting room. After the meeting, one of the bosses came to her register on the main floor and asked to visit with her. In a short time, MaryAnn became the store decorator and ultimately improved several of the stores in the region.

Thinking wild and crazy is fun and if appropriate, done with other people. The use of such thinking becomes possible as you add the restrictions of reality to the scenarios.

**Psychomotor Meditation:** While you are jogging, walking, driving, ironing, taking a shower, doing routine chores, or doing some other form of repetitive physical movement, you can let your thoughts wander to ideas to build energy for venturing. Your body is distracted to free your mind and spirit to create when doing repetitive nonthinking exercise.

**Readiness Using Metaphors and Similes:** You can increase your energy and creative nature by using metaphors and similes. You may remember from high school English that metaphors and similes are very similar but not quite the same. A simile is a figure of speech that draws a comparison between two different things, especially using a phrase containing the words *like* or *as*. A metaphor is used to describe somebody or something with a word or phrase that is not meant literally but by means of a vivid comparison expresses something about him, her, or it. For example, "That Suzie is a snake," is a metaphor, whereas "That Suzie leaves a trail like a drunken snake" is a simile. As we begin to look at examples of metaphors and similes with resiliency or resilient drives, we may find a metaphor such as "Childlike resilience is a breath of fresh air." A simile example is "My character resilience is like a lighthouse along the shore."

Although there are many applications of using metaphors and similes, the purpose in this experience is to put you into a state of mind to have more courage. The metaphor or simile will help you imagine beyond the traditional rut of normal thinking and expand your options. With your selected challenge in mind, go through this metaphor and simile activity.

## ACTIVITY #48: PICK YOUR FAVORITE METAPHOR OR SIMILE

There are numerous metaphors and similes in literature and in everyday conversations. Pick one of your favorite metaphors or similes and put it in context of your selected venturing challenge. Think about it for a few minutes. Be aware of your new thinking, your openness, and your receptivity to new insights.

For example, in relation to your personal resilience, you may think about the metaphor "My challenges leave me aboard a stormed-tossed ship at sea, but I will keep a firm grip on the helm and stay true to my course." Another example may be "The chaos I am going through is a dark night waiting for the light of dawn." If you have trouble thinking of some metaphors, a search on the Internet will provide some examples.

Ponder your venturing situation in the context of these metaphors or similes. An example of what you might be pondering is trying to reconnect with a loved one. The simile you use might be "My mind is like the dark of night waiting for the light of dawn." As you ponder this simile, you may talk to yourself about patience, knowing that people will change and forgive. You may consider what the light is and how you could begin to create some of that light. Is the light a message, a gift, some music, or a smile with gentle conversation?

Be sensitive to some of the thoughts and feelings you may have and remember them. Write your sense of openness and new thinking here.

_____

_____

## ACTIVITY #49: FIND THE METAPHOR OR SIMILE IN YOUR WORLD

As you ponder your venturing challenge, another approach to creating metaphors is to look around your home or office and select any object. Pair your life challenge with the functioning or representation of the object. For example, in school or work, you may come across a water fountain. If your challenge is "like a water fountain," then you may ponder the energy or effort it takes to push the water button before the refreshing water streams from the fountain. Maybe you will see a trash can and ponder how your challenge is like a trash can. You may begin to think "Are there things in my life that I need to get rid of?"

As you identify your own creative approaches to venturing, ownership breeds motivation, which results in energy. You have more energy than you think. There is more evidence that you are being successful and positive than not, which helps to tip the scales of balance toward courage.

## ACTIVITY #50: COURAGE BUILDING THROUGH A RESILIENCE FORCED MATRIX

Discovering energy to take leaps of faith into new ventures can be facilitated by using a forced matrix. A forced matrix simply encourages you to think about the meaning that will come by pairing two different concepts. Enjoy the ideas that come to your head as you think about the energy or creative approach to taking leaps of faith into your next venture. On the top row, write the venture that you are contemplating—to which you have resonated. On the column to the left, think of the Qs that come from each of the drives that we have discussed in this book. You can actually feel your energy and confidence as you think about job hunting (as the example) and your childlike nature. You think of this as an adventure or a game that you want to win. You will feel courage when you connect with your universal source of strength to help you take the jump. Continue with each of the resilient drives.

| | Job Hunting | | |
|---|---|---|---|
| Childlike | | | |
| Noble | | | |
| Character | | | |
| Ecological | | | |
| Universal | | | |
| Essential | | | |
| Intellectual | | | |

## Transforming Fear into Courage

> When fear shows its terrified face, long to know it, dissect it, and then finally love it. Fear will become your ally and your motivation.

When the fear of venturing comes to you, look at it as a positive. As the fear fills your soul, you will be able to make the transition to act.

1. As you prepare to take the leap of faith, you will need to remember and focus on the resonation of rightness you have felt. You will focus on the positives. You will feel the energy of excitement as you jump into the new experience.
2. Remember you have disarmed your fears—you can cope with the worst outcomes. The benefits far outweigh the risks. Remember that we are talking about proactive and life-enriching fears. Fears that are life threatening should bring caution.
3. Feel the energy of fear, and in your mind, change it to excitement.

## Do It: Just Jump

There is that magical moment of control when the right feeling (resonation) and rewards are stronger than your fear and you just take the jump. Here's a true but light story of when I was a Boy Scout.

> I loved being a Boy Scout. Every summer we'd go on a high adventure camping trip to one cool place or another. When I was thirteen, our troop left from San Diego and went up into the High Sierra Mountains for a weeklong camp. Although there were many fun things we did, the most memorable was the compass course. My dad was one of the Scout leaders, and he loved to send us on long compass courses. Our little patrol of four guys would orient our maps, set the direction with our compasses, and then pace off the designated distance that was usually between four hundred and one thousand yards. We would then reset our course with the compass and step

off another distance. At the end of the compass course, we were to find the treasure of candy bars. Our patrol had nicknames for each other, so I'll use the nicknames to tell this story.

Chips, Hogwash, Caveman, and I (Buzzard) took off with great confidence on our course. Before the trip, we had practiced in the parking lot of the building where we held our Scout meetings. We thought we were pretty good, but when we faced the mountainous terrain, our confidence began to fade. After about an hour and a half and just before our last bearings were set, we were pacing by a pit that was about ten feet long and about six feet wide. In this pit seemed to be quicksand. It had been covered by pine needles and dirt, but we stopped and tossed a rock into it, and the quicksand slowly swallowed the rock up. This was the coolest thing that we had seen on the trip, so we quickly abandoned our compass course to play by the quicksand.

After tossing a few rocks in, I began to wonder how deep the quicksand went and realized that someone had to volunteer to jump in and find out. So I told Chips, Hogwash, and Caveman to get some poles so they could pull me out after I jumped in. Chips was the scholar of the group and told me how stupid it was to do it. He was more interested in completing the compass course, and when I told him I was going to do it anyway, he started to worry. "What if it sucks you in so fast that we can't get you out? How are you ever going to get your Scout uniform clean if you go under?" The questions were endless, so after a while, the rest of us just ignored him. (Chips grew up to be a child psychiatrist.)

Hogwash was cool and went after some branches from a nearby fallen tree. We began to plot the strategy to get me out. Caveman was a jock and just stood there saying, "This is soooo cool!" over and over. We needed his strength to make sure I got out. When the preparations were made and all three of my friends were ready with branches, I eased my way in, shoes and all. I sank fairly quickly into the quicksand. I had held on to Caveman's branch with one hand and Hogwash's in the other. When it got to my waist, I hit solid ground, so I let go of the branches. I was really excited to be in this quicksand and shouted to the other guys to come in with me. Without hesitation, Caveman and Hogwash jumped in. What an adventure. As we tried to move around, we noticed that the quicksand had a horrible odor. The more we moved, the stinkier it got. We couldn't figure it out until Chips, standing on the edge of the pit, said, "Uh, guys, look!" We looked and experienced a moment of truth—a moment when you receive sudden enlightenment that clarifies your life situation. Hogwash and I, and even Caveman, suddenly looked at each other and froze. For as our eyes followed the direction of Chips's pointing finger, we saw in the brush a pushed-over outhouse and some tracks that indicated that it had been sitting over our pit perhaps years before. The reality that our "quicksand" was not traditional quicksand infused our souls, and the three of us simultaneously yelled and scrambled to get out. We pulled on each other and tried to climb on top of each other in our desperation. In the *Three Stooges*–like chaos, we got ourselves covered even more with "quicksand." Chips was laughing his face off. We finally got out and sprinted to the stream that was fifty yards away and jumped into the ice-cold water. We never finished that compass course.

The venture into "quicksand" followed the proper readiness preparations. Sticks were obtained to help pull me, and the strongest Scouts were there to help. The spirit of adventure helped to take the leap of faith.

The lesson here is to look at as many circumstances as you can. Studying it out is critical. In this case, the Scouts only studied the option of going in with the assumption that it was quicksand. A complete understanding of the nature of the "quicksand" would have likely thwarted the adventure. But the Qs that were harvested were rewards of an adventure and a great story to tell. Great ventures always result in stories.

# In Summary

- Venturing is the experience of actually working your way through the resiliency process. The disruptions will cause some chaos. You enter the world of the unknown, the unpredictable, yet this process shows us options. Leaving homeostasis is the experience of venturing.
- You can overcome fear through disarming fear through understanding, desensitizing yourself, and momentary catastrophizing.
- You can build courage through progressive resilient reintegration, courage through stories and heroes, and creative approaches to problem solving.
- You increase your courage by maximizing your resilient drives.

Venturing prepares you for your next experience, which is readiness for the Q-nexus. You can begin to practice some skills to assure you receive insights as to what you need to do and who you need to become.

# READINESS SKILLS FOR THE Q-NEXUS

> *Readiness skills for the Q-nexus include several experiences that prepare the mind, body, and spirit to be receptive to resonating and quickening messages.*

After venturing, whether you have been blindsided or whether you are taking a leap of faith into a new experience, you will find yourself in unfamiliar territory. You may feel some confusion, some fear, and potentially some loss, but all that is normal. Even with the formation of your dream and supportive goals, the experience of doing something can be challenging. You are in the disruptive portion of the resilient journey. The disruptive location on the resiliency model is #4 in the model below.

## Figure 24. Disruption

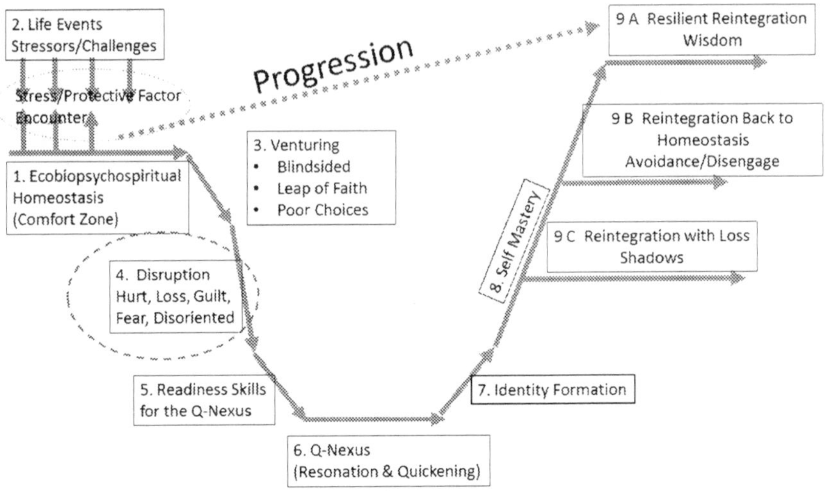

The positive part of disruption is that you will find yourself in a better state to receive inspiration, hope, and guidance as you travel through the resilient journey. When you find yourself wondering what to do or how to feel, you become more open to insights that are softer than your normal thinking. The positives of negative emotions are that they force you to be more open, humble, and needy to receive enlightenment. During the disruption, you look to find meaning, purpose, or order in the wake of the chaos.

During the disruption, you find yourself more open to receiving strength beyond normal capacity. The wise answers and motivation for all life's questions come from the greater wisdom within each soul. The skills to access the best answer come through a variety of modalities that will be described later in this chapter. Each skill is designed to help you listen to the prompts that come from all your childlike, noble, character, ecological, universal, essential, and intellectual yearnings and drives.

In preparation for the Q-nexus experience described in the next experience, it is important to attain a certain level of readiness to receive the prompts, guidance, and strengths you desire. When you are open and receptive to messages from your soul (body, mind, or spirit), you are in a state of submissiveness and humility. I have been advised regularly to avoid using the term *submissiveness* in that the word connotes a state of subjection to someone else. In this case, with our source of universal strength or Great Spirit, we are in a state of receptivity, openness, devotion, and humility. Submissiveness becomes strengthening in this light.

It is also vital that you believe that these modalities will work for you. I cannot overstate the importance of the postulate of self-efficacy or faith. All the good ideas, all the desires, and all the good intentions will fall by the wayside if you do not have the faith or belief that you can make it happen.

The art of faith is initiated with resonation to the modality that feels right for you. Some people resonate to music as a means to find enlightenment. Other people meditate. Others pray. Others go to the mountains. The expectation that you will find answers to life's challenges by using one of the techniques is important. The techniques you choose should lead you to the humble, receptive, and submissive state of openness.

> Submissiveness and humility are not states of weakness
> but rather states of strength, power, and connection.

## Figure 25. Readiness Skills

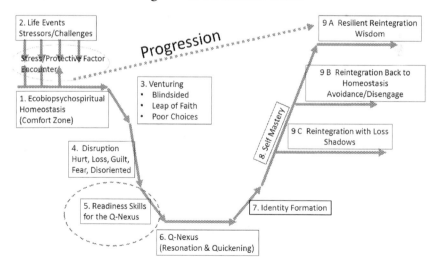

213

# ADAPTING INTEGRATIVE HEALTH SKILLS FOR Q-NEXUS READINESS

We will briefly describe several of the skills that you can use to ready yourself for the Q-nexus. These skills are helpful whether you have taken the leap of faith or have been blindsided by life events. Books have been written about each of these skills, and professionals are available to provide training to help you develop the skills, but you can adapt some of these skills to fit your needs for the Q-nexus without reading a specialized book or receiving specialized training. It should be obvious that these skills can also be adapted to energize yourself in all the stages of the resiliency process. The skills upon which we will focus include internally generated skills in the form of imagery as well as externally triggered skills, such as ecological enrichment.

## READINESS THROUGH INTERNALLY GENERATED IMAGERY

Imagery is your ability to fantasize or daydream about sounds, images, experiences, smells, tastes, or touches. When you are planning, you use your intellectual resilience to visualize how the plan will unfold. When you smell one of your favorite dishes, you imagine what it might taste like. Imagery is a foundation skill that will help you through the entire resilient journey.

- When you rediscovered your childlike nature, you imagined yourself on adventures, playing, and energetic.
- When you identified your noble nature, you created images of your service to other people.
- When you pondered your universal resilience, you imagined your sources of spiritual strength.
- When you were creating your dream, you envisioned new identities for yourself.

# ACTIVITY #51: DEVELOPING IMAGERY SKILLS

You used imagery throughout all your resiliency experiences. This imagery experience is only to help you increase your imagery skills, including all your senses and feelings. Go through the following exercise to see if you can visualize the following in your mind. If you can't visualize the images initially, recognize that with practice, you can develop better imagery skills.

1. Get into a comfortable position, relax, and close your eyes.
2. Try to image a ball—make it a blue ball (visual imagery).
3. Now try to visualize yourself moving—that you are walking. Imagine what it feels like to move your body (kinesthetic imagery).
4. Change the imagery to now imagine that you can hear your favorite music in your mind. You may want to listen, in your imagination, to the sound of a train. Hear the sounds (auditory imagery).
5. Increase your imagery skills by being able to smell things in your mind. Imagine the smell of campfire smoke or the perfume/cologne of a person close to you. If that is not working, try imaging the smell of a skunk (olfactory imagery).
6. Imagine that you see a lemon—it is sliced—you bring the lemon to your mouth, and you bite into the lemon. Imagine the pungent taste. You should not only be able to taste the lemon in your mind but will feel yourself salivating (gustatory imagery).
7. Increase your imagery skills by imagining your sense of touch. Imagine what it feels like to rub your finger over sandpaper. You might try imagining the feel of holding hands with a loved one (tactual imagery).
8. Now try to imagine the emotional feeling of love for someone or a pet. Imagine how that really feels (emotional imagery).

As you practice these skills, you can apply them to acquiring any desirable state of the soul that you desire. You may want more energy or to acquire an emotional state that is more conducive to communication. In this case, you are going to use imagery and all the imaginary senses to attain a state of readiness for the Q-nexus. Try the following imagery strategy to help you attain a state of readiness. It should be noted that this is an example and that you can create an imagery strategy that best fits your thinking.

## ACTIVITY #52: IMAGERY TO BE READY FOR THE Q-NEXUS

> After getting into a comfortable and relaxed state free from outside distractions, create a situation in your mind that will ready you for insight and inspiration. Imagine the place that best allows you to be past your routine-driven thoughts, away from external distractions, and a place that will give you peace. The location can be imaginary or real in your mind. You may want to see yourself in a hammock on a beautiful deserted island. You may want to see yourself in a favorite room of your house. You may want to be sitting on a mountaintop or any other place that is peaceful. Imagine the view that you have. See the colors, smell the scents, and listen to the sounds around you in this special place in your mind.
>
> Now focus on how you are feeling. Recognize your humility and your need for insights. Rid yourself of any preconceived ideas or plans, and open your mind and heart to inspiration beyond normal. You feel confident in receiving the insights. Imagine that you are growing into your energy field or potential and that images of the next steps for fulfillment will come. Continue to expect answers and feelings. Then be still and reject nonrelated thoughts.

## READINESS THROUGH MEDITATIVE IMAGERY

Meditation is a mind-body skill that focuses on the present moment and living life fully in the here and the now. It is an imagery method to help you tune into and connect with your universal source of strength. It allows you to contemplate, reflect, and introspect. Optimally, meditation allows you to empty your mind (which is metaphoric for developing a calm state of mind and keeping an *open* mind and heart), perceiving yourself and life deeply in the present moment. It is removing any intellectual or cognitive thoughts, allowing space for universal inspiration. Most people can't empty their minds; rather, they have thoughts crash into the empty space. Meditation practitioners have developed other ways to meditate that are somewhat easier to master. Many practitioners advocate the use of mantras (where the word *mantra* refers to an anchor word that has personal meaning to the person) and/or concentrating on one thing, such as breath to aid in spiritual development or relaxation. The other popular form of meditation is mindfulness or being in the present moment. With mindfulness, you focus on your breathing or noticing the thoughts and perceptions within yourself and the pleasantness of your surroundings.

In contemplative forms of meditation, a mantra is a meaningful word, phrase, chant, or image that is continually repeated in your mind until it is viscerally felt and its meaning understood in body, mind, and heart. Here are three examples that will help you be ready for the Q-nexus:

1. Repeat the word *love* in your mind over and over. *Love* means connections, and you feel connected to your resilient drives. You love that part of you that makes you happy—you love those yearnings and drives in their purest forms. Continuing to repeat the word *love*, you will feel connected to others you love—people, pets, and your living space. You will feel connected to your universal source of strength as you repeat the word *love* over and over.

2. To create a readiness for the Q-nexus, you may want to focus on a meaningful and relevant mantra, such as repeating the words *humble, receptive, submissive,* or *open.* You will feel any unhelpful pride slip away, and you can become receptive and submissive to a wisdom beyond yourself—the Q-nexus.

3. Readiness may be reached by paying attention to an object that has meaning for you. The object can represent your source of enlightenment. Perhaps you can light a candle and focus on the flame and the many metaphors for the flame. Perhaps a religious symbol, a picture of a hero, a clock, or other image to focus on for a period of time will help with your readiness.

As mentioned earlier in this section, mindfulness is a form of meditation that allows you to focus on the present and pay attention to the here and now. Some forms of mindfulness teach you to use your imagery skills to focus on your breathing or on your environment. You can imagine that with each breath inhalation you will receive insights.

Walking meditation is to pay attention to walking if you are able to walk. Any other continuous physical movement, such as swimming or driving, will also provide an opportunity to focus. The purpose of these forms of meditation is to help you to escape your troubling feelings, regrets of the past, and worries of the future by focusing and appreciating the present walking experience. I recognize that some of you may not be able to walk, but you can focus on any kind of movement. The movement allows your mind to connect to deeper thoughts and perceptions and possibly answers.

To create a state of readiness for the Q-nexus, you can be very mindful. Try the following imagery strategy to ready yourself for the Q-nexus using mindfulness. You will be instructed to see little bits of light. Before you do this, reflect upon what those bits of light might be as per your beliefs discussed in the experience on universal resilience. The bits of light may be qi, strings (quanta), the collective unconscious, or God's Spirit.

## ACTIVITY #53: READINESS THROUGH MINDFULNESS

In a relaxed position and free from distractions, imagine your present situation in life. You see yourself looking out of your own eyes and being able to see a world around you full of particles of light. You can imagine that within you, from your unconscious mind, you can also see little bits of light as well. You can sense that these little bits of light contain wisdom and insights that are beyond your normal capacity. Take a moment to clearly see the sea of particles around you. Look at the colors in your environment and experience the pleasant smells in this wonderful sea. As you breathe in, you can see the little particles of wisdom, light energy, peace, or other Qs enter your body. Now you can feel the energy and peace preparing you for enlightenment. This is a condition in which you are continually living. Celebrate this wonderful state.

There are other forms of meditation that could also be resiliently adapted, which you can do on your own. Skilled practitioners may meditate for up to an hour and remain focused. Most people find benefits from fifteen to twenty minutes of meditative imagery. During that time, you may receive the insights you need.

## READINESS THROUGH IMAGERY AND PRAYER

Prayer is also a form of imagery. Prayer is an effort, and therefore a skill, to communicate with God or a universal source of strength. Prayer is about goodwill for oneself and others. Prayer is the hope to receive insights and answers to life's challenges. I recognize that some of you who are reading this book may not believe in God, but still there are the other sources of universal strength, and each source can provide the wisdom and energy beyond your normal capacity.

This portion of the book is not written to debate whether God exists or not. This section will be helpful for those who believe in God, and those who do not can skip this section and go to the next section. For those who do believe in God, it is important to use prayer as a skill in preparation to have Q-nexus experiences. Using imagery in your prayers will help to personalize God. Whether God is in a human form, a light form, or whether you perceive your God in one of the forms discussed in the experience on universal resilience (qi, the collective unconscious, strings, nature, or the Great Spirit), you can use imagery to connect with God. The most powerful prayers are those where you see an image in your mind and feel as though you are enjoying God's presence, wisdom, and power.

People pray differently. Some recite written or scriptural prayers, some chant, and some pray from their own hearts. Feel free to adapt the following exercise to fit your belief in God or other source of spiritual strength.

## ACTIVITY #54: READINESS THROUGH PRAYER

Try the following five stages to use imagery in prayer as a form of readiness to have a Q-nexus experience:

1. Prepare: Get into a comfortable position and adjust your thinking to allow yourself to be in a spiritual frame of mind. That mind-set is one of openness and a need for blessings, comfort, peace, courage, or other Qs from God.

2. Create an image in your mind: As you think about the origin of God's Spirit with its accompanying Qs that you desire, what image comes to mind? Is God in the form of a man, a woman, a light, or other image? Whatever you believe, form that image in your mind. Imagine that you are in the presence of God. Imagine and feel the love you are receiving. Imagine what God may look like. Bring in all the senses to enhance the image. Feel the spirit of being in the presence of God.

3. Assume a state of gratitude and humility: In the presence of your God, first reflect upon those things that are good in your life. Feel gratitude and appreciation. Confirm that you recognize the greater wisdom and be aware of your sense to be humble.

4. Ask for answers and direction: Have a conversation with your God. Express your needs. Make your God as personable as you want so that it is like visiting with a trusted friend, but at the same time feeling the majesty.

5. Listen: Upon completion of your asking for direction, continue the imagery of a conversation with God. You may be able to hear answers and insights.

## READINESS THROUGH IMAGERY AND JOURNAL WRITING

To help prepare you for the Q-nexus, you may want to start writing about your situation and need for enlightenment. By recording your current disruption, whether it be a leap of faith or being blindsided, you have the ability to view the situation from a different perspective. A new view will help you be open to gaining insights into otherwise hidden facets of your life situation. You can also see extremely subjective scenarios from an objective point of view. You can then write about how you feel about the situation. As you are writing, you will naturally create images in your mind. You can then describe the images as well.

There is a point in journaling or writing therapy when you get into a zone or a state where you are accessing the wisdom of your unconscious mind. This is usually longer than ten minutes. As you reach that flow state, continue to write your thoughts.

When you naturally come to an end of the writing session, you can review your writing. Either during the writing or upon reflection, you will find yourself ready for a Q-nexus experience.

Much like journal writing, some people prefer to ponder and think differently by drawing, painting, or just doodling. As you ponder your challenge and need for guidance, think about the situation and the accompanying feelings, and then begin to draw. Again, to get into a flow state or zone, it may require ten minutes or more. Don't force the drawing; just let it happen. When you write or draw, the process of accessing wisdom beyond yourself for the Q-nexus is effective.

## READINESS THROUGH LITERATURE

Reading scholarly literature helps you to ponder and think beyond your own conscious thought. Two types of literature will help you expand your thinking and ready yourself for the Q-nexus. Some literature is targeted to deal with your specific need for guidance. If you are trying to deal with a body weight issue, there are hundreds of books and articles about how to make that happen. If you are dealing with depression, then there is also literature to help. Studying and learning new information will open options, and you will resonate to some concepts that become part of the Q-nexus.

Literature in the form of fiction, biography, history, classics, or religious works will fill your mind with numerous ideas. You will identify with heroes, self-help methods, and religious concepts. You will be exposed to many ideas during the reading and will likely encounter wisdom with which you will resonate.

# READINESS THROUGH OTHER FORMS OF ECOLOGICAL ENRICHMENT

In Experience 5 on ecological resilience, several elements of the world you live in could be enriched and could help you to thrive through adversity and challenge. Those same ecological elements can be used to ready you for the Q-nexus experiences. We have previously discussed music, water enrichment, cinema, nature, historical sites, animals, aromas, and art. Many of you have special places you go to feel refreshed, inspired, or to make decisions. Some go to a natural setting, such as the mountains, the beach, or a park. Some of you have a place in your home that is your place for enrichment. Others go to a church, synagogue, or temple. If you don't have a place, then creating an environment with pictures, music, comfortable furniture, plants, or other triggers to help you get into a readiness state for the Q-nexus is recommended. The following are some other suggestions to help you ready yourself.

The Internet and literature include guidance on how to use aromas, stones, colors, and water to help you physically and spiritually. In this experience, we are trying to help you acquire a state of openness and readiness for the Q-nexus. If you put meaning into a smell, stone, color, or water experience, it can help in readiness. I will briefly describe how these ecological triggers are used, and then it will be up to you to consider if you can use them to help in readiness.

## AROMAS

Aromatherapy is the practice of using natural oils extracted from flowers, bark, stems, leaves, roots, or other parts of a plant to enhance psychological and physical well-being. We discussed earlier how aromas can help you acquire Qs, but they can also be used to be ready for the Q-nexus. When you are ready for enlightenment, perhaps you can associate one of the smells with the desired state. The smell is the trigger to get you prepared. You can create your own positive experience with aromas. You may want to choose a smell that helps you to be spiritual or humble—perhaps a scented candle. You may want to create a smell that helps you to be more creative and energetic, such as a particular cologne or perfume. The experience, when you need insight, is to believe that the smell will put you into the desired state of readiness.

# STONES

Worry stones are popular with some people in dealing with stress. When stress occurs, the polished stone is placed between the thumb and finger and then rubbed to reduce the stress. You can use stones as psychospiritual anchors to transition you to a state of readiness.

Some popular stones are quartz, jade, agate, jasper, granite, and obsidian. If you choose to select stones to help you contemplate, select a stone that by looking at it makes you think of a desired state of mind and spirit. The stone then will transform you into a state of readiness. So when you need guidance, you can use the stone that you have selected to almost hypnotically trigger a state of readiness. Rub the stone between your thumb and fingers, trusting that you will be able to get into the right mind-set in preparation for the Q-nexus.

# COLORS (CHROMO THERAPY)

Colors are sometimes used in therapy and other practices to create moods or acquire Qs. Colors that are visible to humans range from just under four hundred to just over seven hundred nanometers. Sensitivity to these waves may stimulate different moods in your mind and spirit. Again, the color association with a desired readiness state may be from previous experiences, or it can be learned. Color therapy often associates colors with different moods based upon frequency in the following ways. Some say that red is thought to increase pulse rate, blood pressure, and breathing rate. Therefore, it is often used for circulatory conditions. Blue is believed to cause relaxation and calm. Therefore, blue is used for headaches, pain, cramping, stress, and other conditions.

# ACTIVITY #55: READINESS THROUGH COLORS

These colors and their associations are common. To discover what Qs result from looking at colors, simply take some time and do the associations. Take some time to ponder your feelings as you look at these colors. What Qs do you feel?

- Red _____

- Orange _____
- Yellow _____
- Green _____
- Aqua _____
- Blue _____
- Indigo _____
- Violet _____

It would be a good practice to consider your bedroom, office, or other areas where you want a certain mood. Perhaps your environment can be enriched to help you acquire desirable states of mind as per the colors you choose.

## WATER

Water therapy (hydrotherapy) was briefly mentioned as an ecological resilience strategy—the longing to be in water. Water is used in the treatment of numerous physical health problems but can be used to promote states of mind and spirit to receive Qs. Hydrothermal therapy (variance in temperature of water) additionally uses its temperature effects, as in hot baths, saunas, wraps, and so on. Hydro- and hydrothermal therapy are traditional methods of treatment that have been used for the treatment of disease and injury by many cultures, including those of ancient Rome, China, and Japan. Water therapy has been practiced for centuries. The ancient Greeks took therapeutic baths. Water is an important ingredient in the traditional Chinese and Native American healing systems.

A Bavarian monk, Father Sebastian Kneipp, helped repopularize the therapeutic use of water in the nineteenth century. At the end of the nineteenth century, Father Kneipp preached that nature had endowed man with everything he needed for a happy, healthy, and fulfilled life. He bathed in the pure streams of his native Bavaria and developed a science of water therapy. After curing himself of a serious case of tuberculosis—considered incurable at that time—he began intensive work on the healing powers of water. People practice many dozens of methods of applying Kneipp hydrotherapy, including baths, saunas, wraps, and packs. We have learned that warm water relaxes and soothes the body. It reduces stress, which helps with sleep and also relieves sore muscles. We also learned that cold water, in contrast, stimulates and invigorates for a push start in the morning. It activates the lymphatic and immune systems, as well as endorphins that help in fighting disease and overcoming mild depression (Parsons 2002).

If you are experiencing tense muscles and anxiety from your stress, a hot shower or bath is in order. If you are feeling tired and stressed, you might want to try taking a warm shower or bath followed by a short, invigorating cold shower to help stimulate your body and mind.

When you submerge yourself in a bath, a pool, or a whirlpool, you experience a kind of weightlessness. Your body is relieved from the constant pull of gravity. Water also has a hydrostatic effect. It has a massage-like feeling as the water gently kneads your body. Water in motion stimulates touch receptors on the skin, boosting blood circulation and releasing tight muscles.

Consider those water sources that may help you relax and feel enough peace to ready yourself for the Q-nexus. Whether it be in the ocean, lakes, showers, bathtubs, hot tubs, or swimming pools, this may be a place that distracts you from cognitive functions and readies you for spiritual prompts and messages.

## READINESS THROUGH ART ENRICHMENT

Readiness can be facilitated by pondering artwork to which you resonate. Pondering paintings, sculptures, photography, and other art forms may help you acquire the desired state of the Q-nexus. As you view the artwork, ponder the message of the art and consider how it might apply to your situation. You may also draw images of your source of spiritual strength as a readiness strategy.

## READINESS THROUGH MUSIC ENRICHMENT

Listening to music to which you resonate can conjure numerous thoughts. If you need energy, then you can listen to lively music that you like. If you want to be romantic, then you choose mood music. For preparing for Q-nexus moments, you may want to choose religious music, themes from movies that are meaningful, classical music, or other soft sounds to which you resonate. The approach is to take time, select the appropriate pondering music, and allow yourself to be guided by it.

## RESILIENT ANCHORS

Other people have reminders or triggers to help them bring their Qs to their conscious thinking. Such anchors as wedding rings, certain articles of clothing, and crucifixes all represent ecological anchors to remind people of loyalty and spirituality. The concept is evident given that as you look at a wedding ring, you think of fidelity and love. When you look at a religious symbol, you ponder your spirituality. The key point is that something from the world around you will trigger thoughts that can lead to readiness for the Q-nexus. There may be some natural associations that you have based upon past experiences—as per the wedding ring or religious symbol—or you can create associations from scratch. The important concept here is the association between your optimal state of readiness and the ecological object.

## READINESS THROUGH ESSENTIAL CHANGE

Essential or physical change often leads to states of humility and openness to directions and answers to life challenges. Essential change includes repetitive exercise and fasting, among many others.

## REPETITIVE EXERCISE

Regular aerobic exercisers (walking, swimming, jogging) find that rechanneling the mind to focus on psychomotor centers when doing aerobic exercise frees the spirit to ponder deeper thoughts than when you are at rest. Many regular exercisers take pencil and paper along their walk or jog to be able to write down the thoughts and feelings that seem to flow much faster during the activity. Perhaps for those who do exercise, the best skill may be to go out with your quest for guidance and Qs and discover them during your exercise.

## FASTING

Fasting is essential change that can help ready yourself for the Q-nexus. Fasting often accompanies different forms of imagery, meditation, and prayer. Fasting is depriving oneself from food for a period of time. It seems that no more than twenty-four hours is an optimal time for fasting. Some suggest depriving oneself from food *and* water, but I do not recommend that. The benefits of water with fasting outweigh any benefits that may come from water deprivation. Proponents of fasting cite the following benefits:

- It rests the digestive system.
- It allows for cleansing and detoxification of the body.
- It creates a break in eating patterns and helps to appreciate healthier food consumption.
- It promotes greater mental clarity and cleanses and heals "stuck" emotional patterns.
- It promotes an inner stillness, enhancing spiritual connection.

Fasting is *not* for everyone. Fasting may be detrimental for some health conditions or scenarios, such as diabetes, pregnancy, lactation, kidney disease, AIDS, cancers, and cardiovascular diseases, among other conditions. Fasting is generally for healthy people.

If you choose fasting as a means to ready yourself for inspiration, my suggestion is that you fast and still drink water. Some fasting practitioners suggest drinking only juices. The water fast seems to optimize the physical benefits while readying yourself.

## READINESS THROUGH COUNSELING/ MENTORS/FAMILY

This book is devoted to the personal resilience and resiliency experience. Subsequent literature will discuss how to enhance relationships by embracing resilience principles. It does seem appropriate here to mention that discussions with friends, family members, or trusted counselors may help you ready yourself for the Q-nexus experiences.

## In Summary

- The skills briefly described in this experience are intended to help you gain an acquired state that will allow you to receive the guidance, direction, strength, and qualities you really want in life (Qs).
- The skills can be quickly adapted to use in other stages of the resiliency process. The optimal state of body, mind, spirit, and your ecosystem is a state of openness, humility, and belief that you will be able to receive answers to your life's challenges.
- Integrative health skills, such as imagery, music, art, literature, prayer, and meditation, can be used to ready yourself for the Q-nexus.
- The indicators of readiness are that your body is in a relaxed or nondistracting position, your mind has to let go of any unhelpful pride or concerns, and your spirit is in a state of receptivity, submissiveness, and openness to wisdom beyond your normal consciousness.

The next experience will present the nature of the Q-nexus experience.

# Part 5

# The Q-Nexus

Part 5 is the Q-nexus. It is the moment of knowing what to do, when to do it, and having the energy to make it happen.

The Q-nexus includes two similar experiences. One is the subtle Q-nexus, or what we have called *resonation*, and the second is the more compelling Q-nexus called *quickening*.

The *subtle Q-nexus* is the experience of resonating to desired virtues and qualities, being aware of their subtle companionship, and knowing that you are following a path of personal progression.

The *compelling Q-nexus* is the quickening moment when infusions of qualities and virtues fill the soul, enabling one to progress through life's disruptions. Quickening is felt as joy and comes as a peak experience of well-being, success, bliss, or energy.

We can see how resonation and quickening motivate people to accomplish amazing feats. One example comes from the journal of William R. Palmer, who described his journey pushing a handcart from Iowa to Utah in 1856. The quiet resonation in his life was that it was right for him and his wife to cross the plains to be able to have religious freedom. He

Glenn E. Richardson, PhD

wanted to join like believers in Utah. The handcart company left a little late in the season, but the subtle reassurance of rightness of the journey motivated him to go. During the trip, where he pushed the handcart all the way, he suffered greatly. Years after Mr. Palmer arrived at his destination, he spoke to a group of listeners who were criticizing the decision to cross the plains so late in the season. This account was given in an April 1979 Latter-Day Saint General Conference talk by James E. Faust.

> I ask you to stop this criticism. You are discussing a matter you know nothing about. Cold, historic facts mean nothing here for they give no proper interpretation of the questions involved. A mistake to send the handcart company? Yes. We suffered beyond anything you can imagine and many died of exposure and starvation, but did you ever hear a survivor of that company utter a word of criticism? I have pulled my handcart when I was so weak and weary from illness and lack of food that I could hardly put one foot ahead of the other. I have looked ahead and seen a patch of sand or a hill slope and I have said, I can go only that far and there I must give up, for I cannot pull the load through it. ... I have gone on to that sand and when I reached it, the cart began pushing me. I have looked back many times to see who was pushing my cart, but my eyes saw no one. I knew then that the angels of God were there. Was I sorry that I chose to come by handcart? No. Neither then nor any minute of my life since. The price we paid to become acquainted with God was a privilege to pay, and I am thankful that I was privileged to come with that company.

In this dramatic story, we find resonation to make the journey. We also see the quickening moments where the handcart seemed to push itself. Most of you do not have such physical challenges, but the experience of receiving a boost of strength and resilience may come during difficult times. Experience 12 will describe the Q-nexus.

230

# THE Q-NEXUS: RESONATION AND QUICKENING

> *The Q-nexus is the experience of having quickening moments of increased wisdom that guide someone to know what to do, when to do it, and how to do it.*

Remember, from the experience on universal resilience, you learned about the universal energy units (UEUs) and the following quote:

> In essence, we can say, "We are walking, living, and breathing in a universe full of infinitely small vibrating energy packets (strings) that define and energize everything. The infusion of strings into our souls results in feeling desired Qs."

When UEUs are infused into your body, you can feel the transformation as you enjoy the Qs of peace, courage, wisdom, or other qualities and feelings you need.

The Q-nexus is the almost magical experience of connecting to and receiving Qs from the sea of universal energy units (strings, spirit, qi) in the world in which you live.

The two intimately related mechanisms for accessing the UEUs with resulting Qs are *resonation* and *quickening*. In order to progress in life, you need to be in a ready state of body, mind, and spirit so that you can be aware of resonating experiences. You resonate to music that makes you feel good. You resonate to nature that makes you feel peaceful. You resonate to projects that you enjoy. Resonation is the soft and gentle assurance that you are progressing to fulfill your life blueprint and following a path with heart.

Quickening is a more impactful infusion that comes to you from the sea of UEUs. If you are confused, a quickening moment will give you direction. If you are on the wrong path, quickening will redirect you and give guidance. If you are discouraged, quickening will give you energy. If you are associating with a person you shouldn't, quickening will tell you to end the relationship. Quickening is to receive infusions of Qs along your resonating journey in the form of epiphanies, omens, and other forms of personal revelation. It is the jolt or jump start that creates defining moments and energizing discoveries.

> The potential to have resonating and quickening moments is within the soul of every human being. You have the capacity to discern what to do, know when to do it, feel the confidence that it is the right thing to do, and have access to the energy to make it happen.

Experience 12 is about the Q-nexus as the pivotal point on your resilient journey through life's challenges. Each disruption brings an opportunity for progression. The pivotal point of the Q-nexus is at the bottom of the resiliency trough where you receive the refreshing and enlivening infusion of Qs for which you yearn. You can see that the pivotal and life-changing peak experience paradoxically is at the low point of the resiliency process trough. It is shown as the low point because you are in a state of humility and openness. In the resiliency model, the Q-nexus is circled below to show where in the disruptive and reintegrative process the Q-nexus is positioned.

# Figure 26. The Q-Nexus

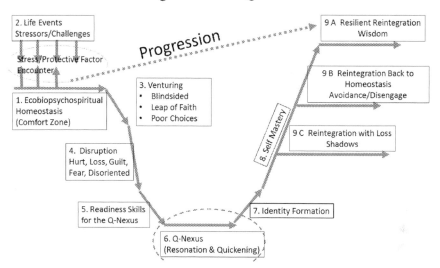

We will explore this powerful Q-nexus moment in this experience and later suggest activities that will help you to experience the infusion of Qs that you need when you are in the resiliency trough. Whether it be patience, courage, hope, enlightenment, guidance, or any of the other Qs you need during disruptions, you have the capacity to acquire those Qs in the trough of the resiliency process.

Experience 12 will describe the range of Q-nexus experiences, including the subtle Q-nexus as well as quickening or the compelling Q-nexus. It will be important to learn the art of discernment to know what is wise and what is misguided. Lastly, this experience will present the idea of the timing of the Q-nexus.

As we begin the discussion of the Q-nexus, it is assumed that you have practiced skills (Experience 11) to which you have resonated to assume a sense of readiness for the Q-nexus. You will want to find a place that is nurturing, be in a relaxed physical state, have a mind-set of openness, and embrace a peaceful spiritual state.

## RESONATION: THE SUBTLE Q-NEXUS

Resonation (the subtle Q-nexus) is the experience of resonating to desired virtues and qualities, being aware of their subtle companionship, and knowing that you are following a path of personal progression.

Resonation, which we addressed briefly in Experience 1, is the subtle Q-nexus that is the infusion of softer Qs, such as peace, a sense of rightness, and confidence. It is felt as a softer resonation that may or may not be part of your awareness. It is the peace and sense that you are on the right path, making the right decisions, and in harmony with your optimal life blueprint. It may be felt as awareness of subtle guidance and power from a source beyond your own cognitive capacity.

In the literature, we read of this subtle guidance using such descriptors as *flow*, the *path with heart*, and *God's Spirit*, among other views. Let's briefly review a few of those perspectives of the subtler Q-nexus.

- Mihaly Csíkszentmihályi (1990) speaks of *flow* as a state of concentration or complete absorption with the activity at hand and with the situation. It is a state in which you are so involved in an activity that nothing else seems to matter. The idea of flow is identical to the feeling of being in the zone or in the groove. Csíkszentmihályi (1990) described flow as "being completely involved in an activity for its own sake. Any unhelpful pride falls away. Time flies. Every action, movement, and thought follows inevitably from the previous one. Your whole being is involved, and you're using your skills to the utmost." For example, you may experience a flow state when you are dancing, rock climbing, playing a game, or reading a book. Flow states are fulfilling your resilient drives.

- In the King James Bible, John 16:13, we read:

  Howbeit when he, the Spirit of truth, is come, he will guide you into all truth: for he shall not speak of himself; but whatsoever he shall hear, that shall he speak: and he will show you things to come.

  The "Spirit of truth" will let you know what truth is and let you know what is forthcoming.

- In the Book of Mormon, there is a story of one of the heroes, Nephi (Nephi 4:6), who was seeking answers as to what he should do.

  And I was led by the Spirit, not knowing beforehand the things which I should do.

- From the Eastern philosophies, there is a sense of moving within the field of energy or qi. Lao Tzu, in his book *Tao Te Ching*, states:

  One who lives in accordance with nature does not go against the way of things. He moves in harmony with the present moment, always knowing the truth of just what to do.

And to confirm this common belief and philosophy, we can read from the fascinating field of theoretical physics (string and quantum theory) and as quoted at the beginning of this experience that:

  In essence, we can say, "We are walking, living, and breathing in a universe full of infinitely small vibrating energy packets (strings) that define and energize everything. The infusion of strings into our souls results in feeling desired Qs."

The resonation, subtle Q-nexus, then, is the ability to follow an energy/spiritual field (UEUs). It will enliven us with confidence that we are doing what we should be doing and feeling peace along the journey. The subtle Q-nexus path is enriched with peace and rightness, fulfilling your resilient drives and your dream. Resonation embraces the concepts of following a path with heart, being led by the spirit, or being in harmony with nature.

## ACTIVITY #56: RESONATION

Try to remember what it feels like to resonate as you walk your subtle Q-path. Remember the feelings of rightness or peace when you are feeling, thinking, and doing in harmony with your life blueprint or your dream.

Remember a time, or even perhaps now, when you felt the subtle peace and guidance of being on a Q-path.

1. Can you feel the peace and rightness of your career? Does it seem that you were made to do what you are doing? Are you resonating to that choice?
2. Can you feel the peace and rightness of your chosen religion or your choice not to have a religion? Are you resonating to that choice?
3. Can you feel the peace and rightness of choosing a friend, spouse, or partner? Does it feel natural and part of your Q-path?
4. Think about where you live. Does it feel like home? Feeling like home suggests that as you walk in you will feel desired peaceful Qs.
5. Do you feel like your life has purpose and meaning as described in Experience 3 about noble resilience? If not, you may want to consider your direction in life.

In all likelihood, there were quickening or compelling Q-nexus moments that helped you to choose your career, religion, partner, location, and life path. If there is little peace or comfort in these choices, it may not be your best Q-path. That is not to say that you do not experience disruptive experiences that may result in guilt, anger, and frustration during the Q-path, but the big picture of progression should reflect a Q-path with heart.

## ACTIVITY #57: REFLECTION

Another way to feel a boosting experience that confirms your Q-path is to enjoy the feeling of reminders of your choices.

- If you are or were an athlete, reflect upon the feelings and warmth of fond memories of when you chose to try out for a team. You will still feel that feeling when watching a sports movie or event.
- If you chose a partner/spouse at some point in your life, hopefully you will remember the experience and rightness of your choice.
- You may feel the rightness of your choices as you resonate to particular forms of music, entertainment, books, or speeches reminding you of good choices with careers and family.

## ACTIVITY #58: SUBTLE Q-NEXUS PLANNING

As you begin your day, try to create a vision of the Q-field you could live that day. Using one of the readiness skills (listening to a type of music, meditating, walking in nature, praying), think about your day of progression. Think of the responsibilities and opportunities your day presents, and ponder each of your resilient drives. Imagine that you are walking in a field of energy and Qs that your resilient drives will provide for you.

- Childlike: Imagine how in your day you can feel the infusion of Qs from making your activities/opportunities in the day childlike— adventurous, fun loving, genuine, curious, teachable, and willing to take responsible risks. For example, perhaps you could make an adventure of the responsibilities you have. Write your thoughts here.

  _____

  _____

- Noble: Imagine how in your day you can feel with the infusion of Qs from making activities/opportunities in the day to feel important, valued, respected, and with purpose and meaning through the actions of service, compassion listening, and believing in someone. For example, perhaps you could imagine yourself finding something and returning it or dropping by and doing some service for a family member, neighbor, or friend. Write your thoughts here.

  _____

  _____

- Character: Imagine how in your day you can feel the infusion of Qs from making your opportunities in the day with the feelings of honesty, integrity, honor, fairness, loyalty, appreciation, and kindness. For example, perhaps you think about your responsibilities for the day and consider how you will feel guilt-free because of your integrity and honesty. Write your thoughts here.

  _____

  _____

- Ecological: Imagine how in your day you can feel the infusion of Qs from the peace, energy, and comfort from your environment. For example, perhaps you could imagine in your day that you take a moment to smell the roses, and be in nature, appreciate art, and listen to Q-enriching music. Write your thoughts here.

  _____

  _____

- Universal: Imagine how in your day you can feel with the infusion of Qs such as peace, courage, wisdom, guidance, enlightenment, truth, and miracles from a source beyond normal consciousness. For example, imagine yourself going throughout your day with the comfort of feeling your source of spiritual strength on your side the entire day. Write your thoughts here.

  _____

  _____

- Essential: Imagine how in your day you can feel the infusion of Qs by sensing the energy from adequate sleep, nutritious foods, and exercise. For example, imagine yourself going throughout your day being sensitive to your essential prompts and responding accordingly to maximize your energy through the day. Write your thoughts here.

  _____

  _____

- Intellectual: Imagine how in your day you can feel the infusion of Qs from learning, understanding, planning, and considering good decisions. Write your thoughts of learning and understanding through the responsibilities during your day. Write your thoughts here.

  _____

  _____

## QUICKENING (THE COMPELLING Q-NEXUS)

> The compelling Q-nexus is the quickening or enlivening
> moment when infusions of qualities and virtues fill the
> soul, enabling one to progress through life's disruptions.
> Quickening is felt as joy and comes as a peak experience
> of well-being, success, direction, bliss, or energy.

Quickening, in pregnancy terms, is the moment in pregnancy when the mother feels the baby move for the first time. Quickening as a Q-nexus experience is the moment when the infusion of enlivening Qs gives you direction, energy, and power. Quickening, as the more compelling Q-nexus experience, is the mechanism to fulfill your needs and purposes. Quickening is felt as bursts of joy. Joy is the jolting emotion that vibrates the spirit, which carries energy to the mind and the body. When quickening is experienced with soul-shaking Q-infusions, you will feel a peak experience of well-being, success, bliss, or exultation.

- Quickening carries your needed answers.
- Quickening is the jolt of energy.
- Quickening is the testimony of a truth.
- Quickening is a burst of confidence.
- Quickening guides you when you are off your path with heart.

Stirring moments of enlightenment can give you goose bumps. The literature is replete with descriptions of quickening or what we are calling the "compelling Q-nexus." You can be happy in life and content with what you are doing as per the subtle Q-nexus, but sometimes you receive some great news and your whole body is filled with energy and excitement as per the compelling Q-nexus.

> Resonation gently infuses your mind with assurance
> or reassurance, while quickening awakens your soul to
> action.

Assuming you are practicing one or more of the readiness skills described in the previous experience, you can have the experience of quickening. Using a sailing metaphor, there are moments when you may need to adjust your course. Quickening is the infusion of what you need to do to adjust your sails and reassume a better route to fulfill your dream. On the extreme end, it may require turning your ship around to avoid a tempestuous storm.

When we speak of quickening, there is a potential for "opening a can of worms," which should be avoided. We will speak of quickening using such terms as *epiphany* and *gut feeling*, to which most of you will be able to relate. There is a part of literature that describes quickening concepts that go beyond scientific justification or at least may seem mysterious to many. Many people are skeptical of psychics, mediums, or those who purport of having out-of-body experiences. Those areas of skepticism are beyond the scope of this book. The quickening sensitivities described here can be experienced by everyone.

Descriptions of quickening are abundant in academic and popular literature. The terminology varies, but the essence of the experience is the same. Let's explore views of quickening from a variety of perspectives.

1.  Reoccurring thoughts: Sometimes your innate resilience sends messages to your conscious mind (intellectual resilience) over and over again until they are heard. The experience of having reoccurring thoughts is often a message of great importance coming from your greater wisdom. When reoccurring thoughts occur, it is a good time to stop and ponder to discover meaning in the reoccurring thoughts. You should anticipate a Q-nexus moment of understanding.

2.  Epiphanies (aha moments or the eureka effect): Sometimes you feel energized when new ideas jump into your mind. An epiphany is a sudden new perception or insight into the meaning of something. It is a burst of understanding. The epiphany is more than just an idea and is accompanied with a stirring of your whole soul (quickening), confirming the importance of the idea. It is a sudden burst of understanding where previously your thoughts lacked focus. As you are pondering your disruption in life as part of the resilient journey, an epiphany may jump into your head, and if it is accompanied with the resonating confirmation, it is something

that you should consider. The classic example in history is the story of Sir Isaac Newton, the famous mathematician and physicist, who observed an apple falling from a tree. He noticed how the apple seemed to accelerate as it fell. The epiphany of the falling apple in 1687 led to Newton's discovery of the universal law of gravity.

3. Synchronicity/coincidences: *Synchronicity* is a term coined by the great psychologist Carl Jung. Synchronicity is when you put meaning to coincidences that occur in your life. For example, perhaps you have been thinking about a friend you have not talked to for some time, and you unexpectedly run into him or her at a store. Perhaps you have been pondering a challenge in your life and you happen to be watching a movie that is a metaphor for your own life situation. You leave the movie with an approach to deal with the challenge. When you are open to synchronistic events, they can help you make choices in your life because they are a form of guidance from a greater wisdom than your conscious mind. Synchronicity is a quickening moment.

4. Spiritual prompts: A spiritual prompt is a soft quickening moment that is sometimes referred to as *inspiration, intuition,* and *gut feeling.* Spiritual prompts are quickening moments that provide you with answers to life challenges and problems. The prompts come with sudden resonating vibrations and energy. It feels very right and very good. When choosing a direction in life, if you study something for a while and it is accompanied by a strong resonating feeling of joy and rightness, it is a good path. *Intuition* or *gut feelings* are terms that also describe spiritual prompts as the ability to sense or know something without a rational reason. When your intellectual resilience is soft as per the skills described in the previous experience and the greater wisdom is instilled into your mind from your spiritual source of strength, it is felt as a feeling of rightness. It is the ability to sense or know immediately without reasoning. For example, the feeling you get when you first meet someone may be an instant sense of trust with accompanied joy. Conversely, you may get an instant feeling of distrust, caution, or fear. A softer term for the spiritual prompt is a *hunch.* As you

make decisions about your life choices, you will intuitively feel the confirmation of rightness as a Q-nexus experience.

> I believe in intuition and inspiration. Imagination is more important than knowledge. For knowledge is limited, whereas imagination embraces the entire world, stimulating progress, giving birth to evolution. It is, strictly speaking, a real factor in scientific research.
>
> —Albert Einstein

> It is through science that we prove, but through intuition that we discover.
>
> —Immanuel Kant

> Intuition will tell the thinking mind where to look next.
>
> —Jonas Salk

5. Gestalts: A *gestalt* is the ability of your mind to create a big picture inclusive of the many individual dimensions of your life. It is a moment when all the pieces of a complex problem come together. It is the climax of the life disruption or chaos when suddenly all the parts of the puzzle make sense. It is the magical moment of clarity. On a larger scale, it is a Q-nexus moment when you have a vision of your life. You see how your profession, your family, your religion, your hobbies, and your friendships form a picture of you being able to fulfill all your resilient drives through your lifestyle. On a smaller scale, you may be considering how you want to decorate a room in your house—say, a family room. You want a television, comfortable couches, perhaps a game corner, a reading area, some family pictures, and quick access to the kitchen. As you ponder these elements in your family room, you have a Q-nexus moment when you have an image of where everything will fit comfortably.

6. Dream impressions: We all dream. The interpretation of our dreams varies with each individual as well as from the perspective of academics. Some people infrequently remember their dreams. Psychologists have varying opinions about the value of dreams. Some suggest that they are merely our minds sorting through the barrage of stimuli that they receive each day from our senses. Dreaming, then, is the process of forgetting unimportant memories and storing the more important information. The forgetting-and-sorting process combined together may result in weird dreams.

Other academics suggest that dreams can have great meaning in your life. Sigmund Freud taught that dreams may be wish fulfillment. As you have an impressionable dream, you may want to consider which of your resilient drives may need to be fulfilled. Freud's therapy describes how you can do "dream work," which is an attempt to explore how you can bring many ideas into one or what he calls "condensation." Freud also suggested that dreams may hide emotions, and as we ponder, we may be able to discover those emotions as a process he calls "displacement."

Some dreams may be symbolic. Carl Jung felt that dreams originated from the collective unconscious mind and that dreams were the expressions from that source of greater wisdom. He also suggested that dreams were prompted from identities (Jung calls them "archetypes") housed within our conscious and unconscious minds. During the resilient journey, we learn to cope with new life situations by forming new identities (described in more detail with Experience 13). Consequently, we have an arsenal of effective coping identities, and dreams may be a means to have the identities express themselves.

To simplify, dreams are a quickening experience that can help you to direct your life. Let me make two suggestions. First, if your dreams are easily forgotten or seem random, then don't worry or think about them. Second, if your dream is accompanied by resonation or a feeling that there might be meaning, then ponder it. If it is clear that the dream can correct a course in life, then you should consider acting upon the quickening moment. If it is about a person you haven't seen in a while, then you may consider contacting that person. Pondering may bring epiphanies for thoughts and action. Career choices, partner selection, caring for children, or how to solve problems may come through your dreams. New identities (more courage, more compassion, or more spiritual) can be prompted through dreams. The Q-nexus experience may be to see an identity or hero in your dream and you feel the quickening power of the insight that you need to formulate the identity in your life.

7. Spiritual experiences: More profound than gut feelings or intuitive prompts are spiritual experiences. A spiritual experience is an enthralling experience where you find yourself immersed in a connection with your universal source of strength. This may be manifested as you are listening to a spiritual leader. Each word that the leader says quickens your entire soul, and you experience infusions of Qs with every word. Perhaps you are meditating or praying and you find yourself captivated with a burning in your bosom catching a vision or image that you are in the presence of and being guided by your universal source of strength. It is a moment when the Qs of enlivenment, inspiration, and personal revelation are clear and consuming. Some have "conversions" or "rebirths" to a new philosophy of life or new line of spiritual thinking based on a significant quickening experience.

8. Other quickening experiences: Many people have unique gifts, and there are many other similar concepts. For example, the classic Greek philosopher Socrates possessed a personal daimon. "The favor of the gods," said Socrates, "has given me a marvelous gift, which has never left me since my childhood. It is a voice which, when it makes itself heard, deters me from what I am about to do and never urges me on." He spoke familiarly of this daimon, joked about it, and often generally followed the indications it gave, mostly warnings of danger. Eventually, his friends would consult the daimon before taking important steps in their lives. Some people have their own daimon or inner voice. For the inner guide to be valued, the messages should be accompanied by resonation and confirming quickening. Many people claim to have extraordinary quickening gifts. Some people have extrasensory perception (ESP).

Some have reported that they have been visited by angels. Others report visitations from people who have already passed away. Some report out-of-body experiences, such as those who are close to death. Some claim to be psychics and others mystics. Some claim to be prophets. It is not the place of this author to question or confirm those experiences, but if they do happen to you, then they can be viewed as quickening experiences.

## RESONATION AND QUICKENING CONTINUUM

In light of the fact that the intensity varies with quickening experiences, the range of sensations is presented as a continuum below. Conscious thinking is a more normal occurrence exemplified by reoccurring thoughts or epiphanies. Resonation is the comfort of being on a path with heart. Quickening is impactful discovery of answers to life situations. The gifted Q-nexus is an experience with major impact.

### Figure 27. Resonation and Quickening Continuum

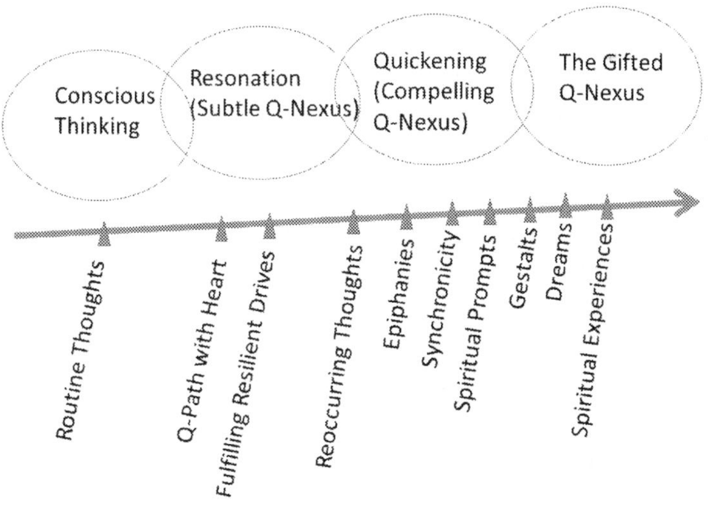

Although indicated as a progressive line of intensity of experiences, the reality is that any of the experiences can be accompanied with powerful resonations that make an impact on your life. The purpose of discussing each of these is to heighten your awareness that these prompts are common if you make yourself aware. In all likelihood, you have had these subtle and compelling Q-nexus moments, and hopefully you will become more aware of them. As you have these experiences, ponder carefully the purpose of the prompt and consider what the meaning could be for you. As you make daily steps toward progression, you can know you are on the right track to maximize your potential if you listen to the Q-nexus moments and act upon them.

> I never made one of my discoveries through the process
> of rational thinking.
> —Albert Einstein

## DISCERNMENT

Once you have experienced a Q-nexus moment or at least a perceived Q-nexus moment, it is important to discern whether the insight you have received is genuine or not. Discernment was explained in Experience 8, but now that the sensing experiences for receiving answers have been described, we approach a most difficult challenge. How do we discern between a choice of our own gratification with accompanying short-term physical pleasure or quick fix as compared to a resonating and quickening moment that will allow for progression and enrich our lives over time? Consider the standards of POPICS to confirm the genuineness and rightness of your answer.

*POPICS* represents some considerations to assure that your insight is genuine, including six checkpoints: progression, outcome, peace, infringement, character, and staying power.

1.  Progression: Remember that progression is the accumulation of Qs throughout your lifetime. Ask yourself the question, "Am I harvesting qualities that I really want by adopting this plan of action?"
2.  Outcome: Consider the immediate outcome of your insight. Does it make sense for you? If you still have a stupor of thought, then perhaps you should either wait or explore other options.

3. Peace: As you ponder the action or thought, is there an accompanying peace? If it does not have peace, then it may not be a genuine Q-nexus.

4. Infringement: Do your actions or thoughts unjustly infringe upon the rights or peace of others? If they do, then they may not be genuine.

5. Character: As you consider your character resilience, ask yourself the question about the insight you have received: "Does it fit within my character code of thought and action?" Does the insight embrace integrity, honesty, honor, fairness, loyalty, fidelity, and kindness and lie within your moral framework? If not, it may not be genuine.

6. Staying power: Genuine Q-nexus insights will continue over time. Reflection upon the insight will continue to feel good. As you ponder the insight, you will continue to feel peace. Imagine how you will feel after time has passed. Will you still feel good about your decision?

## PRIMARY AND SECONDARY EMOTIONS

Part of discerning is to become aware of actions that harvest qualities and virtues you really want (Q-actions) as compared to actions that bleed you of Qs (shadow actions). In an attempt to help you to contemplate the difference between a genuine Q-nexus experience and a masked moment of enlightenment (shadows), let's first focus on the Q-path. We have actually been talking about the Q-path, the positive path, throughout this book. Sometimes, when positive messages that come from your resilient drives reach your conscious mind (intellectual resilience), you try to figure out a way to respond favorably to those messages. The message is a prompt telling you to enrich or protect your resilient drives. But your intellectual resilience buries the message in light of negative memories of past experiences, feelings of self-doubt, and disturbing fear that dominate your thinking. Courage goes out of the window.

In order to discern the Q-path from the shadow path, let's review what these are. Primary emotions are the Qs associated with the resilient drives. These are pure longings, hopes, and intentions to fulfill your dream. They are the qualities that have been the focus of this book. The figure below displays the dimensions of your soul and the world in which you live. You have innate resilient drives to be childlike, noble, and live with character. You live within an ecosystem that can be nurturing. You are walking and breathing in a sea of Qs—your universal resilience. The figure below is the essence of your spiritual life.

### Figure 28. Essence of Your Spiritual Life

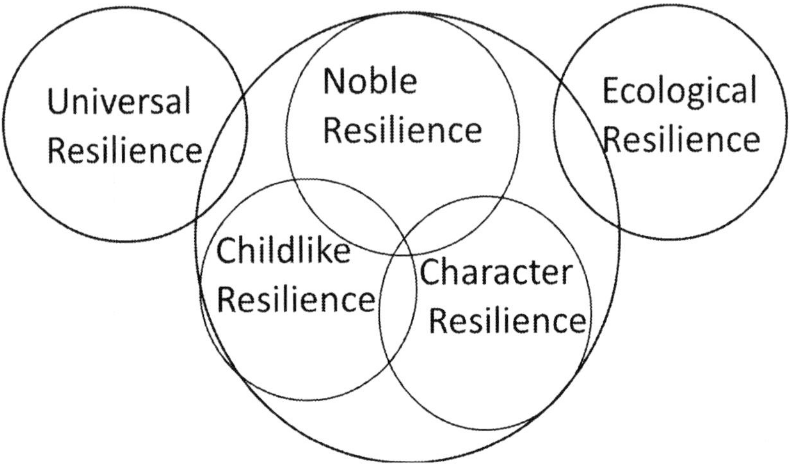

When your life experiences frustrate the acquisition of Qs from your resilient drives, then you experience unfulfilled emotions. These pure, unfulfilled emotions are still primary and are manifest as hurt, loss, guilt, or fear. Your conscious mind feels the pain from the frustrated primary sources and tries to create an action or thought pattern to fix the pain. Your mind is less wise than your universal or spiritual wisdom, so you often allow the primary emotions to turn to secondary emotions, such as anger, jealousy, envy, hatred, lust, or greed. Acting upon these secondary emotions (shadows) will, in all likelihood, frustrate progression and divert you from genuine pathways.

Many people choose to act upon the shadows and try to find immediate pleasure by taking pills, overeating, acting out anger, or escaping into Q-less activities. As you think about this, if your nobility is threatened, then the potential loss or frustration of your noble drives may result in you acting on your shadows of anger or jealousy. Again, if you feel frustrated because of a lack of progression (fulfilling your need for Qs), then you may try to find joy (temporary bursts of Qs) through other undesirable means, such as quick fix pleasures and experience a pseudo (false) rush only to result in increased guilt and unpleasant feelings later.

The figure below shows how frustrated resilient yearnings can turn to shadows.

- **Resilient yearnings** as shown in figure 29 are the yearnings and drives from your universal, ecological, childlike, noble, and character resilience.

- **Primary emotions from unfulfilled yearnings** are the result of thoughts and actions that are not fulfilling resilient drives and yearnings. As seen in the second box, the primary unfulfilled emotions are hurt, loss, fear, and other emotions.

- **Shadows** are the secondary emotions that spring from hurt and loss and other primary emotions. The feelings of anger, jealousy, and denial are shown in the third box.

**Figure 29. Unfulfilled Emotions and Shadows**

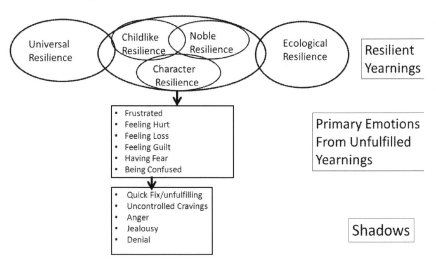

A critical part of discernment is to recognize the difference between your primary emotions and your secondary, shadow emotions. Acting on shadows like jealousy rarely turns out positively. More will be explained in Experience 15.

## TIMING

In many cases, with proper preparation, you will receive either a good feeling or a bad feeling about your resonating experience and can plan to take action immediately. In crisis situations, you may not have time for readiness, and answers may come very quickly.

> When my little brother, Victor, was about four or five years old, an experience happened that confirmed the power of resonation—mother's intuition. One day, as Mom was hanging out the clothes on a clothesline, an intuitive prompt—or, more accurately, a bolt of warning—consumed her whole being. She suddenly felt fear for Victor, and her heart started to race. On the little five-acre homestead, she could have gone anywhere. She could have gone into the house, to the horses, to the cows, or to the neighbors', but her quickening moment prompted her to run the one hundred yards to the south part of the property to the nutria cesspool. (We raised nutria animals for their pelts.) When she got there, little Victor had just fallen and was struggling to get out. He was slipping each time he tried to get out, but kept falling back into the smelly, watery nutria crap. Victor was in trouble, repeatedly sinking below the surface. Mom arrived just in time to pull him out by the hair of his head. As she dragged him out, she hosed him down and put him in a bathtub for a thorough cleaning. When Victor was finally safe in his room, Mom went to her room and burst into tears. She was so grateful she had listened to her mother's intuition and acted in the nick of time.

Sometimes answers come within a reasonable amount of time. Perhaps you have prepared yourself and sought an answer, and as soon as you listen to the music, do the meditation, or have a prayer, you may feel a quickening moment.

Sometimes answers require patience—sometimes a little patience or sometimes a lot of patience. You may have done all that you can do, and the next day when you are driving your car, you have the quickening moments. With a lot of patience, we may need to consider the natural order of things.

> Faith in God includes faith in his timing.
> —Neal A. Maxwell

You are progressing every day as you listen to resilient prompts. You continue to harvest Qs throughout your life. For some of the bigger rewards, you have to wait for nature's timing. A thirteen-year-old child may discover an attraction and love for another thirteen-year-old. They want to have the fruits of marriage in their hearts and minds. You may want to enjoy the fruits of helping people by becoming a physician but only have a high school education. Answers come with patience, and in some cases, hard work or maturity. Let's review the metaphor of planting the seed.

> In order to harvest the fruit from a garden, you have to trust in the timing of nature. You need to assure that it is the growing season and the environment is right (ecological resilience). You need to prepare the soil and assure it is nurturing. Then you plant the seed and cover it with some dirt to protect it from the sun and other elements. You need to provide water to stimulate growth and over time let it be the life source for the plant. You need to protect it from the weeds (shadows). Over time, the plant will break through the surface of the soil. You continue to nurture until the plant becomes full grown. Then, after weeks of nurturing, the buds of fruit begin to appear. Again, patience is necessary to assure ripening. Picking too early will result in a bitter fruit. When nature tells you it is time, the fruit will be ripe and ready to enjoy. The same is true with the timing of some Q-nexus experiences.

Consider the following messages of great thinkers:

- Do you have the patience to wait till your mud settles and the water is clear? Can you remain unmoving till the right action arises by itself?

  —Lao Tzu

- Adopt the pace of nature: her secret is patience.

  —Ralph Waldo Emerson

- To lose patience is to lose the battle.

  —Mahatma Gandhi

- Patience is power; with time and patience, the mulberry leaf becomes silk.

  —Chinese proverb

- Patience is bitter but its fruit is sweet.

  —Jean-Jacques Rousseau

## SOMETIMES NO ANSWER IS THE ANSWER

If you are seeking confirming Qs to accompany a decision or to take an action and you continue to be confused, you may have received an answer from a universal source of strength. If none of your choices are accompanied with resonation or quickening, then your answer may be either to do nothing or be patient for the right time. A stupor of thought generally indicates none of your options is the right option or the right time for the option. If you are confused about a relationship and you don't know whether to make a commitment, the time is not right. If you are wondering what to say to someone in order to clear a disagreement and you are confused, then you should likely wait until you connect to a resonating approach.

All human knowledge thus begins with intuitions, proceeds thence to concepts, and ends with ideas.

—Immanuel Kant

# Sometimes Life's Puzzle Comes a Piece at a Time

If we follow a Q-path, there are steady resonation and peak quickening moments as you go along. I think of my own career path.

> I loved playing football, so after high school I had a quickening moment when I received an athletic scholarship to a university (Step #1). Studies were a necessity to be able to be eligible to be on the team. In an amazing biology class in my junior year, a professor quickened my area of study (Step #2), and I adjusted my course to enjoy studies as much as football. The path felt right until I graduated with a BS in zoology on my way to studying medicine. With my first visit to a medical school and witness of a pulmonary surgery, I was quickened (sickened) with the realization that I did not have the stomach for medicine (Step #3). Having a gestalt one day, I thought, *What if I were to marry my love of sport with my love of physiology?* Consequently, I received a master's degree in exercise physiology (Step #4). When I finished the degree, I also realized that I enjoyed teaching, so the gestalt vision (Step #5) was an identity as a high school teacher and coach. While coaching, I was assigned to teach a high school health education class. Teaching that class turned into an epiphany (Step #6) of what I wanted to do. I went back to school and completed a PhD in health science, which galvanized my career Q-path. I had no clue that I would be a university professor when I starting playing football right out of high school.

Life comes a resonating and quickening piece at a time. You may resonate to an experience with no idea as to how it will benefit you. Over time and step-by-step, you will see the value of following the Q-path, piece by piece.

# In Summary

- The Q-nexus is the almost magical experience of connecting to and receiving Qs from the sea of universal energy units (strings, spirit, qi) in the world in which you live.
- Resonation (the subtle Q-nexus) is the experience of resonating to desired virtues and qualities, being aware of their subtle companionship, and knowing that you are following a path of personal progression.
- The compelling Q-nexus is the quickening or enlivening moment when infusions of qualities and virtues fill the soul, enabling one to progress through life's disruptions. Quickening is felt as joy and comes as a peak experience of well-being, success, direction, bliss, or energy.
- The Q-nexus is the experience of receiving answers to all of life's questions, problems, and challenges.
- The Q-nexus guides you in making judgments, choices, plans, and confirmations of truth.

Experience 13 will focus on your choice to act upon the insight from the Q-nexus. It will then guide you as to how to act and create a new identity to expand your arsenal of identities—each with a Q-based coping skill.

# PART 6

## SELF-MASTERY

Self-mastery is assuming control of your entire soul—
body, mind, and spirit. It is sensing resilient yearnings,
celebrating the enlightenment from the Q-nexus,
and then acting upon the guidance with grit and
determination.

One of the most fascinating journeys in nature is the life cycle of the salmon. The salmon demonstrates amazing grit and persistence after being prompted by Mother Nature. From the salmon life cycle, we will see many parallels in our lives.

My undergraduate degree was in zoology. I loved animals and studying their life cycles. One of the most fascinating life cycles to me was that of the salmon. Adult females spawn and deposit eggs in the sands of creeks in the tops of the mountains. The eggs hatch, and in a few weeks, the little salmon, called alevin, initially feed from the yokes of the eggs from which they are hatched. When the nourishment from the egg runs out, the tiny fish change their identity again and become a fry. Fry learn to feed on the carcasses of adult salmon who have already spawned and died. Over time, a new identity emerges—that of a smolt. The smolt experiences a physiological change to prevent salt water from entering its blood. The smolt has the amazing capacity to live in both fresh and salt water. With that potential, the smolt journey downstream. The creeks grow into small streams, and the streams grow into rivers. The smolt become salmon, and after drifting for hundreds of miles, they enter their ocean life. It is fascinating how salmon can live in both fresh water and salt water. The salmon stay in the ocean for a couple of years doing whatever teenaged salmon do and maturing into adult salmon. The adult fish have finished growing in the ocean when something magical strikes their intrinsic wiring. They have a powerful urge to return to where they were hatched in the mountains. They seek out the mouth of the rivers from which they emerged years earlier and begin the journey back home. It is interesting at this time that the salmon experience physical changes from bright silver to a deep red and bold color as mature adults. The drive of Mother Nature, analogous to the human spirit, is so powerful that they will fight against great odds to complete the life cycle. At first, the rivers are gentle with currents of only three or four miles an hour, but as the elevation rises toward the mountain, the water comes faster and faster, and the salmon have to fight to make progress. Perhaps the biggest challenge comes from the waterfalls that salmon have to jump. This is where we see the famous salmon runs and watch these fish jump, fight, and climb the falls because of the power of their drive—their self-mastery—their spirit. Finally, the survivors are beaten, exhausted, and near dead, and finish their journey by finding the place of their birth in the small creeks. Their remaining energy is put solely into the production of eggs for females and milt (sperm) for males. The mature adults, with all the energy they can muster, lay and fertilize their eggs and die shortly thereafter. Their carcasses fertilize the algae and become the food for the little salmon (fry) to eat, and the cycle starts all over again.

Granted, salmon are simple and act mostly on instinct, but still the quickening moments that help them evolve and form new identities throughout their life cycle parallel your life. To magically leave their adult and mature life in the ocean and turn back to spawn and die at their place of origin high in the mountains is an amazing example of quickening. The powerful quickening moment compelled them to swim upstream with a mission and purpose. I recognize that I am reading too much into the instinctual nature of a salmon, but the choice to head back upstream rather than live in the comfort zone of the ocean is amazing. If they had the capacity to choose, how many salmon would choose to stay and play in the vastness of the oceans? We, too, have the agency to fulfill our greater mission in life based upon our quickening experiences. We, too, can change our identities from a playful salmon in the ocean to becoming the dogged and relentless salmon that swims upstream to fulfill a purpose.

Experience 13 is about how to form identities that will best deal with life challenges. Experience 14 will help you follow a path with heart. Experience 15 will describe a process to rid yourself of your shadow actions—bad habits that stop or limit your progression.

# SELF-MASTERY PART 1: IDENTITY FORMATION, PERSISTENCE, AND GRIT

> *Identity formation is the experience of creating and assuming optimal identities to deal with unique life challenges adding to one's existing treasury of identities created in the past by resiliently reintegrating after disruptions.*

With quickening, you receive impressions or images of answers to life's challenges. If the image continues to feel right with resonation, then you can move forward with all the energy you can muster from your resilient drives. At this point in the resiliency process, you now emerge from the trough of the resilient journey that has taken you from your disruption with an aching heart to some inspiration and hope. On the resiliency model below, you can see where identity formation lies along the resilient journey.

## Figure 30. Identity Formation and Self-Mastery

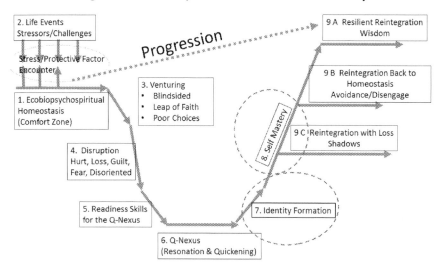

You are now ready to act upon the insight you have received at the Q-nexus to resiliently reintegrate and become stronger through the resiliency process. Whether the disruptions are minor or major, each experience allows you the opportunity to increase your self-mastery and become stronger and more resilient.

> Quickening gives a magical glimpse of your new identity that will thrive in the wake of your current disruptive challenge, but the embodiment of that identity is conceived in persistence and grit.

A simplified look at the resilient journey is to imagine that each time you face a disruption in life, you have the opportunity to harvest such Qs as courage, understanding, peace, and others. Reflecting upon the postulate of progression, each disruption is an opportunity to gather more resilient Q-gems. You do this again and again as per figure 31.

### Figure 31. Harvesting Qs from Each Disruption

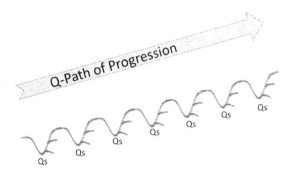

With the quickening experience, you have captured a glimpse of optimal recovery, growth, and correction to your Q-path. Self-mastery is the art of (1) creating the image of new identity, (2) exercising your agency to choose the identity, (3) becoming the new identity, and (4) mustering the grit to persist with the identity.

## THE IMAGE OF THE NEW IDENTITY

The Q-nexus inspires you to do, become, or think in a way that best resolves your disruption. With insight and by paying heed, an image of what the next phase of your resilient journey can look like and an image of a new identity will be formed in your mind. The transition of acting upon the inspiration you received from your Q-nexus moment to seeing an image of what you need to do is almost instant. You will see the new identity in your mind. You will catch a glimpse of an image of someone who is successfully coping and thriving with your life challenge.

Please note that we are not talking about personality as in changing your personality. We are talking about a character, an archetype, or dimension of your complete resilient nature (consisting of a variety of healthy identities) that you can access that will most effectively deal with a particular challenge. For example, in a particular situation, you may need to be more assertive, but the same identity may not be required in another situation when you might access another identity, such as being more compassionate.

In Experience 1, it was suggested the Q-nexus would help you to fortify your life in a number of ways. Let's review a few of those statements and ponder the identity you would need to pull from your arsenal of identities.

- "When you are afraid, the Q-nexus will help you to channel the energy of fear into the power of courage." Quickening will help you identify the courageous warrior in you and shed the coward.
- "When encountering stressors, the Q-nexus will help you embrace those stressors as springboards for growth." The new identity is that of an optimist and will look to see how the stressors can be a positive in your life. You will be able to see the entire resilient journey with growth and wisdom upon completion.
- "When feeling confused at a time of important decision making, the Q-nexus will help you discern, choose, and gain confidence in your choice." The quickening moment in this case is from an identity that is confused to one who now has confidence.
- "When feeling down and discouraged, the Q-nexus will help you discover jewels of hope in the mire of depression." Quickening can change your identity from being depressed to an optimistic and hopeful identity.
- "When you are held captive by addictions, the Q-nexus will empower you with strength and control." One identity may be that you are addicted to tobacco, drugs, pornography, or electronic devices. The Q-nexus will help you form an identity that is free from those addictions.

You have the potential to formulate any helpful identity that comes to you through the Q-nexus experience. To repeat, and to make sure that we are clear, the identity we are going to create is one of many identities that are within the treasury of your experience. This is not your personality but rather a coping identity to deal with a selected challenge.

There are no negative identities that you can adopt if you have experienced a confirming resonation as it pertains to a specific situation. Some identities may appear questionable, but in the right situation, they need to be formulated. For example, the "rebel" identity may be considered negative, but in the situation where you have to get away from negative influences, then the rebel identity is the resonating identity you will want to become. Some identities are behaviorally related, such as changing your identity from a smoker to a nonsmoker or a nonexerciser to an exerciser. Other identities refer to qualities as you resonate to being a patient person in a particular situation or being more energetic in another. Consider a disruptive challenge you may be facing and consider which of the following identities may be part of your quickening moment.

- Do you need to be more of a believer or a skeptic?
- Do you need to be more of an optimist or pessimist?
- Do you need to be more patient or demanding?
- Do you need to be more humble or confident?
- Do you need to be more powerful or vulnerable?
- Do you need to be more of a conservative or liberal?
- Do you need to be more of a planner or spontaneous?
- Do you need to be more flexible or steadfast?
- Do you need to be more of a warrior or a peacemaker?
- Do you need to be more of a giver or a receiver?
- Do you need to be more of a teacher or a student?
- Do you need to be more fun-loving or more serious?
- Do you need to be more romantic or more distant?
- Do you need to be more of a leader or a follower?
- Do you need to be more loyal or rebellious?
- Do you need to be more of an introvert or an extravert?
- Do you need to be more of a creator or a destroyer?
- Do you need to be more practical or wild and crazy?

## ACTIVITY #59: PONDERING A NEW IDENTITY

Consider what identity would be helpful for you as you face a challenging situation. For example, is the quickening telling you to be humble? Is your moment telling you to have more fun—wild and crazy? Describe your new identity here as it pertains to a current life situation.

_____

_____

_____

_____

## EXERCISE YOUR AGENCY TO BECOME THAT IDENTITY

Many people catch glimpses of new identities that will help them become stronger through their adversities, yet in the wake of life's routine, the quickening moment fades. You have a choice to do what you have to do to form that identity. If you have resonated to an identity, then it is important for you to choose to become that new identity. You have a choice to act or not to act.

> Agency is a great human freedom that allows you to choose what to think, how to feel, and what you want to do in life's situations.

I hope we do not forget the great messages and inspiration that come from Viktor Frankl after the wisdom he harvested from his experiences in a Nazi concentration camp during World War II. Dr. Frankl was an Austrian neurologist and psychiatrist as well as a Holocaust survivor. In the trough of despair and suffering, Dr. Frankl had a major Q-nexus experience and received great insights into the human experience. Dr. Frankl's book *Man's Search for Meaning* chronicled his experience and horrific suffering in the concentration camp. He cites how he watched those that had purpose and meaning survive and those that did not have purpose fail and die. He realized that agency is the ultimate human freedom. He defined it as choosing your attitude in any given situation.

> The last of the human freedoms is to choose one's attitude in any given set of circumstances ... to choose one's own way. And there were always choices to make. Every day, every hour, offered the opportunity to make a decision, a decision which determined whether you would or would not submit to those powers which threatened to rob you of your very self, your inner freedom ...
>
> —Viktor Frankl

If you get insight into what you should do in your life situation, the choice to do it is based upon the value you put on it. It is like the scales of balance.

## Figure 32. Agency and the Scales of Balance

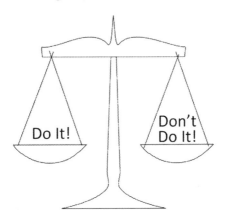

The confirming rightness of a Q-nexus moment should weigh much more than getting sucked back in to your normal routine. You will want to ponder, plan, hope, and become consumed about responding to the inspiration you received. You will be able to imagine that your resilient drives will be fulfilled as you ponder the identity you create. You will sense the art of becoming more skilled at thriving and coping with life situations. You need to make the identity shift much more important to your soul than not making the change.

## BECOME THE NEW IDENTITY

You will want to call upon your intellectual resilience to help you become the new identity. In your conscious mind, you can now formulate the identity by using imagery. In preparation, be sure you have your disruption or challenge in life clear in your mind and also an idea of the identity you need to form.

It is clear that there are varieties of disruptions in the lives of the readers necessitating that this imagery strategy be described in very general terms with the hope that you can fill in the detail. If the identity you are going to formulate is something that you develop within yourself and others are not involved, then the imagery scenario will be with you alone in a comfortable place. For example, you may be trying to overcome a bad habit or adopt a more positive identity. Your identity may be to become more studious or spiritual. You can consider the identities listed earlier in this experience.

If your new identity has to do with relationships and social situations, then you will need to imagine the setting where you need to adopt the courageous, compassionate, assertive, or humble identity depending upon the situation in light of your Q-nexus moment. In the interdependent situation, the imagery scenario will include other people at home, work, or in the community.

I am going to assume that your belief to become the new identity may be a little weak at this point, so we will go through three progressive imagery strategies, beginning with the easiest. It is best to read the imagery strategy and then close your eyes and live the suggested scenarios. In a comfortable position, when there are no distractions, try the following:

## ACTIVITY #60: HERO OBSERVANCE

I want you to imagine that you are in a movie theater all by yourself. As you watch the screen, you will see a movie of the challenge you have in your life, and to deal with it, you need to acquire a quality or new identity. You see the life challenge on the screen. Take a moment and imagine a hero or heroine that is going to take on the same challenge that you are facing. The hero can be a real-life person who handles situations like you want to, or it can be a fantasy figure from a movie. You may imagine George Patton for his quality of courage, Mother Teresa for her nobility, or a parent for her or his loving nature. The hero will demonstrate the key quality you need to deal with a particular situation. Be sure that the figure is someone who exemplifies the quality. You will watch this person as he or she does and thinks what you need to do and think. The observance is to watch in this movie the person deal with a situation in an ideal fashion, whether it be to struggle to overcome an addiction or to resiliently cope with a life challenge. Watch the hero acting, behaving, and doing what you wish to do. (This is vague, but you will see exemplars of how to fight and conquer your battle, make the change you have to make, and become what you have to become.) In social situations, you see this person studying, learning to develop a skill, and forming the new social identity. Watch this person over and over again in your mind, demonstrating the quality you want to acquire in your new identity.

Take a moment to reflect upon what you saw. What were the key qualities from the modeling that you saw? Write that here.

_____

_____

## ACTIVITY #61: THIRD-PARTY OBSERVER

Now you will change the scene. Imagine now that you are that hero in the movie you just watched. Watch yourself becoming the identity. Watch your courage, your humility, your social skills, and your persistence or whatever quality you want or need. Watch yourself doing what the hero did, whether it is struggling to overcome a bad habit or becoming more compassionate. Rehearse this scene over and over in your mind, making the image of you with the identity as clear as possible, including sounds, colors, and movement in your imagery. Continue to watch again and again as you demonstrate that identity.

Again, write your thoughts here as you watched yourself as an observer. How did it make you feel?

_____

_____

## ACTIVITY #62: THE ART OF BECOMING

Again, in the same situation, after watching your hero and witnessing your own self becoming the new identity, now you will become that identity.

> Imagine now that you are in your life situation that you have just witnessed, but you now see the situation out of your own eyes. You are actually there in the situation. You can feel your inner emotions and resilient drives from your soul as you now become the identity. Your body feels the strength to do what you need to do. Your human spirit is reminding you of the quickening moment, energizing you to do what you need to do. Your mind has a vision of what you need to do. Walk through the situation and become the identity you need to become. Rehearse the scene over and over in your mind.

Write your thoughts and feelings about your experience.

_____

_____

The last step is obviously to go out and be the identity in real life. Feel it and act upon it. It will require grit and persistence over time to have the identity become a part of your arsenal of identities.

## MUSTER GRIT TO PERSIST IN THE IDENTITY

Thomas Edison was believed to have said, "Genius is 1 percent inspiration and 99 percent perspiration." Much has been said about the importance of persistence and grit. Grit is the stick-to-itiveness or work required to adopt a new identity. It is so easy to quit or give up. Persistence over time becomes a habit and therefore an identity of finding grit in all your challenges. Persistent grit facilitates the experience of becoming what you want to become.

> That which we persist in doing becomes easier to do, not that the nature of the thing has changed, but our power to do so is increased.
> —Ralph Waldo Emerson

With good parents, great lessons are learned early in life. You are given responsibility, and good parents reward when the task is done.

> *Grit* is the perseverance of effort to accomplish a long-term goal, or in this case, assume a new identity, no matter what obstacles or challenges lay in your path.

One of my lessons as a child came from working on our little mini-ranch.

> Living on a small five-acre homestead allowed us to raise some animals and raise vegetables and fruits in a garden. The curse of curses to our huge garden was what we called devil grass (Bermuda grass). This nasty weed would grow

all over the ground and put down long and strong roots even in the heat of summer without water. When you pulled the grass out, it would break and the roots would grow more grass in several days. I hated devil grass. After the garden was going pretty well, devil grass would always creep in, and Dad's gentle nudging on a Saturday morning would be, "Buzz [my nickname], could you get that devil grass out of the garden today?" Make me mow the lawn, shovel manure, take out the trash, dig ditches, but please don't make me do the devil grass. I would start weeding on a row in the dry dirt and, predictably, the tops of the grass would break off and I would have to dig down and get those roots out. I would celebrate each inch that I was able to clear. It seemed like forever for me to be done with one row and then there was another row to do. Amazingly, using most of the day, the garden would be free of devil grass. I have reflected again and again about the battle with devil grass. I would sometimes wonder why I didn't give up. The prevalent theme was because I loved and valued my father's opinion so much that I would even endure devil grass to make my dad proud. This is the great lesson that my gentle father taught me as a child— that you can accomplish almost anything with grit and persistence. That lesson has carried me through athletics, academics, and my professions. I still hate devil grass.

The identity that my father wanted me to have was that of a hard worker. He gave me an experience where I would have to access all my spiritual resilient drives to accomplish what I had to accomplish. Let's review how you can harness the energy to weed the devil grass.

- Childlike resilience: I used to make a game of seeing how fast I could weed a foot of dirt of the garden. I'd start and begin counting until the foot was clear of devil grass. It became a game of sorts trying to beat my time.

- Noble resilience: I loved my gentle father so much that I would do just about anything to get his praise, praise he always gave when I'd finished the job. I felt noble.
- Character resilience: I had promised Dad that I would do it, and I knew I just had to get it done to avoid guilt.
- Ecological resilience: I loved being outside and was grateful that I wasn't indoors having to clean my room or something.
- Universal resilience: With a spiritual upbringing, I remember being so discouraged, and I would offer simple prayers to help me get through a row.
- Essential resilience: When I knew the battle against the devil grass was looming, I knew I had to prepare for the day by getting enough sleep and a good breakfast to survive.
- Intellectual resilience: I kept trying to figure out a way to make the weeding easier—sometimes I would try watering the ground to make it softer. Sometimes I'd try a shovel, a hoe, or a pick.

The drives that were used to weed the devil grass are the same drives that you need to develop the grit and persistence to create a new identity. Ponder how these resilient drives will help you to act upon the creation of the new identity you formed in the previous section of this book.

## Activity #63: Grit Exercise

As you ponder the identity that has emerged from your Q-nexus experience, how can your resilient drives help you to have the grit and persistence to become that identity?

Childlike resilience _____

Noble resilience _____

Character resilience _____

Ecological resilience _____

Universal resilience _____

Essential resilience _____

Intellectual resilience _____

*Glenn E. Richardson, PhD*

## ARSENAL OF IDENTITIES

With each new life experience, you have the opportunity to formulate a new identity. Some of the identities you will continue to use throughout your life. With a new identity, you add to your arsenal of identity weapons for coping with life situations. Each time you reuse one of the identities, it becomes stronger with increased capacity.

For example, it is easy to remember how hard it was to train as a high school and college athlete. I remember running hills, doing wind sprints, working out with weights, and working out until we almost dropped. We all had to develop the "go until you drop" identity. What was remarkable for me was that years after I finished my playing days in college, the feelings of "go until you drop" still come over me. When I started this book, I shared the experience of getting hit by the car and found myself in a wheelchair with pins sticking out of my legs, I wanted to get better. After getting clearance from the physicians and counsel from physical therapists, I brought out the "go until you drop" identity. A quote from my journal follows.

> I didn't want people to feel sorry for me. I didn't see myself as a victim. I had had a marvelous experience that changed me forever, and I just wanted to be physically functional again. I had caught a glimpse of my life purpose, and I wanted to have the thinking and communication skills so I could better fulfill that mission. Suddenly it felt like my freshman year at college conditioning for the football team. The "go until I drop" identity consumed my soul as I worked as hard as I could on my rehabilitation. I had experienced a quickening confirmation that I would heal. I was determined to walk again. Many times, I would use my arms to lift off my wheelchair and try to take a step but my legs were so weak they could not hold me. I would collapse in my chair—I had many moments of frustration and depression. I tried to hide my tears of discouragement from my family.
>
> One day, our neighbor Bill came over to visit me to see how I was doing. He had visited regularly throughout this ordeal. He had seen me struggle for almost three months

trying to get around in my wheelchair. On this visit, in our living room, I asked Bill to watch. With all the strength I could muster, I lifted myself from the wheelchair and took one step and then another without any support. I was shaky as a newborn calf, but I moved my legs. I took about six steps. As I sat down again, tears streamed from my eyes. I could see tears on Bill's cheeks as well. As I have reflected upon that experience of taking my first steps, I compared them to other events in my life. I reflected how the "go until I drop" had resulted in celebrations carrying the football, long jumping, and completing my graduate work. None of these celebrations can touch the joy and exuberance of taking those first precarious steps.

# In Summary

- Self-mastery is a complex and powerful quality that helps you persist and find peace as you thrive through life experiences.
- For each disruption, you create a new identity to best deal with life events and disruptions.
- You can create new identities in three steps: hero observance, observations of self in the situation, and becoming the identity.
- You can muster the grit to become the new identity by activating your innate resilient forces.

The next experience will help you learn the skills of following a path with heart.

# Self-Mastery Part 2: The Path with Heart

> *Self-mastery 2 is the experience of putting all the dimensions of resilience and resiliency together to create a clearly marked Q-path (path with heart).*

Through the experiences of this book, you have had a journey of self-discovery to find your strengths and drives. You have learned skills to ready yourself for the Q-nexus. As you have felt intuitive or resilient prompts about the answers to life challenges, you have been able to form an image of a new identity to help you become what you need to become. You have practiced assuming the identity to deal with the life challenge you may be facing. It takes time and persistence to have the identity become a part of your soul. Experience 14 will help you persist, maintain the identity, and guide you on a path that Carlos Castaneda describes as the path with heart.

> A path is only a path, and there is no affront, to oneself or to others, in dropping it if that is what your heart tells you ... Look at every path closely and deliberately. Try it as many times as you think necessary. Then ask yourself

> alone, one question … Does this path have a heart? If it
> does, the path is good; if it doesn't, it is of no use.
>
> —Carlos Castaneda

We could also call the path with heart a Q-path, which is living your life each day with a purpose of harvesting Qs as directed by your resilient drives.

If you embrace and nurture all the concepts, skills, and plans we have discussed to this point, you will feel more capable than you ever imagined that you could. You can generate Qs innately and from the world around you. All of these constitute the path with heart.

> Your wise guide along the path with heart is your integrated
> soul (body, mind, and spirit) sending messages through
> the language of resonation and quickening.

Although the only real guide you need for the Q-path is resonation and quickening, still the experiences we have covered in the previous chapters are markers along the path. You know that there are several key markers that will assure that you are on the right path.

1. You know that the path with heart requires leaps of faith into new experiences and that you will have Q-nexus moments to be able to do resiliency mapping.
2. You know that path with heart will be confirmed as you fulfill you childlike, character, and noble resilient yearnings and drives.
3. You know that along the path with heart you will be the recipient of ecological and universal energy that clarifies and enlivens your journey.
4. You will know that the path with heart is one that optimizes your mind and body.
5. You will know that along the path with heart your dream will resonate constantly while you strive to accomplish supportive goals.
6. You will know that along the path with heart it fills your soul with the courage required to venture and take leaps of faith while you progress down the path.

7. You will know that along the path with heart you will learn skills that ready you to experience the Q-nexus.

8. You will know that along the path with heart you will have quickening moments that will let you discern what to do, know when to do it, feel confident that it is the right thing to do, and experience an infusion of energy to make it happen.

9. You will know that along the path with heart that you will need to self-master as you demonstrate persistence and grit as you live your dream and accomplish goals.

## CYCLIC PATTERN OF THE PATH WITH HEART

The path with heart, or Q-path, is a positive cyclic pattern. We have described the resiliency process when we have faced one life event, but when that journey is completed, then we face more. So with multiple events, we can show the process as cyclic and repeated over and over. In some cases, we ideally grow and progress, but we don't always find fulfillment. So let me present a new model below that shows the cyclic pattern of resiliency. We will proceed a step at a time and label the model by number with a description for that number.

#1: Yearnings and drives: The cycle begins with innate resilient yearnings and drives. You long to be childlike, noble, and have character.

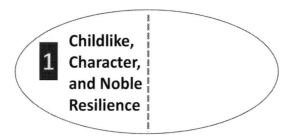

#2: Strength from beyond yourself—ecological and universal resilience: Hopefully, you will be walking a path with heart comforted by the peace and assurance that comes from the world around you. This is homeostasis or the comfort zone.

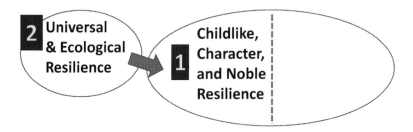

#3: Intellectual resilience: It is the function of your mind to listen to the soft resilient messages that are sent to your intellectual resilience to help you become aware, discern, and choose wise paths to fulfill the yearning of your innate resilience.

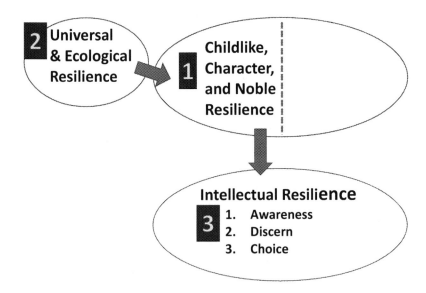

#4: Wisdom: When you become aware of your resilient drives, you will hopefully use wisdom. You will use your intellectual resilience and learn what to do, create options, make wise plans, and form the new identities that will fulfill your yearnings and drives.

#5: Venture and take Q-actions: To implement the plan and new identities, the whole soul (body, mind, and spirit) ventures to take Q-actions (as per resiliency mapping described in Experience 1).

#6: Fulfillment: Hopefully, the Q-action will fulfill the resilient yearnings and drives. You have the yearnings. You make a decision to do something about it. You do it and then you reap the Q-harvest from the action. This is the cycle that leads to fulfillment, happiness, and progression. Ideally, you live your life this way.

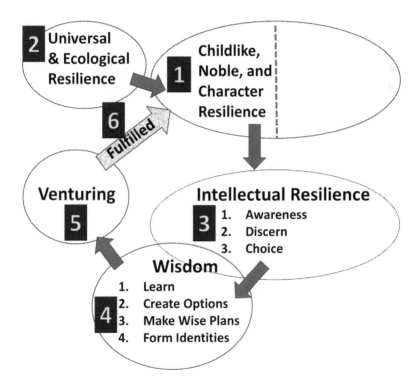

This is the path with heart. You can gather Qs for the rest of your life following this model.

## MAKING EACH DAY A PATH WITH HEART

With your understanding of who you are and where you want to go in life, you can live a path with heart every day. Remember the model that shows all your resilient drives and shows how they are interdependent. If you fulfill one yearning or drive, it will affect all the drives. It is the ripple in the pond. If you toss a pebble into the pond, it has a rippling effect. The path with heart is the same. If you have a spiritual experience, it will affect your whole soul. If you fulfill your childlike nature, it will fill your soul. You can toss the pebble into any one of the dimensions of your human condition and you will feel a positive rippling effect. Consider the story of finding a path with heart for Dirk.

> As a child, Dirk faced enormous challenges. His father was abusive in many ways, including physically and sexually. He regularly abused Dirk and his five siblings. Every month or two, the family would move so that the father could escape creditors and law enforcement. At the age of thirteen, Dirk knew he had to get out of the house, so he ran away. He learned to survive in many ways. He slept in an open field in a sleeping bag and hid it when he went to school. For food, he would go into hotels that served complimentary breakfasts, and he would say to the hotel staff that his parents were still asleep. He got on a free meal program at the school. He would shower at the school during the junior high physical education classes. He would go in the back of grocery stores and rummage through trash Dumpsters looking for food. For clothes, he would shoplift or go to charitable organizations. His scavenger lifestyle continued unnoticed through his years of high school.
>
> At seventeen, he met a girl at school who had a similar abusive background but was still living at home. Dirk convinced her to run away with him—as time passed, his girlfriend became pregnant. Dirk felt obligated to marry her, so they went to a justice of the peace with no best man or maid of honor. The couple had the child, which began the quickening moments for Dirk. He felt a stirring of nobility, and he committed to making a life for his wife and child without abuse. The young couple was able to convince a man in his senior years to let them live in a bedroom over

a garage, and both Dirk and his wife did chores to pay for the rent. Dirk got a minimum-wage day job.

The owner of the home with the detached garage where they lived was concerned for the young couple. He witnessed them sleeping on a bug-infested mattress that they had rescued from the trash. The owner mentioned the couple's situation to a religious organization, and one day, Dirk and his wife came home from work to find their room over the garage furnished with a new bed with linens, a crib, a couple of chairs, and a portable stove. The tiny bathroom now had towels, washcloths, and a variety of bathroom items. At first, Dirk's nobility (pride) was hurt, and he became angry, but it soon softened in appreciation. A representative of the religious organization came to visit Dirk and his wife and shared Christian values. Dirk was overwhelmed with gratitude. He felt another quickening moment with an accompanying dream of being able to be in a stable position so that he could feel the joy of helping others. Over time, he took steps to fulfill the dream. He applied for scholarships, went to school at night, and with diligence followed his path with heart to become a social worker. Dirk is now working in a county program to help children in abusive families find their dreams. He is invited regularly as a guest speaker to share his story and inspire others to find their path with heart.

Much like Dirk, we all can pursue a path with heart as we infuse Qs into our soul. In Dirk's case, it was essential drives to live and then his noble drive to help his family. Later, spiritual values gave him more Qs with sufficient energy to follow his heart.

The dimensions of your human condition will each provide a portal or avenue for you to energize your whole soul. The portal that you choose to use to energize the entire human condition will depend upon which area is struggling and which areas are strong. The struggling areas are losing Qs, or Q-draining. If possible, you will want to do something favorably in the designated portal. If not, then you can use the other portals to soften the experience and prevent the Q-draining.

> The human system is like tossing a pebble into the pond. When the pebble hits the surface of the water, the rippling affects the entire pond. It doesn't matter whether the pebble is a good thing or a bad thing—it still creates the ripple.

As you look at the model, know that each dimension is interdependent. One dimension will influence the other and infuse the qualities and virtues you really want and need (Qs). The integrated human system is one fluid entity. You can't have something negative happen in one area and not have it affect the other. Conversely, you cannot have something good happen in one area and not have it benefit the others.

The entire human condition will depend upon which area is struggling and which areas are strong. The struggling areas are losing Qs or Q-draining. If possible, you will want to do something favorably in the designated portal. If not, then you can use the other portals to soften the Q-draining.

## Figure 33. The Integrated Human System

280

As you begin your days, you may want to ponder some of the following questions that will help you have a day with heart.

1. How can I make my day more adventurous? (Childlike)
2. How can I have more fun in my responsibilities today? (Childlike)
3. Is there room for spontaneity or cautious risk taking today? (Childlike)
4. How do I behave and think so that I will not feel guilty today? (Character)
5. How do I demonstrate honesty and integrity today? (Character)
6. What acts of kindness can I do today that will make me feel good? (Noble)
7. How will I respond to my physical body's need for movement today? (Essential)
8. How will I listen to my body telling me what to eat, when to eat, and how to eat today? (Essential)
9. How will I assure that I listen to the sleep messages my body sends me today? (Essential)
10. What do I want to learn today? (Intellectual)
11. How do I assure I make the right choices today? (Intellectual)
12. What can I do to create an energizing or peaceful environment at home, work, driving, or play? (Ecological)
13. What can I do with listening to music, singing, or other sounds today to feel more enriched? (Ecological)
14. Where can I go today if I need to think or feel peace? (Ecological)
15. What practices can I do today to connect with a force that is beyond my normal consciousness today? (Universal)

A day involving the path with heart is a day when you listen to your resilient yearnings and drives and take opportunities to fulfill them. When you face life challenges, you can find peace if you will use your resilient drives to help deal with life issues.

You can also look at the Integrated Human System Model in figure 33 and see where you are hurting or lacking Qs. If you are tired of studying because your intellectual resilience is exhausted, perhaps you could take a break to energize your mind by accessing the ecological portal and listening to some energizing music. Perhaps you could access the childlike portal and play an active game or do something adventurous.

# In Summary

- The path with heart is a daily journey of feeling the resonating rightness of what you are doing each day.
- The cycle begins with recognizing your resilient yearnings and drives as well as the strengths beyond normal capacity.
- You then use your intellectual resilience to listen to the resilient messages and help determine the wisdom of your path.
- You then venture to implement the plan and new identities, the whole soul (body, mind, and spirit) ventures to take Q-actions.
- When you take those Q-actions, you will feel fulfillment, happiness, and progression.

The next experience is about shadows, which are thoughts about doing things that are self-defeating. If you respond and act upon those shadows, then you will end up doing something your heart tells you not to do. These actions we call *shadow actions*. Most people have habits they would like to break, and in Experience 15, you will learn the process of dissecting the shadow, going to the origin of the behavior, and re-creating a new pathway that is free from the shadow.

# SELF-MASTERY 3: ESCAPING THE PATH OF SHADOWS

> *Self-mastery 3 is the experience of using the resources of the Q-path to dissect and eliminate shadows and shadow actions.*

Most of us have undesirable thoughts and habits. In fact, many of us struggle with obsessions, addictions, time wasting, and character-compromising habits. You may be suffering from thoughts and habits that, as hard as you try to be resilient, you still find yourself doing that result in guilt, discouragement, anxiety, and depression. To this point in the book, we really haven't addressed those problems because the intent has been for you to discover, nurture, and act upon your strengths to find joy, happiness, and life progression. We have spent the first fourteen experiences in this book with the intent of helping you discover and nurture your innate strengths, gifts, and energy to be able to live a path with heart and progress throughout your lifetime. Life isn't completely blissful and problem-free for most of us. Sometimes your best planned actions do not result in fulfillment but rather in unhappiness and distress.

A path strewn with obstacles and pitfalls reveals itself over time as stepping-stones to strength, happiness, and progression.

When we are blindsided by life events, we recover from the disruption with emotions that, if acted upon, will lead to unhappiness and digression rather than progression. With disappointment or hurt, sometimes our emotions turn to anger and jealousy—which, if acted upon often—can result in damaged relationships. Sometimes people try to escape the unhappiness by engaging in unhealthy behaviors, such as the overuse of alcohol and drugs.

In our lives, we witness and can read about the tug-of-war between opposing forces. For example, we read about:

- Good and evil
- Pleasure and pain
- Anima and animus
- Virtue and vice
- Yin and yang
- Positive and negative
- Male and female

The list can go on, but the context surrounding opposites is that opposites enrich life. Positive protons and negative electrons attract and make a solid bond. From the resiliency model, disruption is necessary to experience resilient reintegration, allowing you to grow stronger and progress.

Experience 15 will build upon the path with heart model discussed in Experience 14 and add a path of shadows to complement life's journey. We will explore how to transform bad habits into strengths and how to jump from the shadow path back to the path with heart.

But first, let's review the placement of the path of shadows on the resiliency model. The addition to the model will be the large arrow that is labeled SHADOWS that stretches between "Disruption" and "Reintegration with Loss."

## Figure 34. Shadows in the Resiliency Model

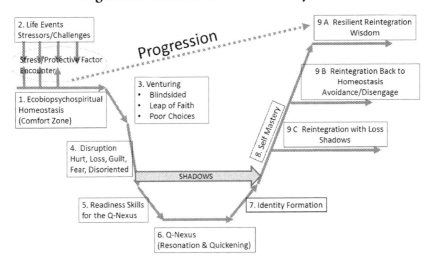

Rather than exploring the trough of resiliency where you are humbled and open to insights and inspiration, some people feel a disruption (hurt, guilt, loss, and fear) and quickly take on secondary emotions, such as anger or jealousy. They bypass the opportunity to grow and progress but instead react and do things that they often regret. The path of fighting, yelling, using drugs, and engaging in activities outside of your character framework is called the path of shadows.

This experience is designed to help you embrace and overcome undesirable thoughts and actions. We will call these thoughts *shadows* and the actions *shadow actions*.

> *Shadows* are the thoughts and cravings to do things that are Q-draining or self-defeating.

> *Shadow actions* occur when you act upon the shadows (undesirable thoughts and cravings) and do what your character resilience does not want you to do. When you do shadow actions, the aftermath will result in guilt, shame, and other unpleasant emotions.

Initially, let's simplify the essence of how you can do this as we consider shadow actions as a simple choice of direction in the road of life.

## The Postulate of Agency: Heart or Shadows

You have essentially two choices when occasions arise for you to act. One choice is to do what your resilient spirit tells you to do, and the other is do what your shadow is telling you to do. Your resilient spirit wants to follow a path with heart. Your heart (resilience) tells you to think and do things that will help you fulfill your childlike, character, and noble yearnings without compromising your character. The other choice is to follow the path of shadows, which is to do reactive actions that will, in the long run, result in shame, guilt, and other unpleasant emotions.

**Figure 35. The Choice: Path with Heart or Path of Shadows**

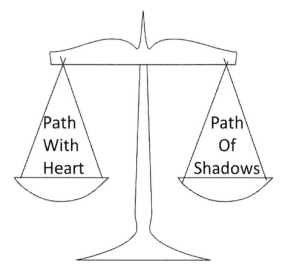

If your desire to follow a path with heart is stronger than the drive to follow shadows, then you will likely follow the path with heart. This is a path that will help you harvest Qs by fulfilling your drives. The choice to follow the path with heart is called a Q-path.

On the other hand, if your cravings or uncontrolled emotions are stronger than your desire to follow your path with heart, then you will find yourself doing things that sap your energy and result in a Q-drain. Again, the simple view of how to overcome undesirable thoughts and habits is to determine a way to make the path with heart more desirable and dominant in your life and at the same time make the path of shadows less desirable. This concept reminds us of the famous Cherokee chief who was teaching his grandson about life found at http://www.firstpeople.us/ FP-Html-Legends/TwoWolves-Cherokee.html.

"A fight is going on inside me," he said to the boy.

"It is a terrible fight, and it is between two wolves. One is evil—he is anger, envy, sorrow, regret, greed, arrogance, self-pity, guilt, resentment, inferiority, lies, false pride, superiority, self-doubt, and ego." He continued, "The other is good—he is joy, peace, love, hope, serenity, humility, kindness, benevolence, empathy, generosity, truth, compassion, and faith. This same fight is going on inside you—and inside every other person, too."

The grandson thought about it for a minute and then asked his grandfather, "Which wolf will win?"

The old Cherokee simply replied, "The one you feed."

With that simple formula in mind, we will first discuss how to make the path with heart weigh more than the path of shadows. We will feed that wolf by strengthening the path with heart with as many Qs as possible.

From Experience 14, we followed the cyclic path with heart from the resilient yearnings and drives (#1) to intellectual resilience (#3) to wisdom (#4) to venturing and taking Q-Actions (#5). The hope is the actions then result in fulfillment and progression. But what if the actions you take do not work? What if after you act, you feel unfulfilled?

Stage six in the cyclic model is either actions that result in being fulfilled or actions that result in being unfulfilled. If you are unfulfilled, the outcomes of your actions are the primary emotions of hurt, loss, guilt, fear, and guilt. The unfulfilled yearnings are then communicated back to your mind "#3.) On the cyclic path with heart, we find ourselves at unfulfilled yearnings (#7) as shown in figure 36 and described next.

## Figure 36. Unfulfilled Resilient Yearnings and Primary Emotions

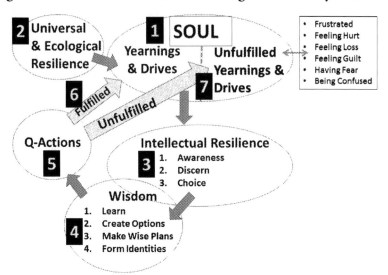

#7. Unfulfilled yearnings: Sometimes our actions don't work out and we feel the aching of unfulfilled yearnings. The unfulfilled yearnings can be felt as hurt, loss, guilt, fear, and confusion as shown in the model. Once again, the unfulfilled messages are sent to the control center—our intellectual resilience.

#3. Intellectual resilience: The unfulfilled yearnings are received by our conscious mind, and again we become aware of the unfulfilled yearnings. The messages of the aching heart are usually louder than the gentle resilient yearnings. The mind is now in danger of activating the shadows, but if we want to stay with the path with heart, the mind will again go to wisdom (#4) and learn more, create more options, make wiser plans and re-create new identities to try to fulfill the resilient yearnings. Your mind makes the choice to follow wisdom or the shadows.

## THE PATH OF SHADOWS

Sometimes the hurt, loss, fear, and confusion arrive at your intellectual resilience and you quickly turn to your shadows. You react rather than think wisely. You make quick fix decisions. You decide to use substances that will help you escape the hurt. You get angry and jealous. That is when our minds choose the shadows.

## Figure 37. Shadows to Shadow Actions

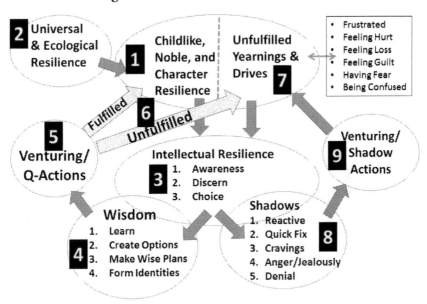

#8. Shadows: Your mind sometimes deals with unfulfilled yearnings in an unwise, short-term, and Q-draining fashion. Shadows include the following descriptions:

- Shadows are secondary emotions, such as anger, jealousy, or aggression.
- Shadows are also addictions, obsessions, and cravings for immediate pleasure.
- Shadows are thoughts and feelings that lie outside of your character code.

You feel unfulfilled—a void in your soul. You get frustrated, which turns to anger and aggression. You may crave some kind of high from alcohol, drugs, pornography, or other means to escape the hurt. The cravings and secondary emotions are the shadows. We will see that this is a possible point for your mind to intervene before you act on the shadows.

#9. Shadow actions: Shadow actions are the result of the cravings and uncontrolled secondary emotions of the shadows. You find yourself doing what you really don't want to do. You let the shadows overrule your wisdom. In other words, when you resort to shadow actions, in all likelihood you will reintegrate with loss as per the resiliency model.

The following list includes some of the shadow actions that people do that rarely have positive outcomes:

- smoking or chewing tobacco
- overusing alcohol
- uncontrolled gambling
- swearing
- overeating
- not getting enough sleep
- electronic device addictions
- other entertainment addictions (TV, sports)
- procrastinating and being lazy
- overusing prescription drugs
- using illicit drugs
- overuse of caffeine
- watching pornography and other undesirable sexual habits
- offending others (arguing / fighting / yelling / being overly critical)
- physically hurting other people or animals
- gossiping
- body obsessions and eating disorders
- overspending
- being dishonest or lying
- illegal activity (shoplifting / cheating on taxes)
- rudeness

After doing shadow actions, you find yourself back to an intensified #7 (see figure 37 on the previous page). Your mind, your intellectual resilience, then discerns and makes another plan of action.

#7. Unfulfilled yearnings: The cyclic path of shadows brings you back again to unfulfilled yearnings. When time has passed, after you have engaged in shadow actions, you find yourself feeling guilty for your actions. You feel a loss of hope that you will ever be able to overcome your undesirable habit. These new unfulfilled feelings compound the initial unfulfilled yearnings, and now the aching heart is crescendoing.

#3. Intellectual resilience: What goes around always comes back to your intellectual resilience. You are even more aware of the crescendoing screams of your aching heart or unfulfilled yearnings. The guilt for having engaged in the shadow action racks your mind. The scary thing about this cycle is that it can be never ending. The more guilt you feel, the more you reach for the action that you are trying to eliminate. The postulate of agency seems to weaken, and one just doesn't seem to learn. The cycle continues again and again. You drink alcohol excessively or use drugs and then when the effect wears off, you go to the substances again to try to wipe out your guilt and other unpleasant emotions.

Now you know the two cycles. The path with heart is when your mind is wise and your actions are fulfilling or unfulfilling. But you continue on the path until you find a way to fulfill those yearnings. The other cycle is the path of shadows when you find yourself doing the things you regret. At any point in time, when you are able to use your intellectual resilience to learn, discern, plan, and create a new identity, then it is time for you to eliminate shadow actions. We do that first through the dissection of shadow actions and then put the elements on trial, as per the scales of balance.

## DISSECTION OF SHADOW ACTIONS

To dissect your shadow actions into their component parts, simply start with the shadow action that you would like to eliminate from your life.

## ACTIVITY #64: SHADOW ACTIONS AND WHY?

On the following line, write the shadow action and why you don't want that habit anymore.

| Shadow Action | Why You Want to Eliminate It |
|---|---|
|  |  |
|  |  |
|  |  |
|  |  |

You can superimpose your shadow action on the shadow path model as number nine. Let's go through the dissection one number at a time as shown on the model. This dissection will be helpful when we put your shadow actions on trial and eliminate them. So, briefly, here is the dissection:

- #9: The shadow action: The undesirable and self-defeating behaviors
- #8: The shadow: Secondary emotions, such as anger or jealousy, cravings for immediate pleasure, or thoughts to do things outside of your character resilience.
- #3: Intellectual resilience: Your conscious mind senses the prompts from the unfulfilled yearnings, discerns, and makes decisions to do something that is unwise.
- #7: The unfulfilled yearnings: When your resilient yearnings and drives are thwarted and frustrated, you will feel the hurt, loss, guilt, or fear.
- #1: The resilient yearnings of your soul: Your yearnings and drives to be childlike, to be noble, to have character, to be enriched in your ecosystem, to be connected to a universal source of strength, and to fulfill essential and intellectual needs.

To provide a couple of examples of the dissection, we will follow two stories. One story will follow Jamie's story of ridding herself of an addiction, and the other will follow Scott's story of overcoming the shadows and shadow actions stemming from a fight that happened during his college years.

Jamie was a student at a major university. During the summer just before school started, Jamie was on vacation with her family. While cliff jumping at a lake, she slipped and fell short of the deeper water in the lake. She landed in about seven feet of water, which was enough to buffer her fall, but her left foot landed on a rock, and she broke several bones in her lower leg. After several surgeries, she was in a cast and able to return to school. In order to deal with the pain, especially at night, Jamie was given a prescription for pain reliever—a narcotic, which was a potentially addicting substance if overused. It helped her sleep without pain. She found that the opiate seemed to improve her mood in school and helped her cope with stress.

After a couple of weeks, her prescription expired, and on a follow-up visit, she asked her doctor for another prescription, complaining of night pain. Reluctantly, the doctor provided the prescription. Jamie began to use the opiate more than once a day because she wanted the good feeling during the day as well. Her prescription again ran out, and when she requested more of the opiate from her physician, he refused. Jamie went one night without the opiate, and she felt horrible. She knew that her father had some painkillers remaining from a surgery he had had. On a visit to her parents' home, she went into their bathroom and took the pills. Soon, she had used all her father's pills. She found a friend at her college that had ways to get more painkillers as well as other "feel-good" prescription drugs. Over time, Jamie gradually found herself dependent upon a variety of painkillers, which began to have an effect on her studies and social life. She also found that a significant part of her paycheck was going toward the pills.

Let's dissect Jamie's shadows.

1. #9: The shadow action: Taking pain pills well beyond the prescribed time.
2. #8: The shadow: Having a craving for pain pills she felt she needed to make it through a day.
3. #3: Intellectual resilience (conscious mind): As much as Jamie didn't want to take the pills, her mind could not think of any other way to feel good. The mind chose to take the path of shadows rather than the path with heart.
4. #7: The unfulfilled yearnings: Jamie became unhappy and dependent. The only way she thought she could fix the unhappiness and energy drain was with painkillers.
5. #1: The resilient yearnings of the soul: Jamie just wanted to be happy and enjoy life. She wanted to fulfill her noble drive to be successful in school and to have a profession. She wanted energy from her resilient yearnings and drives.

Now let's consider Scott's story.

Scott worked for a reputable company and after several years received a promotion as an associate director. This required him to move back to the city where he grew up. He was thrilled to be back home. On his first day on the job, he met with the director with whom he would be working very closely over the next few years. His heart sank. The director was David. The last time that Scott spoke to David was when they were in college together. They had been friends in the same fraternity. But David developed an interest in Scott's girlfriend and began to flirt with her. Scott's girlfriend responded by encouraging David to continue. Scott accused David of trying to steal his girlfriend, and a huge argument ensued. The argument escalated into a fistfight, and David threw a punch that broke Scott's nose. To compound the animosity between the two, David continued to court Scott's girlfriend and, in the end, married her. Scott and David put an end to their long friendship and became bitter enemies. Scott was still single, having lost the love of his life. At their first meeting, Scott put on a facade that all was forgotten and that the old fight was the foolishness of college kids. Inside, he was burning up with hatred and dread for having to work with the boss that had stolen his girlfriend.

We can also dissect Scott's story and his path of shadows.

- #1: The shadow action: Scott was superficial and distant with David, causing meetings to be uncomfortably stiff. He wasted time and productivity, resenting his situation.
- #2: The shadow: Scott was angry and renewed the intensity of the jealousy he had felt nine years earlier. The feelings had faded over time, but the emotions were now rekindled each time he was around his new boss. It poisoned his heart.
- #3: Intellectual resilience (conscious mind): As much as Scott wanted to take the high road and forgive David, he couldn't bring himself to do it. The choice was to decide whether to follow the shadows or the path with heart. Right now, he was following the shadows.
- #7: The unfulfilled yearnings: He had enjoyed the friendship with his ex-friend. He missed having fun with and confiding in David. He needed to trust his boss, but after the betrayal in college, there was little chance of that happening. He felt a sense of loss of his friendship, loss of trust, as well as the loss of the love of his life. The hurt was rekindled, and he was worried that this would force him to leave his job.
- #1: The resilient yearnings of the soul: Scott had wanted to enjoy his promotion and enjoy his new coworkers. He wanted to enjoy being back in his hometown. Although the urge had waned over the years, he wanted to be friends again with David.

I'll add a couple of other dissections, unrelated to the stories, to assure that you can see the nature of each shadow action. It is important to understand dissection in order to conquer the shadow actions.

**Dissecting backstabbing, gossip, bitterness, and anger at work:**

1. The shadow behavior would be the actual backstabbing with accompanying bitter and angry comments.
2. The shadow would be anger, jealousy, envy, or frustration.
3. The mind determines that the best way to deal with the hurt would be to hurt back.
4. The aching of the heart could be the frustration of several possible situations, such as feeling a loss of control, feeling devalued, or being disliked by colleagues.
5. The yearning of the heart is to feel valued and of worth.

**Dissecting mentally or physically attacking a loved one:** When the heart's yearning to love and be loved is blocked, then the mind quickly goes to the shadow behavior.

1. The shadow action is verbally or even physically attacking a loved one.
2. The shadow is anger or jealousy.
3. The aching of the heart is generally feeling emotional hurt or unloved.
4. The yearning of the heart is to love and feel loved.

**Dissecting overeating** (attempts to medicate the aching heart):

1. The shadow behavior is overeating.
2. The shadow is your mind craving food to medicate the aching of the heart through the pleasure of food. This may be conscious or more likely subconscious thinking.
3. The mind knows that food gives you a quick fix pleasure rush.
4. The aching of the heart can come from any source of sadness or disappointment of unfulfilled yearnings. You may be trying to fix

the guilt for stepping outside of your character code, hurt from a loved one, loss of control, or a number of other reasons.

5.  The yearning of the heart is to feel peace for living within your moral framework, feeling control in an area other than food, or feeling loved by those we love. As far as overeating, it also wants to listen to your essential resilient drives to eat intuitively.

## ACTIVITY #65: DISSECTING YOUR OWN SHADOW ACTION

Think of your own undesirable shadow action. Then proceed to dissect it into its component parts and describe the parts of the shadow actions below.

## THE SHADOW ACTION

_____

_____

## YOUR SHADOW

_____

_____

## YOUR CONSCIOUS MIND

_____

_____

## YOUR RESILIENT YEARNINGS

_____

_____

## TRIAL OF THE SHADOWS

The path of shadows model provides a mechanism where you can eliminate your shadow actions. The dissection of the shadow action allows you to seriously consider what is prompting you to do things that, in the long run, you really don't want to do. Although there are many approaches to eliminating shadow behaviors in your life, the trial of the component parts of the behavior serves as a good example of one way to eliminate the behavior. We will have a trial for each of the accomplices that contribute to the shadow actions. From the model, we know that the potential accomplices to the crimes of the shadow actions include (1) the shadow action, (2) the shadow, (3) the mind, (4) the unfulfilled yearnings, and (5) the resilient yearnings. Let's first do the trial, and then we will do the sentencing of all five contributors to the shadow action.

## #1: TRIAL OF THE SHADOW ACTION

The shadow action is the actual behavior that is the product of the integrated mind, body, and spirit. It is the action that, after you do or think it, will likely make you feel shame, guilt, and remorse. Remember, when doing the trial, the shadow action is only the behavior and nothing else. It is not the thought or emotion—just the action. Trial questions might be like the following:

Question #1: Is the shadow action innocent or guilty of making you feel like you have violated character resilience? After you take the action, does it make your heart ache by making you feel guilty, sad, or remorseful?

Question #2: If the shadow action is guilty, then what kind of sentence are you going to give it? Are you going to eliminate it? Do you want to destroy it?

Question #3: If you want to eliminate it, how will you get rid of this shadow action?

There are many ways to eliminate the undesirable behaviors, but we will defer to how to do that at the sentencing of the shadow action. We have found the shadow action is guilty. We are going to skip #2, #3, and #4 for now from figure 37 and put the resilient yearnings on trial (#5).

## ACTIVITY #66: WRITE THE OUTCOME OF YOUR TRIAL WITH YOUR SHADOW ACTION HERE

_____

_____

# TRIAL OF THE RESILIENT YEARNINGS (THE HUMAN SPIRIT)

The prominent forces that come from your very core are the resilient yearnings. The drive to be childlike, be noble, have character, have an enriching ecosystem, and be close to a source of spiritual strength is part of everyone's yearning spirit. Through the dissection, we have seen that energy, yearnings, and drives from this innate source are within you. Let's put the resilient spirit on trial by asking the trial questions.

Question #1: Is feeling the yearnings to fulfill your resilient drives right or wrong?

Question #2: Is your resilient spirit guilty or innocent of wanting to be noble, childlike, and to live within character?

If your resilient spirit is something you want and need, then the drive is innocent. It is who you are. You want to continue to nurture and determine ways to fulfill those resilient yearnings and drives wisely.

## ACTIVITY #67: WRITE THE OUTCOME OF YOUR TRIAL OF YOUR RESILIENT YEARNINGS HERE

_____

_____

Let's move to #7 on the model (figure 37).

## TRIAL OF THE UNFULFILLED YEARNINGS OR ACHING HEART

When your resilient drives are frustrated and unfulfilled, you feel hurt, loss, guilt, or fear. These are the emotions that amplify the unfulfilled yearnings of the heart and alert your mind to your spirit's needs. Let's put them on trial.

Question #1: Is it good to have these feelings that alert you to unfulfilled yearnings and drive? Do you still want them? Are they natural, and can they lead to a path with heart? Are your unfulfilled yearnings guilty or innocent?

Question #2: If you think they are innocent, do you want to keep them? Of course you do, because they are red flags of emotion that help you identify needs of your resilient spirit.

Even though these unfulfilled yearnings are difficult to experience, they are positives in your life that help you to know the direction you should take.

## ACTIVITY #68: WRITE THE OUTCOME OF YOUR TRIAL WITH YOUR UNFULFILLED YEARNINGS HERE

_____

_____

## TRIAL OF THE CONSCIOUS MIND

When the unfulfilled yearning messages come from the aching heart, your conscious mind becomes aware of the need. Your mind wants to fix the pain. You will choose to think with wisdom or you will react with shadows. The wise mind will make plans that have long-lasting positive effects (progression), and the shadow mind will react and plan for a quick fix that is Q-draining.

For now, let's assume that your mind makes an unwise decision and chooses revenge, anger, or craving of a substance. Your mind making unwise choices is the shadow. The shadow has the short-range vision. That part of the mind told the body to strike out at someone, take the drug, or do whatever the shadow action is. With your mind in the shadow mode, we will do the trial of the shadows.

## ACTIVITY #69: WRITE THE OUTCOME OF YOUR TRIAL WITH YOUR CONSCIOUS MIND HERE

_____

_____

# TRIAL OF THE SHADOWS

Let's do the questioning for the shadow on trial.

Question #1: Is it right or wrong to crave unhealthy substances or have secondary emotions? Is the shadow innocent or guilty?

Question #2: The shadow did not actually do the shadow action, but it gave the command to do it—the shadow prompted it. You may be thinking that the shadow is guilty of being an accomplice to the shadow action. So the shadow is guilty—as an accomplice.

Question #3: What do you want to do with the shadow? Is it the unwise part of your intellectual resilience? Do you want to keep the good intentions of trying to fulfill the yearnings of the heart but channel its energy into wise actions? Let's put the shadows on probation.

You have determined that the actual behaviors that frustrate your progression are guilty and need sentencing.

# ACTIVITY #70: WRITE THE OUTCOME OF YOUR TRIAL WITH YOUR SHADOWS HERE

_____

_____

# SENTENCES FOR THE SHADOWS AND SHADOW ACTION

The last step of a trial is to determine the sentence or punishment for the guilty parties in the crime. In other words, what are you going to do to your shadows and shadow actions?

In essence, you have determined the following:

1. Your resilient yearnings are innocent. You need them and value them to provide energy and guidance. They are an energy source that you will want to use later after you deal with the shadows and shadow actions.

2. Your unfulfilled yearnings are innocent and are to be viewed mostly as a red flag for attention to be given to the resilient yearnings. Your wise mind values the aching heart.

3. The shadow part of your mind was found guilty of being the instigator or accomplice to the unwanted behaviors. You need a plan to alter the thinking—put the mind and shadow on probation.
4. The shadow action was found guilty and needs to be eliminated.

Now comes the challenging part—actually eliminating the shadow actions and turning your shadows into wisdom. Let's first execute your shadow action.

## EXECUTION OF THE SHADOW ACTION

Eliminating the behavior may be challenging, but your effort will be worth it if you want to enjoy life guilt-free. The energy you have used struggling with the shadows and shadow actions can be diverted into progression and positive actions in fulfilling your dream.

You will want to make the execution of the shadow action a significant event. I would encourage you to have some type of ceremony when you are ready. We are a society rich with ceremony; we wear caps and gowns at graduations and put on rings at weddings. Some people use the ceremony of confession to a spiritual leader or family member to launch a new beginning. Some post signs where they work and live with reminders of blazing a trail of new thoughts and behaviors.

The ensuing ceremony is one you can try to help you eliminate your shadow action. In preparation, be sure you are ready by reflecting upon how you feel in the aftermath of doing the shadow action. Remember the guilt in your resilient heart that results because of what you thought and/or what you have done. This will be a leap of faith, as per the resiliency process model, into a disruption, but the joy of self-mastering and eliminating the undesirable behavior is worth the leap. You may or may not want to include a trusted friend to witness the ceremony and support you. Try the following:

1. Pick a time: Appoint a designated time when you feel prepared and can devote your full attention to the change.
2. Ponder the aftermath: Ponder your sensitivities about how you have felt after you have participated in the shadow action. Focus on the guilt, hurt, or shame you felt by violating your character

resilience. Build your determination from your resilient drives to eliminate the action.

3. Get it on paper: Begin the ceremony by writing all the things you hate about the behavior. Write about your lack of control, the time you waste, and the secrecy. Write about the Q-bleeding of goodness, integrity, and morality that leave your soul when you act on your shadows. Write about the guilt, despair, and discouragement. Write all the things you can about the evil the behavior brings into your life. Keep the paper or print it (saving it on your computer will help you to review this document later if you need it). Note: Another option is to draw a picture of the shadow action that encompasses your feeling.

4. Confirm your readiness: Reread your written expressions of disgust. Add more thoughts and ideas as they come to mind. Feel the revulsion. If you have a trustworthy person you want for support, you may have that person read your thoughts as well.

5. The execution: Find a safe location where you can burn a piece of paper. When you are 100 percent ready and with great heartfelt ceremony, lift the piece of paper in the air. The paper is the shadow action, and you are going to execute it by burning. Light the paper, and as the paper burns, feel the purging of the shadow action from your soul. Feel the shadow action go away. It is no longer part of you. You have executed that shadow identity.

6. Reminders: Continue the ceremony by gathering the ashes, if you can, and burying them or putting them in container that will remind you of your commitment. This will allow you to grieve and remind you of your actions.

7. Grieve: Feel the loss of never being able to do that action again. You may want to create a psychological anchor, such as a jar with the ashes or some other symbol as a reminder. You may want to find a picture or poem that represents the loss of that behavior and your commitment to be free of the shadow action. For some time, you have used the shadow behavior to medicate your aching heart wounds. The reality of not ever being able to resort to it again creates a great sense of loss. The shadow behavior created an identity that is no longer part of who you

are. Spend some time, maybe a few days, to seriously grieve the loss of your behavior.

8. Make amends: If your shadow archetype has offended others, do all you can to make up for it. It may be that a lot of damage was done, and time will be needed. Take whatever time you need to feel remorse and also to make amends.

The shadow action is gone. It is no longer a coping mechanism. You will no longer be able to use the action to cope with life challenges. Let's continue with Jamie's story.

Jamie woke up on a Saturday morning the week before her university spring break. She had a week without needing to attend classes. She started to crave her painkillers, but she had already taken her last pill. Suddenly, Jamie let out a scream of disgust. Her mind started to spin, as it always had, to scheme about how she was going to get more pills. Jamie had been attending a resiliency class at the university, where she had received instruction on eliminating shadow behaviors. She started to reflect upon the time she had wasted and her horrible dependence on the pills. Anger began to boil up inside her, and the disgust reached a fever pitch. She hit her pillow again and again. Exasperated, she resolved to execute her addiction to pills. Jamie packed some food and her camping gear and went up to the Uinta Mountains. Jamie had loved camping all her life. She went to a favorite campground and pitched a tent. In the evening after she had cooked her meal, she was sitting around the campfire thinking about how she would survive without the pills and at the same time was aching for the relief the pills could provide. As she had planned, she grabbed the empty prescription bottle from her last round of painkillers. She saw the bottle as the enemy. She cursed the bottle for all the misery it had put her through. She pleaded with her God and nature to help her overcome this habit. With great ceremony and determination, Jamie took the plastic prescription bottle and placed it on the end of a stick. She then watched it slowly melt and burn in the fire. She wept and wept. She struggled all night long, craving the medication. The next day she went on a vigorous hike in the mountains, which eased her craving. She knew it would be a couple of weeks of hell, but she was determined.

The description of the steps to eliminating the shadow action also came from Scott's story.

Scott wrote all his feelings down on paper. He described the betrayal. He wrote about the fight with David. He wrote a lengthy discourse on how that event had affected his whole life. Professionally, he thrived, but he had lost his best friend. He wrote about his frustration working with a man he hated. He longed to have a supportive work environment. Lastly, he wrote his resolve to forgive David. He wrote a long time about forgiving him. He thought how great the workplace would be if he and David were friends again. He had to eliminate his distancing and rigidity at his work. He wanted to feel not only comfortable with David but also happy about the friendship days. Scott woke up on a Saturday morning and thought about how he would forgive David and become warm again. He pondered how he would feel and behave at work. They had been working together for two months and still they were distant. Finally, Scott, with great resolve, went down to his garden in his backyard. He struck a match and slowly burned his writing. He knew that he could no longer resent David. He watched the paper burn slowly. He buried the ashes and placed a marker on the grave.

In Scott's case, he knew that he would be friendly to David, and he began to imagine himself treating him differently at work. He knew he would be kinder and more conversational, but the feelings were still there. But he also wanted to rid himself of those secondary emotions.

## ACTIVITY #71: DESCRIBE HERE HOW YOU WILL EXECUTE YOUR SHADOW BEHAVIOR, AND WRITE THE CEREMONY HERE

_____

_____

_____

## PROBATION OF THE MIND: WISDOM OR SHADOWS?

Consider for a moment where we are:

1. You still have your blameless and virtuous spiritual core—your resilient drives and yearnings that if your mind listens, you will find joy and fulfillment. You found your resilient core innocent and vital.
2. You still have your alerting mechanism or your unfulfilled primary emotions. When your needs to fulfill your resilient drives are frustrated, a red flag surfaces in the form of hurt, loss, guilt, or fear. You found your unfulfilled yearnings to be innocent and vital.
3. You have just eliminated the shadow action—it is no longer part of your life.

With your intellectual resilience and its drive to understand, plan, mend your aching heart, and fulfill your resilient drives, you find your control center. Part of your control comes by understanding the dissection of the path with heart and path of shadows model where you can see the two key points to transition shadows to wisdom. As you can see in the model, the first warning flag is when the feelings of unfulfilled emotions reach your conscious mind. The second flag is when the unfulfilled yearnings turn to shadows.

## Figure 38. Flagging the Points of Intervention

# THE PROBATION FOR THE UNFULFILLED YEARNINGS

When loss, hurt, guilt, fear, frustration, and emptiness reach your intellectual resilience, a red flag will enter your awareness. Where in the past you may have resorted to shadow emotions or shadow cravings, the red flag now is a sign to stop and ponder where you are on the model. Just stopping and pondering the fork in the path to be wise or foolish will help you reflect upon the postulate of agency and content from Experience #8 about intellectual resilience.

1.  You will become aware of the aching heart. When you feel that awareness, you can condition your mind to see the red flag. An alarm should go off in your head telling you it is time to implement a plan that you have designed.
2.  You will strive to understand the cause of the aching and lack of fulfillment. To better understand, you will use your skills of discernment. You will study it and progress by gaining information and knowledge about the situation. You will resonate to truths that apply to you. You will envision meaning from the information you have gained.

3. You will reflect upon your vision of an ideal life that is your dream. You remember how a Q-path will best fulfill your resilient drives and yearnings. You will feel that burning of rightness.
4. You will remember how badly you feel when you succumb to the shadows.
5. You will create a plan to power load your path with heart.
6. You will remember the scales of balance and know how to tip the scales by nurturing the path with heart and diminishing the weight of the path of shadows.

**Figure 39. Tipping the Scales to the Path with Heart**

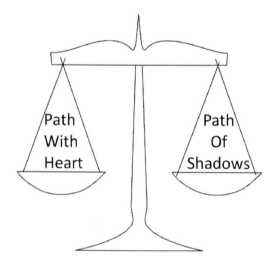

You will load the path with heart side of the scale with the help of your childlike and noble natures. You will receive strength, guidance, and power from your universal source of strengths. You can access strength from your essential resilience. You build it and tip the scales to wisdom.

## PROBATION FOR THE SHADOWS

You need a plan to be able to deal with the shadows before you act on the shadows. Again, when you feel the cravings for harmful substances or to take other shadow actions or if you feel yourself getting angry and jealous, raise the red flag. Stop and dissect the shadow and go back to the sources of the shadows. You will discover unfulfilled yearnings and drives. From that point, you can redirect your path and follow the guidance that you have received throughout this book. If the shadow path is the craving for a quick pleasure, then you need to dive into the deep reserves of your innate, essential, ecological, and universal resilient sources and create a plan that will give you a quick pleasure within your character code. You need to activate and enliven your powerful innate sources of resilient energy.

You will want to attack the shadow probations with a sense of adventure, to find humorous stories to tell about your plight, and to almost make this a competitive game—you against the bad shadow actions. You will want to realize that you are noble and strong. You are an exemplar, and you should feel the energy in this. If there is a chance to help others with similar problems, you will do service and feel an enhancement of your energy.

With the focus on energy, remember that you need to eliminate any thoughts or behaviors outside of your character code. If the shadow action you are struggling with at this time is outside of your character code, then pondering the freedom you will feel should create some courage and hope. Hopefully you have learned some skills to listen to what your body really needs to help generate Qs to help combat the shadow actions. Remember that when you mindfully listen to what your essential resilience is telling you about what and when to eat, how much sleep to get, and how much movement and exercise your body needs, you will be fortified with Qs. To have the strength and energy to overcome shadows and shadow actions, you will need your body to function optimally.

With the focus on your resilience, you will find that you will be able to harness the energy generated by the shadow and use it for positive experiences. Shadows are no longer an option. Let's finish the story about Jamie.

> When Jamie returned from her days camping in the Uintas, she could still feel the cravings for the pills. During her experience in the mountains, she planned her life to avoid the prescriptions and focused on building her path with heart. In the mountains, she had connected with nature and felt its calming effect. She hiked every day and enjoyed the natural rush of endorphins that substituted for the pain pills. Her plan was to go home and create a

pseudo-mountain retreat in her bedroom. She got plants and posters to symbolize the strength she received from nature. She walked and biked daily to get her natural rush. Jamie drew pictures and reminders and put them on her walls to help reflect upon the joys of freedom from her pills. She began to tell her story to trusted family and friends, which helped her to be the drug-free identity she had imagined in the mountains. Jamie became more physically fit and more spiritual. Over time, the cravings lessened and lessened. But each time a minor craving would come, she felt the red flag rise up within her, and she would respond with exercising, meditating, praying, or visiting one of her trusted friends. The energy she had previously put into finding drugs she now used for exercise and friendships, resulting in her becoming more physically fit and being invited to many social events.

We can also continue with Scott's story.

Scott kept telling himself that he had to get past the resentment and blame he had for David. Scott had the opportunity to drive or fly to a city six hours from his home as part of a business trip. He opted to drive to the city. As he prepared for the trip, he planned to have a forgiving experience. He knew he had to rid himself of the blame and resentment he felt for David. During his drive, he imagined what he might look like when he acted cold and distant. He imagined what his coworkers were thinking. He saw his shadow as an enemy inside himself that he had to eliminate. Scott remembered the early days of his friendship when times were good and that David was actually a very good person. He talked in his mind and even out loud to his God to help rid himself of this shadow inside him. He wanted to be free of the angry monster. For hours on the road, he pleaded, struggled, and agonized while he was driving through open country. Even when stopping for gas, he pondered and battled in his heart. About an hour from his destination, feeling exhausted and hungry, Scott pulled over to the side of the road. He wept uncontrollably. He then hung over the steering wheel in deep meditation. Suddenly, he felt a warm tingling sensation in his head. It was a wonderful feeling of peace. The tingling warmth progressed throughout his body. He felt as though a huge burden was being lifted. He could actually feel the resentment and anger leave his soul. He suddenly felt a love for David—the same love that he had felt in their college years. He had the desire to hang out with him. He felt his whole body being purged of the shadow monster that was within him. He kept reflecting upon the moment, and he continued to cry great tears of gratitude.

## ACTIVITY #72: PROBATION OF THE SHADOW

Describe here how you will put your shadow on probation. Also describe your journey and how you will bolster the path with heart side of the scales of balance. Describe how you will create opportunities for your resilient yearnings and drives to overpower your shadows.

_____

_____

_____

## BENEFITS FROM OPPOSING FORCES

The law of nature is that in order to create wholeness, there needs to be opposing forces. In physics, it is the positive charge of a proton coupled with the negative charge of an electron to form an atom. In psychology, it is the anima and the animus for wholeness. In Chinese medicine, it is the yin and the yang. It is also told in biblical theology that Adam and Eve were forced to leave a world with no opposition in the Garden of Eden. There was no progression in the world of only bliss. But to progress, they needed to be cast into a world where they would know good and evil, pleasure and pain, virtue and vice. Developmental theorists speak of the drive for independence but also of the yearning to find comfort and security of companionship. Opposing essential yearnings strengthen your body in cycles, such as alertness combined with sleep. Both are requisite for health. As we look at the year's seasons, we see winter as a time of dormancy, but with spring, we see a drive among plants to grow and blossom.

Shadows are the opposing forces in your life that make you stronger. You become wiser if you learn to master the opposing forces of heart and shadows. You may have had issues in the past that you regret, and you still may have some undesirable habits, but you can eliminate them and harvest the energy for progressive purposes. You can become what you want to become and follow the path with heart that is guided by the resilient drives within you. It is like the Zen story of the samurai warrior.

A powerful and valiant samurai warrior went to see a little monk. The warrior killed many enemy soldiers in his day, and in his older years, he felt a need to consider the afterlife. "Monk!" he said in a voice accustomed to instant obedience. "Teach me about heaven and hell!"

The monk looked up at the mighty warrior and replied with utter disdain, "Teach you about heaven and hell? I couldn't teach you about anything. You're too proud and arrogant. Not only that, you're dumb and dirty. You're a disgrace, an embarrassment to the samurai class. Get out of my sight. I can't stand you."

The samurai got furious. He shook, got red in the face, and was speechless with rage. He pulled out his sword and prepared to slay the monk. He put the sword on the monk's neck and said, "With a flip of my wrists, I could cut your head off!"

Looking straight into the samurai's eyes, the monk said softly, "And therein lies hell."

The samurai froze when he realized the compassion of the monk who had risked his life to teach him and have him feel the nature of hell! Humbled, the samurai put down his sword and fell to his knees, filled with gratitude. He thanked the monk for his wisdom as he felt the magnificent peace of insight.

Then the monk said softly, "And therein lies heaven."

Humbling experiences learned by Jamie, Scott, and the samurai show the power of the softness of Qs. They can help us overcome our shadows and shadow actions.

# In Summary

- The challenge of following your path with heart is to keep undesirable thoughts and actions from derailing you along the resilient journey.
- Shadows are the mind's way of dealing with unfulfilled yearnings in an unwise, short-term, and Q-draining fashion.
- Shadows are secondary emotions, such as anger, jealousy, or aggression. Shadows are also addictions, obsessions, and cravings for immediate pleasure. Shadow actions are to act upon the anger and addictions.
- The means to turn bad habits into strengths is through developing skills to jump from the shadow path back to the path with heart.
- Your mind can dissect the shadow actions to discover the shadows. You can then find the aching heart that triggered the shadows. Finally, in the dissection process, you can dissect the aching heart to find the resilient yearning core and rebuild your path with heart from that point.

The concluding experience will address the final stage of the resiliency process—wisdom.

# PART 7

# RESILIENT REINTEGRATION AND WISDOM

Part 7 is about the positive outcomes of the
resiliency process—wisdom. After you have
experienced a disruption, received insight as
to what to do, and demonstrated self-mastery
in doing what you needed to do, then you can
reflect upon the wisdom you have gained.

Part 7 is about that wisdom. We can see many examples in life
of how people reintegrated time after time and progressed each
time until they accomplished what they wanted to accomplish or
became what they wanted to become. There are numerous quotes about
wisdom to which we may resonate. For example:

Nothing in life is to be feared, it is only to be understood.
Now is the time to understand more, so that we may fear
less.

—Marie Curie

Life isn't about waiting for the storm to pass ... it's about
learning to dance in the rain.

—Vivian Greene

*Glenn E. Richardson, PhD*

The fool doth think he is wise, but the wise man knows himself to be a fool.

—William Shakespeare

Knowing yourself is the beginning of all wisdom.

—Aristotle

The only true wisdom is in knowing you know nothing.

—Socrates

Experience 16 will discuss the resilient understanding of wisdom.

EXPERIENCE **16**

# REFLECTIVE WISDOM AND RESILIENT REINTEGRATION

> *Wisdom is the experience of reflecting upon the harvesting of Qs from past disruptions and seeing the world through Q-eyes.*

We all seek wisdom. Wisdom is having repeated experiences to which we have resiliently reintegrated for which we have gained knowledge, good judgment, and experience. The last stage of the resiliency process is resilient reintegration, which is to have gained from life experiences and increased in wisdom. Wisdom is circled in figure 40 on the resiliency model.

### Figure 40. Resilient Reintegration

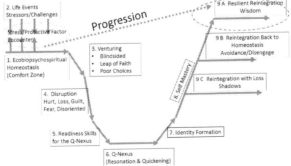

Resilient reintegration is the pinnacle of the process of coping, learning, and becoming stronger through the disruption. It is the wonderful feeling of fulfillment and the infusion of the Qs of accomplishment. Remember that each life experience brings pinnacles of enlightenment, learning, and growth.

The primary quality that results from resilient reintegration is wisdom. Upon reflection of all of life's disruptions, there have been lessons and opportunities for growth. As we come to the final experience of this book, my hope is that you have gained wisdom and insight as to how to embrace life challenges and grow through them throughout your journey.

The great psychologist Abraham Maslow used the term *transcendence* to describe resilient reintegration. Maslow defined transcendence as the human ability to rise above a situation and live on a higher plane. Resilient reintegration allows you to rise above where you were in the comfort zone. This pertains to many aspects of your life.

1. You can rise above time by being so totally engaged in a project that you lose track of time.
2. You can rise above culture and diversity by looking into the eyes of others and seeing their goodness, their heart, their nobility, and their spirituality.
3. You can rise above the past and start anew with a fresh beginning without regret of the past.
4. You can rise above your weaknesses and shadows and turn them into strengths.
5. You can rise above your fears and turn them into courage.
6. You can rise above any unhelpful pride and selfishness and find fulfillment in service.
7. You can rise above your circumstances and see life as good despite conditions.

The energy and power for rising above is derived from the resilient drives of your human spirit. You can reflect upon Experience 6 that described your human condition of universal oneness and interdependence of your body, mind, spirit, and ecosystem. Triggering one part of the system will positively influence the others. Your resilient spirit is the primary trigger that will help you to rise above. Wisdom and resilient reintegration are the experiences of becoming receptive and submissive to that energizing resilient spirit. Wisdom and true power occur when your human spirit assumes control of your soul.

## Qs OF WISDOM

In the beginning of the resiliency process, you encountered a life challenge or took a leap of faith. Through the journey of disruption and reintegration, you may have been disoriented or struggled, but at some point your received insight (the Q-nexus) as to how to best thrive through the experience. Through self-mastery, you created a new identity and resiliently reintegrated. Upon resilient reintegration, you have the opportunity to reflect upon what you learned and the Qs you harvested in the process. Some of the Qs you feel with resilient reintegration include the examples of Qs listed below.

1. Appreciation
2. Gratitude
3. Happiness
4. Confidence
5. Self-Efficacy
6. Faith
7. Joy
8. Peace

Perhaps the most important and inclusive quality you experience upon reflection is wisdom.

## RESILIENT WISDOM

Wisdom has been discussed and debated for centuries. In most circles, wisdom is seen as the judicious application of knowledge. It is the ability to think and act using knowledge, experience, understanding, common sense, and insight with good intentions. In classical writings of antiquity, wisdom was considered one of the four cardinal virtues. The Greek philosopher Plato (400 BC) first described the four virtues as prudence (wisdom discussed in this experience), temperance (self-mastery discussed in Experiences 13, 14, and 15), courage (venturing discussed in Experience 10), and justice (character resilience discussed in Experience 4). These four cardinal themes were debated and taught by Plato's student Aristotle, later by the Greek philosopher Cicero (100 BC), and still much later by Thomas Aquinas (AD 1280), among many others.

The two perspectives of wisdom stem from intellectual resilience and universal resilience. The wisdom of intellectual resilience is a learning, experiencing, and self-actualizing form of wisdom that comes from resilient reintegration and reflection upon progression through life's disruptions. It is the discernment of essential resilient message to know how to care for your body. This is resilient wisdom.

Each of life's experiences or disruptions leads you through a resilient journey of potential learning, understanding, and enrichment. Reflection upon the resilient journey will help you highlight and appreciate how you have grown. You have had the choice to not progress through the disruptions because of your agency. Consequently, the experience may have resulted in stagnation or recovering with loss. As you think about resilient reintegration, wisdom is reflective of a process. The following are thoughts about wisdom from a process perspective:

1.  Wisdom is the product of experience after experience or resilient reintegration after resilient reintegration.
2.  Wisdom is making choices that will allow you to harvest Qs over time.
3.  Wisdom is the magnificent series of revolutions as your human spirit assumes control of your entire soul and you become humbly submissive to the quiet, powerful, and true whisperings of universal Qs.
4.  Wisdom is evidenced by the manifestation of Qs that have been harvested during the Q-nexus path.
5.  Wisdom is continually learning from life's disruptions. With each successful reintegration, you experience the infusion of confidence and self-efficacy/faith.

## ACTIVITY #73: QS OF WISDOM

You may want to reflect upon the Qs and wisdom you have received by reading this book. Write your thoughts here.

_____

_____

_____

## UNIVERSAL WISDOM

The other perspective of wisdom comes from a more universal resilience perspective. In ancient Greek philosophy, the more spiritual wisdom is Sophia, the name of the Greek god of wisdom (Kellenberger 1985). It is wisdom that is gained by being connected to the spiritual. It is a reliance on the compassion, peace, and hope that suggests that life is a journey to be celebrated. The more spiritual experiences we have, the more peace we can find in all of life's challenges. Spiritual wisdom is the sense that you are walking through life with the companionship of an energy that tells you that you are on the right path.

## REFLECTING UPON THE EMPOWERING NATURE OF THE Q-NEXUS

At the beginning of the book, we talked about how the Q-nexus could empower and help you. Let's see how the empowering experiences are fulfilled.

1.  *When you are afraid, the Q-nexus will help you to channel the energy of fear into the power of courage.* In Experience 10, we spoke of venturing and turning fear into courage by tipping the path with heart side of the scales of balance with resilient drives and reducing fears through understanding.

2.  When encountering stressors, the Q-nexus will help you embrace those stressors as springboards for growth. You learned the resiliency process model and resiliency mapping described as the springboard for growth in Experience 1.

3. *When facing great adversity, the Q-nexus will help you find strength beyond normal capacity to thrive.* Experience 6 on universal resilience described sources of strength beyond normal capacity and Experience 11 on readiness for the Q-nexus guided you through skills to access those sources.

4. When feeling confused at a time of important decision making, the Q-nexus will help you discern, choose, and gain confidence in your choice. You will remember that confusion is the precursor and sign of readiness to receive the answers through the experience of resonation and quickening.

5. *When feeling down and discouraged, the Q-nexus will help you discover jewels of hope in the mire of depression.* After experiencing all the resiliency concepts, you know the journey. You can almost celebrate depression because you know this as a disruption and an opportunity to use readiness skills to resiliently reintegrate.

6. *When you are feeling anxious, the Q-nexus will give you calm and peace.* Anxiety produces tremendous energy that you can transform into courage and then experience calm and peace. From the skills you learned in Experience 11, you can have calm and peace.

7. *When you are held captive by addictions, the Q-nexus will empower you with strength and control.* Experience 15 took you through the process of dissecting your shadow actions and described how you can access strength and control.

8. *When you are angry, the Q-nexus will infuse you with deep and mature understanding about the nature of life and the circumstances.* Chronic unresolved anger can become a shadow and therefore fits into the path with heart and path of shadows model described in Experience 15. As you dissect anger, the originating source is oftentimes found in a desire to improve autonomy, vitality, and competence in a desire to be loved and connected—the realization of the sources of anger then helps us develop insight into how to channel the anger into either developing more mature understanding or into constructive action.

9. *When faced with situations beyond your control, the Q-nexus will help you find peace and acceptance.* Although several experiences

will help you find peace, perhaps the most important experience is about universal resilience—the ultimate source of Qs.

10. *When concerned about what is right, the Q-nexus will confirm your truth.* One of the early postulates in the language of the Q-nexus spoke of resonation, but the real confirming truth is found in the Q-nexus experience. Quickening is the infusion of truth.

11. *When tired, the Q-nexus will infuse you with increased capacity to think, perform, and do.* You have discovered a rich source of energy in your resilient drives, and as you ponder the energy from all your resilient sources, you will feel your capacity increase.

12. *When you need to create a turning point in your life, the Q-nexus will infuse your heart and mind with insights on how to know which way to turn.* You will know that the direction you will take will be within your character, noble, and universal resilience. You will be able to discern between a path with heart and a path of shadows. You can be quickened to the right direction.

## THE ACORN THEORY

You have learned that you are growing into an energy field of potential. James Hillman, an American psychologist, proposed what has been called the *acorn theory* in his book entitled *The Soul's Code: In Search of Character and Calling.* He proposes that we are all like acorns, born with the potential to become a huge oak tree. Our entire makeup is designed to be magnificent. If we nurture the acorn with water, fertile soil, and sunlight, it will flourish. You too can nurture your soul with your resilient yearnings and drives to be guided into, metaphorically, an amazing oak tree. You will feel noble and in touch with your sources of universal strengths. The absorption of the water and nutrients is similar to the process of resonation and quickening that enlivens your whole life. The sunlight is like harnessing energy and strength from sources beyond your normal capacity. Your greatness is more than you can imagine. The innate vision or blueprint is housed within you. As you nurture the energy produced by your resilient drives and bask in the light and truth of its sunshine or universal resilience, you will live a creative and meaningful life that will fulfill your potential. Your dream or vision is to become the great oak tree, and you can progress. You walk your path with heart with universal wisdom.

# Q-EYES

As you walk your Q-path, you will see the world through Q-eyes and will picture life differently. With each life event, whether you have been blindsided or made poor choices or whether you have taken a leap of faith, you will live a happier life if you see it with the Qs that come from your resilient drives.

## RESILIENCY Q-EYES

- Reflecting upon the postulate of progression, following a celebration of resilient reintegration, you will create a vision of your next leap of faith.
- You will see all disruptions, no matter how minor or how major, as a journey to acquire new skills, identities, and Qs.

## CHILDLIKE Q-EYES

- See the challenge as an adventure.
- See the challenge as a chance to have fun or be playful.
- See the humor in the challenge.
- See the opportunity to be creative in the challenge.
- Feel the childlike energy as you face the challenge.
- See the challenge as a chance to take calculated risks.

## NOBLE Q-EYES

- See the challenge as part of your purpose and find meaning.
- See the challenge as an opportunity to become better and to learn.
- See the challenge as an opportunity to serve and help others.
- See the challenge as an opportunity for compassion and listening.
- See the challenge as an opportunity to believe in someone.

## CHARACTER Q-EYES

- See the challenge through the eyes of honesty.
- See the challenge through the eyes of integrity.
- See the challenge through the eyes of honor.

- See the challenge through the eyes of loyalty.
- See the challenge through the eyes of fidelity.
- See the challenge through the eyes of fairness.

## ECOLOGICAL Q-EYES

- See the life and energy in all living things.
- Feel the Qs that come from natural things.
- Look for music, art, plants, and other people that enliven your soul.

## UNIVERSAL Q-EYES

- See the challenge through the eyes of a universal spirit and strength beyond normal consciousness.
- See a universal force guiding you through the challenge with healing, insight, meaning, wisdom, and understanding.
- See challenges being overcome with strength beyond normal capacity.

## ESSENTIAL Q-EYES

- See the challenge through the eyes of the amazingly perceptive body. What is the voice and wisdom of the body saying?
- See the challenge as an opportunity to improve fitness, energy, vitality, and overall health.

## INTELLECTUAL Q-EYES

- See the challenge through the eyes of a creative and constructive mind.
- See the challenge as an opportunity to brainstorm and increase thinking, reasoning, and logical decision-making capacities.
- See the challenge as an opportunity to learn and increase in knowledge.

Living resiliently is to see the world with Q-eyes through your big story of life as well as the numerous stories of disruption and reintegration that occur throughout the day. Consider the story that embraces Q-eyes demonstrated one day on a back road in Texas.

> George, an exercise physiologist, and I were driving back from Houston and heading home to College Station after a long day of doing stress-management seminars at an accounting firm. We always loved to take the back roads in Texas because the country was so beautiful. We jumped off the freeway and were heading on this back road when we came to a few cars that were waiting for a truck to recover its load. We were about the fourth car to get there, and we debated whether to turn around or to wait. We opted to wait. It appeared that the truck had jackknifed the trailer that was loaded with telephone poles. Several of the poles had fallen off. The driver had a forklift that had been strapped to the back of the trailer, and he was in the process of lifting the poles onto the now-straightened truck and trailer, one pole at a time. His truck and poles totally blocked the two-lane road.
>
> George and I were only about ten miles away from being home, so we were a little frustrated. We noticed that some of the other people waiting for this guy to finish loading his poles were also upset. They had gotten out of their cars and didn't seem to be too patient about waiting. We saw them walking around mumbling to one another about the wait. As George and I got out of the car, we could hear conversations about the truck driver and his marginal IQ. While all this stress was being put on this poor truck driver, I joked with George and said, "Which of those stress-management strategies we just taught for the accountants would work for this guy?" Then I noticed that the driver on the forklift was smiling and giggling. I said, "George, look at that guy—he's smiling and laughing. Either he's fruit loops or we need to find out how he's dealing with this stress in such a positive way.

When we find that out, we'll bottle it and sell it." George and I got closer. Between the driver's knees, sitting on the chair of the forklift, was a five- or six-year-old boy. The driver and his boy were playing tractor—on our time! The little boy and dad had their hands on the lever and were having a great time loading the telephone poles one at a time. They were totally oblivious to the grumblings of those who waited. Here was the great principle: you see disruptions as opportunities to love, play, and have adventures. When you focus on your strengths as opposed to the external stressors (the irate observers), the problems have a tendency to go away. This driver saw the world with Q-eyes and his disruption an opportunity for childlike Q-eyes.

## ACTIVITY #74: Q-EYES IN AN IDEAL TWENTY-FOUR-HOUR DAY

Your day will be different when you look through Q-eyes. Try the following exercise to create a vision of an ideal twenty-four-hour day using your arsenal of drives and identities. Let's have you imagine tomorrow.

1. Get into a comfortable position and take a few relaxing breaths. With each exhalation, you feel yourself becoming more and more relaxed.

2. Imagine yourself as you wake to start your day. Feel the softness and comfort of your bedding as you wake up. In your imagination, see the colors, furniture, and items in your room. They cause you to be grateful.

    Take a moment to reflect upon your dream in life—the fulfillment of your drives. Imagine yourself doing a ritual of seeking your universal resilience source or spiritual source of strength through prayer, meditation, music, or some other practice.

3. You may want to consider the nature of the day and feel the identities you will need to function optimally.

4. Close your eyes again and go through your morning routine. Feel your mindful and appreciative identity. If you shower in

the morning, focus on how refreshing and wonderful the water feels. As you eat a morning meal, eat it with appreciation and be mindful. If you need to help other people to get ready, feel gratitude for having those people in your life.

5. Imagine the rest of the day when traveling and accomplishing tasks that need to be done. With each task or responsibility, select the best resilient yearnings and drives with resulting identities and visualize thriving during your tasks. See all the tasks through Q-eyes. See yourself accessing the identities you need, whether they be to be compassionate or your warrior.

6. Be sensitive to your need to move and to nurture your essential resilience through exercise. Imagine yourself doing the kind of movement that will be enjoyable for you. You can gain energy from the movement being childlike. It may be an opportunity to be noble as you help others. Maybe your repetitive movement can be a meditative experience for you.

7. You may have had a resolve to do some life-enriching activities that you have not been doing to this point. Are there additional activities that will be part of your ideal day to enrich your life? Are there additional identities that will help you fulfill your mind, your body, and your spirit? Be mindful of all that you do in the day. Feel the energy levels from family and colleagues. You may ponder ways to increase the connections with family, friends, and your environment.

8. After your day of responsibilities, imagine your evening hours (presleep). Are there ways to increase your nobility by helping and serving others? Are there ways to increase your intellectual or essential resilience? Are there better choices that you can make in your free time? Imagine the ideal evening hours.

## Q-NEXUS: THE APPLIED THEORY OF EVERYTHING

The Q-nexus is truly the applied theory of everything from a resiliency perspective. As you walk through life with its accompanying disruptions, you will be faced with choices. You will be faced with a need to feel increased energy, courage, patience, hope, and power to thrive though life challenges. You will need to feel self-worth and value. You will want to have fun and adventures. You will need to know what is right, fair, and honest. Every facet of your life will be enriched with childlike, noble, character, universal, ecological, essential, and intellectual resilient Qs.

The means to make everything optimal will be through the Q-nexus, the magnificent infusion of the Qs, that will help you to know what to do, when to do it, and how to do it. The Q-nexus, whether it be the subtle resonating guidance that you are on a path with heart or whether it is the course-adjusting and course-informing jolt of quickening, is the direction you need to optimize your life. In a moment of resonation, you will be able to see and feel your life story in your resilient spirit, which will be relayed to your conscious mind.

## BE THE HERO IN YOUR STORY

As you envision your life growing into a grand oak tree as per the acorn theory, you will have an amazing story and legacy of your life. Your life story began at birth like the acorn. When you die, you will have become a great oak tree. You will be noble. You will have touched many lives. You will have accomplished many personal goals. Right now, you are somewhere between birth and death. After all the discussion we have had in this book, it is now time to write your own story starting with today and projecting into the future.

You are the hero in your story.

You are the crowned humble ruler in your kingdom or queendom.

## ACTIVITY #75: WRITE YOUR STORY

Write your story from now to the future. This is not a quick exercise but one that you should write over time. One way you could do it is by imagining your future creative self talking to the present self about what it could be and become. Part of your story will be your own personal journey. The other part of your journey is to "learn it, live it, and teach it." Hopefully you will embrace the principles described in this book. It is my sincere hope that you will benefit and that, as you learn and experience the lessons of the Q-nexus and resilience, you will be moved to share what you have learned with others. Lasting change occurs when you become a role model or a teacher. When you teach a spouse, a child, a parent, or a friend, it forces you to remember, better understand, apply, and live the principles. Walking the Q-path will be noticed by others, and they will want to be part of your vision and wisdom. Write a few thoughts to trigger your mind as you write your story.

_____

_____

_____

_____

_____

_____

Stories are brief moments in time or significant life events that take some time. Let me close this book with my reflection a year after my accident.

> After months of rehabilitation, I found myself celebrating my forty-second birthday. On the one-year anniversary of the accident, I found myself jogging and reflecting upon the experiences of the previous year. My heart swelled with gratitude that I was able to recover. I was grateful for the skilled medical care I received and for the support of my family. I was grateful to still remember the awe and wonder of the experience that took me close to a place filled with love, joy, and peace. My story of recovery is the big story, but each day on the journey of recovery was a story within itself. Most days, I learned and became stronger. Other days, my hope faltered. But then I would return to that incredible moment in the coma, and my faith was restored.

> As I reflected upon what I had learned, perhaps the biggest change was how I saw the world. Walking across campus, I would look at students and faculty and sense their energy

and countenance. I knew they all had stories—they were in the midst of a story as I passed them on the walkways. I looked at animals differently. I would look into dogs' eyes to try to feel their spirits—they became friends. I could no longer fish or even kill insects.

I had learned that I was walking, living, and breathing in a magnificent sea of energy, wisdom, courage, hope, and power. My academic and professional passion had now become to study resilience and resiliency.

My passion has evolved to try to help people create Q-nexus moments, moments when you receive infusions of the qualities you really want, such as courage, purpose, enlightenment, peace, and fulfillment. An expectation of my job as a university professor is to publish articles in journals. As I pondered my experiences, I decided to write an article about the resiliency process and formulated the metatheory of resilience and resiliency. I published it in the *Journal of Clinical Psychology*. More importantly, I created graduate and undergraduate classes on resilience to try to touch the lives of those wonderful souls I am privileged to teach. It has been a joy to travel to places around the world and try to touch lives by speaking at professional meetings. I have learned so much in this rehabilitation process. The experiences of the coma, in the hospital, and rehabilitation became the foundation of a whole new life and purpose for me.

# References

## Introduction

Bandura, Albert. "Self-efficacy Mechanism in Human Agency." *American Psychologist* 37, no. 2 (1982).

Benson, Peter L., P. C. Scales, S. F. Hamilton, and A. Sesma Jr. "Positive Youth Development: Theory, Research, And Applications." In *Handbook of Child Psychology*, vol. 1, edited by W. Damon and R. Lerner, 894–941. Hoboken, NJ: Wiley, 2006.

Dyer, W. W. *Power of Intentions*. Carlsbad, CA: Hay House, 2004.

Garmezy, Norman. "Stress-Resistant Children: The Search for Protective Factors." In *Recent Research in Developmental Psychopathology*, edited by J. E. Stevenson, 213–233. Oxford: Pergamum Press, 1985.

Garmezy, Norman. "Stress, Competence, and Development: Continuities in the Study of Schizophrenic Adults, Children Vulnerable to Psychopathology, and the Search for Stress-Resistant Children." *American Journal of Orthopsychiatry* 57, no. 2 (1987): 159–174.

Greene, Brian. *The Elegant Universe*. New York: Vintage Books, 2003.

Peterson, C., and M. E. P. Seligman. *Character Strengths and Virtues: A Handbook and Classification*. New York: Oxford University Press, 2004.

Rutter, Michael. "Psychosocial Resilience and Protective Mechanisms." *American Journal of Orthopsychiatry* 57, no. 3 (1987): 316–331.

Rutter, Michael. "Pathways from Childhood to Adult Life." *Journal of Child Psychology and Psychiatry* 30, no. 1 (1989): 23–51.

Rutter, Michael. "Psychosocial Resilience and Protective Mechanisms." In *Risk and Protective Factors in the Development of Psychopathology,* edited by J. E. Rolf, A. S. Masten, D. Cicchetti, K. Nuechterlein, and S. Weintraub, 182–210. New York: Cambridge University Press, 1990.

Werner, Emmy. "Vulnerable but Invincible—High Risk Children from Birth to Adulthood." *European Child & Adolescent Psychiatry* 5 (1996): 47–51.

Kellenberger, J. *Wisdom: Folk, Arcane, Practical, Religious, Philosophical, Mystical.* Lanham, MD: Lexington Books, 2015.

## EXPERIENCE 1

Richardson, G. E. "The Metatheory of Resilience and Resiliency." *Journal of Clinical Psychology* 58, no. 3 (2002): 307–321.

Richardson, Glenn E., B. L. Neiger, S. Jensen, and K. L. Kumpfer. "The Resiliency Model." *Health Education* 21, no. 6 (1990): 33–39.

## PART 3

Padesky, Christine A., and Kathleen Mooney. "Strengths-Based Cognitive-Behavioural Therapy: A Four-Step Model to Build Resilience." *Clinical Psychology & Psychotherapy* 19, no. 4 (2012): 279–362.

Richardson, G. E. "The Metatheory of Resilience and Resiliency." *Journal of Clinical Psychology* 58, no. 3 (2002): 307–321.

EXPERIENCE 2

Csíkszentmihályi, M. *Finding Flow: The Psychology of Engagement with Everyday Life.* New York: Basic Books, 1997.

Fulghum, Robert. *All I Ever Needed to Know I Learned in Kindergarten.* New York: Random House, 1988.


EXPERIENCE 4

Williamson, M. *A Return to Love.* New York: HarperCollins, 1992.

Shah, I. *Tales of the Dervishes.* New York: Penguin, 1970.


EXPERIENCE 5

Cooke, B., and E. Ernst. "Aromatherapy: A Systematic Review." *British Journal of General Practice* 50 (2000): 493–496.

Pert, C. B. *Molecules of Emotion: The Science behind Mind-Body Medicine.* New York: Simon and Schuster, 1997.

Hooker, S. D., L. Holbrook-Freeman, and P. Stewart. "Pet Therapy Research: A Historical Review." *Holistic Nursing Practice* 17, no. 1: 17–23.

Sternberg, E. M. *Healing Spaces: The Science of Place and Well-Being.* Cambridge, MA: Belknap Press, 2009.


EXPERIENCE 6

Ader, R., D. L. Felten, and N. Cohen, eds. *Psychoneuroimmunology*, 2nd edition. San Diego: Academic Press, 1991.

Bandura, A. "Human Agency in Social Cognitive Theory." *American Psychologist* 44, no. 9 (1989): 1175–1184.

Borysenko, J. *Minding the Body, Mending the Mind.* Reading, MA: Addison-Wesley, 1987.

Campbell, J. *The Hero's Journey: Joseph Campbell on His Life and Work.* New York: Harper & Row, 1991.

Castaneda, C. *The Teachings of Don Juan.* New York: Pocket Books, 1968.

Csíkszentmihályi, M. *Flow: The Psychology of Optimal Experience.* New York: Harper Perennial, 1990.

Fuller, R. Buckminster. *Utopia or Oblivion.* New York: Bantam Books, 1969.

Goleman, D., and J. Gurin, eds. *Mind Body Medicine.* Yonkers, NY: Consumer Reports Books, 1993.

Greene, Brian. *The Elegant Universe.* New York: W. W. Norton and Company, 1999.

Harris Poll. "Americans' Belief in God, Miracles and Heaven Declines." 2013. http://www.theharrispoll.com/health-and-life/Americans_Belief_in_God_Miracles_and_Heaven_Declines.html.

Hillman, James. *The Soul's Code.* New York: Random House, 1996.

Long, J. *Evidence of the Afterlife: The Science of Near-Death Experiences.* New York: HarperCollins, 2010.

McTaggart, L. *The Field: The Quest for the Secret Force in the Universe.* New York: HarperCollins, 2008.

Moody, R. A. *Life after Life.* New York: Bantam, 1975.

Moore, T. *Care of the Soul.* New York: HarperCollins, 1992.

Pelletier, K. R. *Mind as Healer, Mind as Slayer.* New York: Dell, 1992.

Pert, C. B. *Molecules of Emotion: Why You Feel the Way You Feel.* New York: Simon & Schuster, 1997.

Richardson, G. E. *Resilient Youth Curriculum Guide.* Utah: Bountiful, 1996.

Roberts, T. "Education and Transpersonal Relations: A Research Agenda." *Simulation Games* 8, no. 1 (March 1977): 7–28.

Rogers, C. R. *On Becoming a Person.* Boston: Houghton Mifflin, 1961.

Shannon-Missal, L. "Americans' Belief in God, Miracles and Heaven Declines." *Harris Poll* 97, December 16, 2013.

Sollod, R. "The Hollow Curriculum: The Place of Religions and Spirituality in Society is Too Often Missing." *Chronicle of Higher Education* 38, no. 28: A60.

Wittine, B. "Beyond Ego." *Yoga Journal* (September/October 1987): 52–57.

## EXPERIENCE 10

Bandura, A. *Self-Efficacy: The Exercise of Control.* New York: Worth Publishers, 1997.

## EXPERIENCE 11

Parsons, K. *Human Thermal Environments*, 3rd edition. Boca Raton, FL: CRC Press, 2002.

## EXPERIENCE 12

Castaneda, Carlos. *The Teachings of Don Juan: A Yaqui Way of Knowledge.* Oakland, CA: University of California Press, 1968.

Csíkszentmihályi, Mihaly. *Flow: The Psychology of Optimal Experience.* New York: Harper & Row, 1990.

Emerson, Ralph Waldo. http://www.izquotes.com/quote/373096.

Frankl, V. *Man's Search for Meaning.* New York: Beacon Press, 1959.

Freud, S. *The Interpretation of Dreams,* 3rd edition. New York: Macmillan, 1913.

Gandhi. https://eagleman6788.wordpress.com/2012/07/04/2572/.

Jung, K. *The Archetypes and the Collective Unconscious,* 2nd edition. Princeton, NJ: Princeton University Press, 1959.

Kant, Immanuel. http://www.inspirationalstories.com/quotes/immanuel-kant-all-human-knowledge-thus-begins-with-intuitions.

Lao Tzu. *Tao Te Ching: Annotated & Explained.* Woodstock, VT: SkyLight Paths, 2006.

Maxwell, Neal. http://iheartinspiration.com/quotes/faith-in-god-faith-in-timing.

**PART 6**

Frankl, V. *Man's Search for Meaning.* New York: Beacon Press, 1959.

# INDEX

**F**

# W

# Y